VENGEANCE

ALSO BY TOM CLAVIN

Running Deep

Bandit Heaven

The First to Go West (with Bob Drury)

The Last Outlaws

Follow Me to Hell

The Last Hill (with Bob Drury)

To the Uttermost Ends of the Earth (with Phil Keith)

Lightning Down

Blood and Treasure (with Bob Drury)

Tombstone

All Blood Runs Red (with Phil Keith)

Wild Bill

Valley Forge (with Bob Drury)

Being Ted Williams (with Dick Enberg)

Dodge City

Lucky 666 (with Bob Drury)

Reckless

The Heart of Everything That Is (with Bob Drury)

The DiMaggios

Last Men Out (with Bob Drury)

That Old Black Magic

The Last Stand of Fox Company (with Bob Drury)

Halsey's Typhoon (with Bob Drury)

VENGEANCE

THE LAST STANDS OF CUSTER, CRAZY HORSE, AND SITTING BULL

TOM CLAVIN

ST. MARTIN'S PRESS
NEW YORK

First published in the United States by St. Martin's Press, an imprint of St. Martin's Publishing Group

EU Representative: Macmillan Publishers Ireland Ltd, 1st Floor, The Liffey Trust Centre, 117–126 Sheriff Street Upper, Dublin 1, D01 YC43

www.stmartins.com

Designed by Omar Chapa

Map by Rhys Davies

The Library of Congress Cataloging-in-Publication Data is available upon request.

ISBN 978-1-250-37450-9 (hardcover)
ISBN 978-1-250-37451-6 (ebook)

First Edition: 2026

10 9 8 7 6 5 4 3 2 1

To Peter Israelson, who believed from the beginning and never wavered

CONTENTS

AUTHOR'S NOTE

Why another book on the Battle of the Little Bighorn? After all, a whole stable of distinguished writers—including, in more recent years, James Donovan, Mark Lee Gardner, Nathaniel Philbrick, and Robert Utley—has tackled one of the most famous topics in American history.

That very fame is a reason. The battle on June 25–27, 1876, is like our version of a Greek myth. It is a story of warriors clashing in the most dramatic way, and it ends in tragedy. With every retelling we reexperience that epic event and we learn new things—or change our opinions—about the battle and its participants.

It makes sense, too, that there is a new book to coincide with the 150th anniversary of the Battle of the Little Bighorn. It reminds us of reports reaching major cities throughout the United States in July 1876 of the defeat of not only an entire army regiment but the demise of George Armstrong Custer, the most charismatic cavalry commander in the country. The anniversary of such a catastrophe—for white America—is reason enough.

"In truth, it was also the last stand of the Sioux and Cheyenne as well, because their victory over Custer led to their own destruction," writes Herman J. Viola in *Little Bighorn Remembered*. "Imagine the shock and embarrassment to citizens of the United States enjoying the centennial year of their independence. The U.S. Army went after Sitting Bull and his allies with a vengeance."

Indeed, because the battle is often referred to as "Custer's Last Stand," where he met his glorious end—as it would be portrayed in scores of illustrations and paintings—such a Custer-centric view obscures that the event hastened the end of independence for the Lakota Sioux and Cheyenne. By the finish of the following year, many of their leaders were dead, in exile, or confined to reservations, sometimes starving thanks to the malfeasance of Indian agents. The experiences and fates of Sitting Bull, Crazy Horse, Gall, and others are crucial to the full story.

Another reason, there is that word again: *vengeance*. That theme is woven throughout the story. In addition to gaining prestige and counting coup, warriors in the Great Plains tribes were always seeking to avenge some previous transgression. When the white settlers and soldiers arrived, the hunger for vengeance intensified—Cheyenne must avenge the Sand Creek Massacre, the army must avenge the Fetterman Fight, and so on. The ultimate vengeance came at Wounded Knee in December 1890—the same month that saw the murder of Sitting Bull. It was the final "battle" of the war against the Plains tribes.

One more: I wanted to tell this legendary tale through my own lens. Having written a number of books about well-known characters and events in the nineteenth-century American West, the thought occurred: Why *haven't* I written about the Battle of the Little Bighorn? And I wanted to write the story in as straightforward a way as I could, without overanalyzing and taking detours. If you keep turning pages, I have achieved that goal.

This story is one that does not get old—it gets retold and retold, as befits an event featuring characters who hold a prominent place in American mythology.

PROLOGUE

WASHITA RIVER VALLEY, NOVEMBER 1868

A foot of snow had already fallen before sunrise on November 23, 1868. The soldiers of the Seventh Cavalry shook the sleep out of their eyes and the flakes off their shoulders as they gathered around flickering campfires struggling to survive the frequent blasts of wind. As they drank weak coffee, the troopers glanced up: The storm showed no sign of slowing.

This was good news to Lieutenant Colonel George Armstrong Custer, the field commander of the regiment.* Only the calendar disagreed that it was winter in Oklahoma. Here was a blizzard at just the right time for an operation against the Indians. Traditionally, the U.S. Army did not conduct winter campaigns, and thus the Indians felt safe in their remote

---

* The official commander of the Seventh Cavalry was Colonel Alfred Sully, but because of a lack of aggressiveness in the field, he had been exiled to Fort Harker.

villages until the first signs of spring. Custer aimed to rattle that complacency sometime during the next few days.

When he was ready, Custer mounted his horse and had his troopers do the same. Even in such challenging conditions, the regimental band managed to strike up the familiar tune of "The Girl I Left Behind Me." The notes were swallowed up by the swirling snowflakes in the predawn darkness, and soon so too were the groggy and shivering men of the regiment. Their destination was the Washita River Valley.

The head man of the Cheyenne village in the valley, Black Kettle, has to be considered as one of the more unfortunate Indian leaders in U.S. history. He, and his wife (Medicine Woman Later) too, had survived the Sand Creek Massacre four years earlier in Colorado—though Medicine Woman Later had been shot nine times—and here in Oklahoma, over five hundred miles to the southeast of that attack, the couple was in the crosshairs of another military unit.

Black Kettle had been born around 1803 in what became South Dakota. Little is known of his life prior to 1854, when he was made a chief of the Council of Forty-Four, the central government of the Cheyenne tribe. The council met regularly at the Sun Dance gatherings, where its members affirmed unity. Black Kettle was a pragmatist who believed that U.S. military power and the number of westbound migrants were overwhelming and could not be successfully resisted. In 1861, he and Arapaho allies surrendered to the commander of Fort Lyon in Colorado, believing that he could gain protection for his people. After a visit to Washington, DC, where he was presented a large American flag by President Abraham Lincoln, Black Kettle and his followers settled in at the Sand Creek Reservation.

At dawn on November 29, 1864, Colonel John Chivington, a former clergyman, and his Third Colorado Cavalry attacked the reservation. Most of the warriors were out hunting. Following Indian agent instructions, Black Kettle flew the American flag plus a white flag from his tepee, but they did not provide protection from the marauding white men, who shot and stabbed 163 Cheyenne to death and burned down the village encampment. Most of the victims were women and children. For months afterward, members of the militia displayed trophies in Denver from their battle, including body parts they had taken for souvenirs.*

Black Kettle escaped the massacre and then returned to rescue the severely injured Medicine Woman Later. Despite the death toll, pragmatism continued to rule over anger, and he continued to counsel pacifism, believing that military resistance was doomed to fail. "Although wrongs have been done me, I live in hopes," Black Kettle said. He added, however: "I have not got two hearts. I once thought that I was the only man that persevered to be the friend of the white man, but since they have come and cleaned out our lodges, horses, and everything else, it is hard for me to believe white men anymore."

But he tried. Black Kettle moved south and continued to negotiate with U.S. officials. In October 1865, he signed the Treaty of the Little Arkansas River. By this document, the United States promised "perpetual peace" and lands in reparation for the Sand Creek Massacre. However, its practical effect was to dispossess the Cheyenne yet again and require them to move to what was called Indian Territory, present-day Oklahoma. There, with life not any better for the Cheyenne, Black Kettle's influence waned. "Dog Soldiers" led by Roman Nose, who was at least twenty years younger, rebelled and waged war against the army.

So, one would think that a sidelined Black Kettle would be out of harm's way, especially after he signed yet another peace document, in 1867. The Medicine Lodge Treaty was a series of agreements further

* One of these bizarre displays was an appearance by Colonel Chivington on a Denver stage where he described the battle as the audience gaped at a display of some one hundred Indian scalps.

establishing reservations in Indian Territory and protecting them from white intruders.

But once again, the star-crossed Black Kettle was at the wrong place at the wrong time. The Seventh Cavalry was inexorably approaching his camp.

Only a few days earlier, Black Kettle had made his way to Fort Cobb to reassure the post commander, Colonel William Hazen, of his peaceful intentions. Hazen was convinced, but he was probably unaware of the campaign created by General William Tecumseh Sherman to further corral the Cheyenne.

On November 26, after three days of struggling through snow, Custer's regiment crossed the Canadian River at the Antelope Hills. Now having a better idea of where he was, Custer ordered Major Joel Elliott to take three companies upstream to find a trail his weary troopers and their horses could follow. Elliott was more successful than his commander had hoped: Not only did he find a trail after traveling just twelve miles, but it had been made by the feet of as many as a hundred Cheyenne heading south. To the major, this indicated an Indian village of some size was in that direction.

A messenger plowed through the snow to bring a communiqué to Custer. The delighted lieutenant colonel sent a message back, telling Elliott to follow the trail. The rest of the regiment, leaving its baggage train to plod along as best it could, hurried to catch up. Soon after midnight, after having reunited with Elliott's companies, the Seventh Cavalry arrived on a ridge behind an Indian camp. After moving forward with his Osage scouts and surveying the area, Custer planned to divide the regiment into four battalions and attack the village.

One of the Osage scouts, Little Beaver, pointed down and told Custer, "Heap Injuns down there." The more the better, thought Custer.

At this time, Black Kettle's camp consisted of about 250 Cheyenne. The headman, not in turn reassured by Colonel Hazen about any protection and with horrid memories of Sand Creek still vivid, was planning to move his camp down the Washita River to join larger Cheyenne encampments and seek safety in numbers. But Black Kettle was in no particular rush, given that the army was not known to conduct campaigns in heavy snow. Thus, his plan would remain only a plan, not a solution.

Custer had his own plan, and in pitch dark, he assembled his officers to tell them of it: Attack at dawn. The colonel was queried about there possibly being many more Indians than the regiment could handle. "All I'm afraid of is we won't find half enough," Custer replied. "There are not Indians enough in the country to whip the Seventh Cavalry."

This scene would be repeated almost identically less than eight years later in Montana overlooking another—and many times larger—Indian village.

By dawn, the regiment was very cold, but ready. The four battalions would attack simultaneously: Elliott and three companies from the northeast, Captain William Thompson with two companies from the south, Captain Edward Myers and two companies from the west, and Custer with four companies from the north. The latter contingent would be accompanied by the regimental band.

Though some fingers were frozen stiff, the band managed to launch into "Garry Owen," Custer's favorite fighting tune. The song was short-lived, however, because the instruments froze too. The buglers managed to blare "Charge," and the columns of the Seventh Cavalry attacked the village. Custer, dressed in buckskin and his face almost obscured by a full, thick beard and a fur cap pulled low, was at the front of his battalion as they burst into the camp of startled Cheyenne.

What ensued was deadly chaos. Half-asleep villagers exited their tepees and ran around each other, some being knocked down. Gunshots resounded, mixed with the screams of frightened women and children. Men searched for weapons and equally frightened horses. In all, close to eight hundred troopers rampaged through the Cheyenne encampment.

There would be no survival this time for Medicine Woman Later. She was shot dead during the charges of the four columns. So too was her husband. Both Black Kettle and his wife were struck by bullets in the back as they tried to cross the Washita River in a desperate search for safety.*

In ten minutes, the "battle" was over. The Cheyenne later claimed only eleven of their men had died. The rest were women and children. In addition, fifty-one lodges and their contents were burned, and the camp's pony herd of roughly eight hundred horses was killed. The Seventh Cavalry suffered twenty-two men killed, including two officers. One was Captain Louis Hamilton, who had the misfortunate of having a bullet pass through his heart a moment after he burst into the village.†

The rest of the stay at the Washita River was a mopping-up operation. Some Cheyenne were spared, and fifty-three women and children were taken as prisoners to be brought to Fort Supply. One of them was Monahsetah. She was the teenage daughter of the Cheyenne headman Little Rock, who had been killed during the assault. She was seven months' pregnant and would give birth in January 1869.

One of Custer's senior officers, Captain Frederick Benteen, as well as Cheyenne oral history, contended that Custer "cohabited" with Monahsetah

---

* Black Kettle's body could not be found. It was assumed that he had been carried to a remote canyon for burial. Not quite seventy years later—July 13, 1934—some Works Progress Administration laborers who were lengthening a bridge over the Washita accidentally uncovered a skeleton dressed in Black Kettle's jewelry. His bones were donated to a local newspaper, *The Cheyenne Star*, which displayed them in a window.

† Louis McLane Hamilton was akin to American royalty. His father was Philip Hamilton, who was the youngest son of Alexander Hamilton. Like his grandfather, Louis's older brother, Philip Jr., died in a duel. Louis Hamilton fought in Chancellorsville, Gettysburg, and other major battles and managed to emerge without a serious injury.

during the winter and early spring and that in late 1869, she bore a son, fathered by Custer. The boy was named Yellow Swallow.

In addition to preparing the captives for travel, the wounds of fifteen troopers were attended to. Before the Seventh Cavalry left, however, Lieutenant Colonel Custer had two mysteries to ponder. One: Where was Major Elliott? His detachment had last been seen pursuing Cheyenne who were trying to reach the Washita River. Elliott had been heard to shout, "Here goes for a brevet or a coffin!"*

Two: Why were the Osage scouts reporting a large number of Indians approaching from downstream? There were too many to be a Cheyenne hunting party returning to the village.

Custer was completely unaware that farther down the Washita River there were three larger encampments. The one Black Kettle had planned to join was Cheyenne, and the other two were Arapaho and Kiowa.

To be on the safe side, though, it was time for the regiment to get out of there. Troopers pushed tepees over, set fire to them, and then threw into the blazes clothing, weapons, saddles, and any other Cheyenne possessions they could find. By the time the Seventh Cavalry left, the village was virtually destroyed.

Because Custer never resolved the second mystery, what he took away from the Washita River Valley experience was that numbers of hostiles did not matter. A swift surprise attack by well-armed and determined cavalry would terrify and confuse not just the Cheyenne but any tribe. Victory went to the bold.

It would be weeks before the first mystery was solved—horribly.

---

* A brevet is a promotion in rank awarded for battlefield heroics. It was rare to have such a promotion carry over to peacetime. Custer, for example, had risen to brevet major general by the conclusion of the Civil War. Though he was no longer one, many of his men and friends, as well as his wife, still often called him "General."

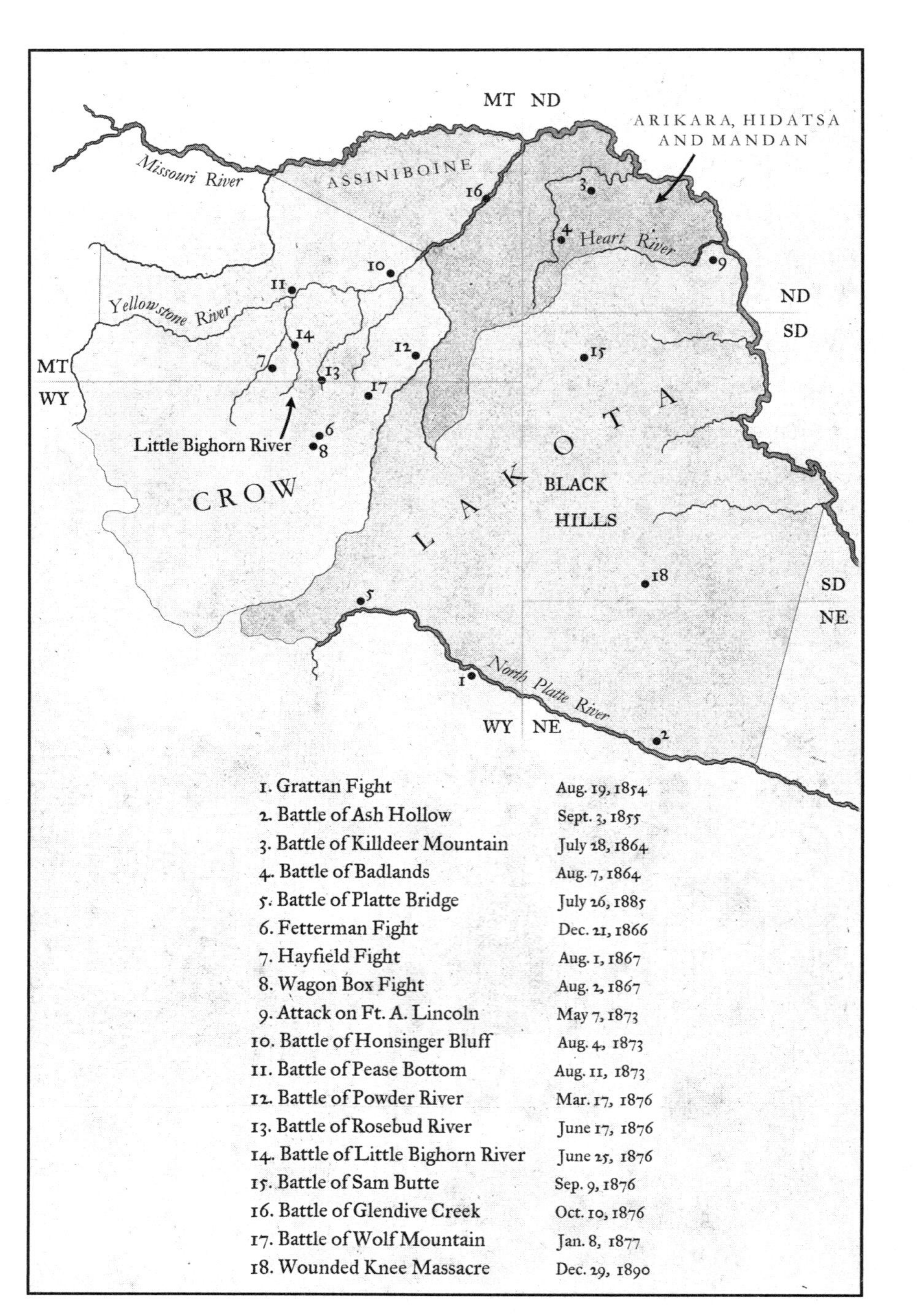
MT ND
ARIKARA, HIDATSA
AND MANDAN
Missouri River
ASSINIBOINE
Heart River
Yellowstone River
ND
SD
MT
WY
Little Bighorn River
CROW
LAKOTA
BLACK
HILLS
SD
NE
North Platte River
WY NE
1. Grattan Fight Aug. 19, 1854
2. Battle of Ash Hollow Sept. 3, 1855
3. Battle of Killdeer Mountain July 28, 1864
4. Battle of Badlands Aug. 7, 1864
5. Battle of Platte Bridge July 26, 1885
6. Fetterman Fight Dec. 21, 1866
7. Hayfield Fight Aug. 1, 1867
8. Wagon Box Fight Aug. 2, 1867
9. Attack on Ft. A. Lincoln May 7, 1873
10. Battle of Honsinger Bluff Aug. 4, 1873
11. Battle of Pease Bottom Aug. 11, 1873
12. Battle of Powder River Mar. 17, 1876
13. Battle of Rosebud River June 17, 1876
14. Battle of Little Bighorn River June 25, 1876
15. Battle of Sam Butte Sep. 9, 1876
16. Battle of Glendive Creek Oct. 10, 1876
17. Battle of Wolf Mountain Jan. 8, 1877
18. Wounded Knee Massacre Dec. 29, 1890

ACT I

THE INVADERS

The white man made me a lot of promises, and they only kept one. They promised to take my land, and they took it.

—**RED CLOUD**

1

THE SIOUX ASCEND

As was true for many of the violent engagements involving whites and Natives in America since the sixteenth century, to some soldiers the Washita River attack in 1868 was an act of vengeance. It was time to pay the Plains Indians back for the Fetterman Massacre in Wyoming two years earlier. It was of little consequence that the revenge was exacted in Oklahoma and the victims were Cheyenne instead of the Sioux led by Red Cloud and Crazy Horse, who had annihilated Captain William Fetterman's eighty-one-man command. An Indian was an Indian, and any diminishing of their population meant more land and riches for the *wasichu*.*

---

* In the Lakota Sioux language, *wasichu* is a term that can be understood as "white people" or "outsiders," but it carries a broader connotation, often referring to a state of mind characterized by greed and a disregard for Native cultures and resources. Today, wasichu is still being used to describe individuals, corporations, and governmental entities that are perceived as exploiting Native American lands, resources, and lives for personal or corporate profit.

Before the invasion of the American West by white people of mostly European descent, Indigenous tribes invaded one another's lands, gaining and ceding territory over decades. The Sioux were more wide-ranging and aggressive than most.

In the sixteenth century, the Sioux migrated up the Mississippi River Valley to the river's headwaters in the forests of northern Minnesota. Their warring abilities enabled them to carve out a wide swath of territory and keep at bay competitors for hunting grounds.

But the Sioux sovereignty did not last. European ships entering Hudson Bay carried crates of guns, powder, and ball ammunition that traders happily exchanged for hides and pelts provided by members of the Cree tribe. The stunning leap in death-dealing arms took the power away from the Sioux. They went into exile, melting into the forests and swampy wastelands, where they could only grub for acorns, roots, and edible plants. Once-proud warriors did more hiding than hunting.

According to Stephen Ambrose in *Crazy Horse and Custer*: "The gun gave eastern tribes great advantages over their western neighbors—its noise had a psychological effect; the bullet had more hitting power than the arrow; the range was greater. With the gun the eastern tribes drove their enemies westward. As the white fur traders penetrated farther into the interior of the continent the process was repeated. Most of the famous Plains tribes were pushed out onto the prairie by military defeats, the Crow, Arapaho, Blackfeet, and Cheyenne among them. The last major tribe to arrive on the plains was the Sioux, trekking out of the woods of Minnesota."

The Sioux did not cross the Missouri River until the summer of 1776. This was a sort of independence time for them too as they migrated to the Great Plains. They found that the horse was there in abundant numbers, and fortuitously, the vast region of the plains, teeming with buffalo, was ripe for conquest. The Mandan and Arikara had been decimated by epidemics of smallpox. The Sioux tribes—Blackfeet, Brule, Hunkpapa,

Miniconjou, Sans Arc, Two Kettle, and Oglala—acted more or less in concert, while the Crow, Cheyenne, Pawnee, and other tribes could not or would not combine their forces for defensive purposes. By 1800, the Sioux had acquired more than enough horses to take control of a vast region stretching from the Missouri River on the east and north to the Black Hills on the west and the Platte River on the south.

And what a beautiful and dangerous region it was. "The Great Plains, on a cloudless day, stretch out forever under an infinity of bright blue sky," writes Ambrose. "During the violence of a tornado or a snowstorm, however, the vision is limited to the length of an arm. The Plains can be hot, dusty, brown, flat, and unfit for life; they can be delightfully cool, abundantly watered, a dozen shades of green, marvelously varied in appearance, ranging from near mountains to level valleys, and hospitable to all forms of life."

The neighboring Arikara (also known as the Ree) played a pivotal role in the ascension of the Sioux by introducing them to horses and demonstrating how to ride them. The Arikara would quickly come to regret this: The hardy Sioux became expert horsemen and fearsome warriors once more. The Crow and Pawnee as well as the Arikara were routinely raided by Sioux hunting parties. Though not nearly destroyed by disease as the Ree had been, the other tribes had to recognize that the Sioux were now the dominant people in the Great Plains.

2

PAHA SAPA

Having successfully invaded the Great Plains and subjugated its other inhabitants, the Lakota Sioux settled in for the long haul. The Black Hills were the center of this relatively new universe. Symbolically as well as practically, the Black Hills served the Sioux well.

"It mattered little to the Lakotas that they had wrested the Black Hills from the Cheyennes, who had taken them from the Comanches and Kiowas, who had ejected the Crows less than a century earlier," writes James Donovan in *A Terrible Glory*. "They did not care that each Indian landgrab had been even more direct than the whites'." What mattered most was the sanctity and possession of the new homeland. And it was worth fighting for.

The Black Hills are one of the oldest mountain ranges in the world, and at Harney Peak they attain a height of over seven thousand feet.* The wooded region is sixty miles wide and one hundred miles long, north to

* It would always be a source of frustration for the Sioux that the highest point

south. Because of the mountainous terrain, the Sioux did not construct any permanent villages there, with the plains being much more suitable for habitation. However, the Black Hills could be a refuge in periods of bad weather and were used for occasional hunting, and the many trees provided the tribe's lodge and travois poles.

Crucial to the Sioux claims of supremacy was that the Black Hills region was a holy place, where spirits dwelled. It was called Paha Sapa, which is often translated as the "Heart of Everything That Is." A big reason why: It was here that an enduring creation story was born.

In the time before time began, the goddess Ite, the mother of the four winds, conspired with the spider spirit Inktomi to create the Buffalo Nation of Sioux people. Together, these deities delivered the nation up from an underground netherworld to the surface of the earth filled with game. The connecting door to this new world was called the Wind Cave.

It is to this day one of the longest caverns in the world—a series of honeycombed tunnels. Because of its deep passageways and the small size of its mouth, only eight by ten feet, the Wind Cave reacts inversely to outside air pressures: It seems to exhale when the outside air pressure is low and to inhale when the pressure is high. The Sioux of the early nineteenth century believed that it was from this cave that the gods had delivered their ancestors.

Even the Sioux holy men and medicine men probably could not have imagined the pressure that would be placed on the tribe to preserve Paha Sapa as a connection to their past or that leaders would have to rise up to resist that pressure. The first great one to be successful against the wasichu was not Sitting Bull.

It was in May 1821 that a baby was born to a Brule Sioux, Lone Man, and his Oglala wife, Walks As She Thinks. Their camp was alongside a

---

in the revered Black Hills was named for William Selby Harney, otherwise known among the Lakota as "Woman Killer" and "Mad Bear."

tributary of the North Platte River called Blue Water Creek in Nebraska. The Native band had just noted a glowing meteor streak across the night sky above their camp. The baby was named Red Cloud.

His early years coincided with the Sioux being at the height of their power and based in the Powder River Country. However, it was unlikely that the boy, who early on showed physical gifts and intelligence, would ascend to become the overall headman. When Red Cloud was five, his father died, and in Sioux society, a fatherless child was at a great disadvantage.* But the child was otherwise fortunate in that Walks As She Thinks returned to her original village and her son received the patronage of her brother, Old Smoke, a particularly powerful and durable Oglala headman.

* Lone Man died of alcoholism. Like smallpox and cholera, this was another disease given to the Indians by Europeans for which they had no natural immunity.

3

DECREES AND DISEASES

By the time of Red Cloud's birth, white people were appearing more often in the Powder River Country. The explorations and reports of Lewis and Clark's Corps of Discovery, Zebulon Pike, Jedediah Smith, and others had heightened curiosity about the land west of the Missouri River.

It was at times referred to as the "Garden of the World," but that favorable impression (or hope) was countered by the report of Major Stephen Long, who was the first to call the territory to the west of the Missouri the "Great American Desert." He further maintained that based on his observations, the Great Plains were "almost wholly unfit for cultivation and of course uninhabitable by a people depending on agriculture for their subsistence."

Such a negative view did not deter mountain men, fur traders, and other hardy souls from going to see for themselves. Doing so, they encountered the Indigenous residents, who for generations had found the land quite habitable. While many of the encounters were peaceful—tribes and wasichus came to appreciate the advantages of trading with each other—another view grew in importance: Wherever the white man went and whatever he wanted from the land, the people residing there were in the way.

In 1823, Lieutenant Colonel Henry Leavenworth led the first U.S. military expedition against Indians west of the Missouri, against the Arikara. Though the campaign was modestly successful, military action was not the first option for the covetous but supposedly principled whites. Treaties and presidential decrees might do the trick without bloodshed. After all, how smart could savages be? An example of the latter was issued in 1825 by President James Monroe that required tribes to pick up and move west to a vaguely designated Indian Country.

Five years later, President Andrew Jackson had Congress pass the bluntly named Indian Removal Act. One of its consequences was the eviction of the Cherokee Nation from Georgia and the subsequent Trail of Tears to Oklahoma. By 1840, with very few exceptions, Indian tribes east of the Mississippi River had been shunted to the West.

The war with Mexico later that decade resulted in large swaths of land in the West and Southwest coming under U.S. ownership. One would think there was enough for everyone. According to the 1840 Census, the U.S. population was just over seventeen million. With the country now extending from the Atlantic Ocean to the Pacific Ocean and the border of Canada to the reconfigured border with Mexico, or a shade under three million square miles, there was no need to take any more land occupied and hunted on by the western tribes.

Everything changed with the discovery of gold at Sutter's Mill in California in 1848. This did not require the taking of land necessarily: It was more about borrowing some to create paths to get to the gold.

The Oregon Trail became the most popular path. It originated in Independence, Missouri, and ended 2,170 miles later in Oregon Territory. The trail crossed what are now the states of Kansas, Nebraska, Wyoming, Idaho, and Oregon.

The circuitous path was first configured by fur traders on foot or horseback who were active until 1840, when the frenzy for beaver fur ended. Four years earlier, a trail that could accommodate wagons had been cleared from Independence to Fort Hall, Idaho. The trail was eventually extended to its last stop, the Willamette Valley in Oregon. Though the journey was arduous and hazardous, the fertile farmland west of the Rocky Mountains was now within reach.

The Oregon Trail and its many offshoots were used by about 400,000 settlers, farmers, miners, ranchers, and business owners and their families. The traffic was especially thick from 1846 to 1869 thanks to farming folk being joined by gold-seekers, those looking for a new life (whatever that may be), and then individuals or entire families desiring to leave the Civil War behind them. Among the trail's tributaries were the California Trail, Mormon Trail, and Bozeman Trail, which shared the eastern half of the Oregon Trail before turning off to their separate destinations. Use of the Oregon Trail declined after the first transcontinental railroad was completed, making the trip west substantially faster, cheaper, and safer.

Before the appearance of rail, however, travelers in their wagons had to pass through areas occupied by Native tribes. As unwelcome as this was, at first tribes did not view the wagon trains as a terrible thing—as long as they kept moving west, Indigenous residents found it best not to impede them. Also, the migrants were often willing to trade with the tribes, exchanging items like coffee and sugar for blankets and buffalo skins. There were skirmishes, but for the most part, warriors left the whites alone so they could focus on the fighting between tribes to win ponies and prestige.

The view of the wagon trains as innocuous would change as "Euro-Americans became a consistent presence and an increasing annoyance," reports Joseph Marshall III in *The Journey of Crazy Horse*. Every year there came a "steady stream of white emigrants moving east to west from late spring to midsummer. Tens of thousands of people, thousands of oxen, mules, and horses, and hundreds of wagons passed through. Those people carried with them many things new to the Lakota, some beneficial and some destructive. Most of all, however, they brought change."

What was terrible, the tribes were to learn, was the emigrants also carried alcohol and disease. Of the two, the latter was more damaging because diseases killed quickly and in bunches. In 1837, soon after the wagons began to roll on the Oregon Trail, at least four different epidemics broke out among the Great Plains tribes.

When they began to learn of these mystifying and cruel diseases, many Indians intentionally avoided contact with the emigrants. But the lure of trade goods, such as metal pots, skillets, and knives, sometimes proved too strong. Some traded with the white travelers anyway and inadvertently spread disease to their villages. The Lakota Sioux called smallpox the "rotting face sickness."

Many tribes suffered high mortality and depopulation, averaging 25 to 50 percent dead from disease. For the larger tribes this was devastating enough—for example, it is estimated that two-thirds of the Blackfeet population died—but some smaller tribes neared extinction after facing a severely destructive spread of disease.

So, the Natives let the wasichus keep moving, for the most part unmolested. There were enough conflicts, though, that the U.S. government was beseeched to build forts and garrison soldiers there to protect the wagons full of nervous white people.

The fate of William Judd Fetterman would be a preview of the defeat George Armstrong Custer would suffer a decade later.

4

DECOY TO DEATH

In 1863, to shorten the journey to gold fields in Montana, the Bozeman Trail was blazed through the heart of the territory of the Cheyenne, Arapaho, and Lakota. From 1864 to 1866, the trail was traversed by about 3,500 miners, immigrant settlers, and others who competed with the longtime inhabitants for the diminishing resources near the trail.

By this time, Red Cloud had become headman of the Lakota Sioux. Spotted Tail was a rival for that position, but Red Cloud was the acknowledged leader by most of the Lakota population. Some historians contend that at the height of his power, the Lakota Sioux controlled close to 20 percent of land in the United States. Certainly in the northern plains, where Red Cloud and the Oglala dwelled, there was no serious rival for supremacy.

Then, with the Civil War concluded and a new surge of migrants, the wasichu leaders in Washington, DC, decided a U.S. Army presence was needed on the Bozeman Trail—enough of a presence that just one fort would not do; there had to be three. Technically, the forts were located on

Crow territory, and that tribe was OK with them: They believed the U.S. Army would kick the Sioux out, which served the Crow's interests best.

Red Cloud saw the situation differently. To him, the passing-through stage appeared to be ending. There was a big difference between a rumbling wagon and a stationary stockade.

Charged with carrying out the fort-building plan was Colonel Henry Carrington. With seven hundred soldiers and three hundred civilians under his command, in June 1866 Carrington arrived in Powder River Country. Three forts were constructed, the first of which, Fort Phil Kearny (near present-day Buffalo, Wyoming), was to be his base of operations. Living at the fort-to-be site were four hundred of his soldiers and most of the civilians.*

During the next few months, while Fort Phil Kearny was under construction, Carrington suffered about fifty Indian attacks, losing more than twenty soldiers and civilians. The Indian warriors, invariably mounted and often led by Crazy Horse, Red Cloud's field general, appeared in groups of twenty to one hundred. Several of Carrington's junior officers pressed him to take the offensive, especially in November, when a cavalry company of sixty-three men arrived to reinforce the post. The company included infantry Captains William Fetterman and James W. Powell. Both officers had been assigned to Fort Phil Kearny from the Eighteenth Infantry's headquarters at Fort Laramie. During the war,

* Philip Kearny was a one-armed, much-decorated army officer who served in the Mexican-American War and early in the Civil War. In 1862, after the Union defeat at the Second Battle of Manassas, General Kearny engaged Confederate forces at the Battle of Chantilly. While scouting positions near his men, Kearny inadvertently rode near Confederate forces and was killed while attempting to escape. General Robert E. Lee, who, along with many other Confederate officers, held great respect for General Kearny, forwarded his remains under a flag of truce to Union lines to ensure that the general received a proper burial.

the thirty-three-year-old Fetterman had put together a distinguished combat record.

Although he had no experience fighting in the West, Connecticut native Fetterman criticized Carrington's defensive posture and was contemptuous of their Indian foes. He boasted, "Give me eighty men and I can ride through the whole Sioux nation." Many other officers shared Fetterman's feelings. Once Fort Phil Kearny was completed, Carrington gave the restless captain permission to attempt a night ambush. However, Red Cloud's wily warriors instead stampeded a herd of cattle on the bank of the Powder River opposite Fetterman's intended trap.

On November 22, Fetterman himself almost fell into a Sioux ambush. He had accompanied an escort guarding a wagon train gathering firewood for the fort. A single Sioux warrior—possibly Crazy Horse himself—appeared, trying to entice the soldiers into chasing him into the woods. Lieutenant William Bisbee, commanding the wagon train, ordered his men to take cover instead of pursuing. A frustrated Fetterman did the same.

Red Cloud, encouraged by the minor successes, decided to undertake a large military operation against Fort Phil Kearny before snow and plunging temperatures forced the Sioux to move their large village on the Tongue River to a site with more protection from the winter weather. After the decoy trick again almost worked on December 6, he and Crazy Horse decided to try it once more, this time with a force adequate to destroy any group of soldiers sent to chase them.

The warriors, possibly numbering more than one thousand, congregated about ten miles north of the fort, reconnoitered, and decided the best place to lay the trap was along the Bozeman Trail north of Lodge Trail Ridge, about four miles from Fort Phil Kearny. Members of two allied tribes, Cheyenne and Arapaho, took up positions on the west side of the trail, and the Lakota were on the east.

The morning of December 21 was clear and cold. About 10:00 A.M.,

Carrington dispatched a wagon train to the "pinery"—about five miles northwest and the nearest source of construction timber and firewood for the fort. Almost ninety soldiers were detailed to guard the wagon train. Less than an hour later, Carrington's pickets on Pilot Hill signaled by flag that the wagon train was under attack.

Carrington mustered up a relief party composed of forty-nine infantrymen, twenty-seven mounted troopers, and five civilians, for a total of eighty-one officers and men under the command of Captain Fetterman. The infantry marched out first; the cavalry had to retrieve their mounts before they could follow and catch up.

According to Carrington's subsequent report, his orders were clear. "Under no circumstances" was the relief party to "pursue over the ridge, that is Lodge Trail Ridge." These orders were given twice, the second time by Carrington from the sentry walk after telling the soldiers to halt as they left the front gate of the fort. On leaving the fort, however, Fetterman took the Lodge Ridge Trail northward rather than the trail northwest toward the pinery, where the wagon train was. Carrington assumed that Fetterman intended to approach the warriors attacking the wood train from their rear.

Within a short time, the signal came that the wood train was no longer under attack. About fifty warriors appeared near Fort Phil Kearny, but Carrington dispersed them with a few cannon shots. Those Indians and others harassed Fetterman as he climbed Lodge Trail Ridge and then disappeared out of sight of the fort.

About noon in the fort, Carrington and his men heard heavy firing to their north. Seventy-five men were placed under the command of Captain Tenodor Ten Eyck and sent out on foot to search for Fetterman. Ten Eyck advanced carefully up Lodge Trail Ridge. Reaching the top at about 12:45 P.M., he and his men saw a very large force of warriors in the Peno Creek valley below. They approached the soldiers and taunted them. Meanwhile, Carrington dispatched another group of forty-two soldiers to join Ten Eyck.

The warriors in the valley slowly dispersed and faded from view. Ten Eyck and his soldiers soon found the bodies of Fetterman and all his men in the valley. Even a dog that had followed the doomed column had been killed.

The dead soldiers had been stripped naked and mutilated. That afternoon, wagons were sent to bring the bodies back to Fort Phil Kearny.

According to Herman Viola in *Little Bighorn Remembered,* "From the condition of the horribly mutilated bodies, it was obvious Red Cloud's warriors intended to make a statement. One corpse, that of a civilian who joined the column to test his new repeating rifle against the Indians, had 105 arrows in it."

The Fetterman Massacre was the largest loss of life suffered by the U.S. Army against an Indian force in the West. And it could have been worse: Down eighty-one fighters, Fort Phil Kearny was even more vulnerable to attack. In fact, fearing that the fort would soon be overwhelmed, Carrington ordered that a trail of gunpowder leading to the fort's magazine be laid so that the remaining soldiers and civilians would die in a massive explosion rather than suffer the monstrous fate of Fetterman and his men.

However, the fort was saved by a fortuitous blizzard that persuaded Red Cloud to hurry to locate and establish a winter camp.

5

SPRING GRASS

Red Cloud's War lasted into 1868, when a frustrated President Andrew Johnson administration proposed peace. In the Treaty of Fort Laramie, the Lakota Sioux and their allies were given legal control of the western Powder River Country, including and especially the Black Hills.

After agreeing to the treaty that November, Red Cloud and his warriors enjoyed the experience of closing down the Bozeman Trail and burning to the ground Fort Phil Kearny and the two other, smaller stockades on the trail, Fort Reno and Fort C. F. Smith. Another happy outcome for the Lakota was their protected territory now included the hunting grounds of the Crow, who no doubt regretted having sided with the wasichu in the war.*

Less than two years later, Red Cloud was at, of all places, the White House, being feted by President Ulysses Grant.

---

* The Lakota leader's war thus became the only one that ended with an Indian defeat of the U.S. government.

During that interval, he had not been active as a war chief. Though only in his late forties, he was transitioning to elder statesman. He had fought and won his battles. To put an exclamation point on this, in March 1869, Red Cloud unexpectedly appeared with one thousand mounted warriors at the gates of Fort Laramie, where he had signed the treaty the previous fall. He was not there to fight, but he could if he wanted to. Fort Laramie could end up like Fort Phil Kearny. After making this dramatic gesture, Red Cloud and his army turned and leisurely rode off to hunt in Wind River Country.

The Grant administration apparently decided if you can't beat them, convince them. In June 1870, Red Cloud and Spotted Tail accepted an invitation to lead a delegation of Oglala and Brule to Washington, DC. The train ride alone, with its powerful steam-belching engine running faster and longer than any horse, must have represented the growing gap between the tribes and white society.

There was much more in store. The Lakota delegation was given tours of the Capitol and army and navy facilities, with extra time spent at the War Department's arsenal, where huge cannons, howitzers, and other imposing weapons were stored. Red Cloud, Spotted Tail, and their entourage were seeing up close the true military might of the United States.

After the stick came the carrot. President Grant hosted a reception for the delegation at the White House. There and in subsequent meetings with government officials, Red Cloud was treated like visiting royalty. Headlines and articles giving a running account of his pronouncements made the Lakota headman even more nationally famous. Large crowds of onlookers gathered at every public sighting of the celebrated Sioux leaders.

The adulation continued in New York City when the group arrived there later in June. Thousands of people lined Fifth Avenue to catch a glimpse of the once-infamous warrior chief who had bested the U.S. Army. In a speech delivered at the Cooper Institute in Manhattan, Red Cloud reiterated his belief that the Treaty of Fort Laramie protected the territory he had fought for. "No one who listened to Red Cloud's speech yesterday can doubt that he is a man of great talents," reported *The New York Times*, further describing him as a "man of brains, a good ruler, an eloquent speaker, an able general and a fair diplomat."

A "man of brains" could not help but realize the futility of fighting the wasichus again and the dimming prospect of Sioux sovereignty in the plains. As Red Cloud told Secretary of the Interior Joseph Cox, "Now we are melting snow on the hillside while you are growing like spring grass."

After his return home, Red Cloud and his people continued to roam Powder River Country, but the end of their lifestyle was as inevitable as the end of the buffalo. Red Cloud recognized that. In 1872, he again traveled to Washington and persuaded the federal government to set aside a rolling swath of land along the White River in northwestern Nebraska that would become the Red Cloud Agency. He and his family and most of his Oglala followers moved to the new reservation.

Once settled in, Red Cloud declared, "I shall not go to war any more with whites."

He was true to his word. But Red Cloud's self-exile left a vacuum of leadership in the Lakota Sioux. Sitting Bull would soon fill it.

6

"FINAL SOLUTION"

One of the consequences of the Red Cloud War was it forced the U.S. government to take some of its attention off Reconstruction in the South and redirect it to the West. And soon after the war ended, there was a reordering of the top U.S. military brass.

Ulysses Grant took the oath of office on March 4, 1869, becoming the eighteenth U.S. president. Replacing him as commanding general of the U.S. Army, a position he would hold for fourteen years, was the forty-five-year-old William Tecumseh Sherman. The Ohio native, one of eleven children raised by the widowed and no doubt exhausted Mrs. Sherman, had emerged during the Civil War as Grant's right-hand general. There could not have been a more loyal successor.*

* Despite the hardship of their father, an Ohio Supreme Court justice, dying while they were still children, several of the Sherman siblings had distinguished lives. Charles Sherman Jr. became a federal judge. John Sherman was one of the founders of the Republican Party and served as a U.S. congressman, senator,

Or one less suited to dealing with the western tribes still clinging to independence. While General Sherman promoted the protection of Indians who resided peacefully on newly created reservations, he was all for punishing renegades of any tribe, especially if they committed crimes. In 1871, for example, Sherman ordered that the leaders of the Warren Wagon Train raid, an attack by a combined Kiowa and Comanche war party from which Sherman himself had narrowly escaped, be tried for murder in Texas. The resulting trial of Satanta and Big Tree marked the first occasion in which Indian chiefs were tried by a civilian court in the United States.*

Sherman regarded the expansion of the railroad system as the "most important element now in progress to facilitate the military interests of our Frontier." One of the main concerns of his postwar service was, therefore, to protect the construction and operation of the railroads from hostile Indians.

Following the Fetterman Massacre, Sherman had telegraphed Grant, "We must act with vindictive earnestness against the Sioux, even to their extermination, men, women and children." In 1867, he had written to Grant that "we are not going to let a few thieving, ragged Indians check and stop the progress" of the railroads.

The railroads could be of some military help too. In an 1872 letter, Sherman advised that the progress of the Northern Pacific Railway

---

and cabinet secretary. Hoyt Sherman was a successful banker. Two of William Sherman's foster brothers served as major generals during the Civil War: Hugh Ewing, later an ambassador and author, and Thomas Ewing, who was a defense attorney in the military trials of the Lincoln assassination conspirators. And Sherman's niece, the pessimistically named Euthanasia Sherman Meade, was a pioneering female physician in California.

* Both were found guilty and sentenced to death but were later paroled.

should be assisted in every way by the military because doing so "will help to bring the Indian problem to a final solution."

His views had obviously not changed the following year when he wrote in a private letter that "during an assault, the soldiers cannot pause to distinguish between male and female, or even discriminate as to age. As long as resistance is made, death must be meted out."

Sherman also believed that bison eradication should be encouraged as a means of weakening Indian resistance to assimilation. He voiced this view in remarks to a joint session of the Texas legislature in 1875. He encouraged bison hunting by private citizens and, when Congress passed a law to protect the bison from overhunting, Sherman helped convince President Grant to use a pocket veto to dispose of the legislation.

"Few people fought harder to maintain their traditional way of life than the Indians of the Great Plains," states Herman J. Viola. "But courage could not overcome the railroad, the telegraph, and, above all, the extermination of the bison. As long as Plains Indians could live off the land, they were invincible. Nobody knew this better than the soldiers chasing them. That is one reason western army officers issued free ammunition to hide hunters who, along with diseases into the buffalo herds by domesticated livestock, helped the United States solve its 'Indian problem.'"

7

LITTLE PHIL

With Commanding General Sherman overseeing the entire U.S. Army, day-to-day operations in the West were handled by another prominent Civil War hero, Philip Sheridan. He had been born in Albany, New York, in March 1831. His parents were Irish Catholic immigrants from County Cavan who were soon on the move again, to Somerset, Ohio.

Small in stature, Sheridan reached only five feet, five inches tall, earning him the unenviable nickname "Little Phil." After first meeting him, President Lincoln described the young officer as a "brown, chunky little chap, with a long body, short legs, not enough neck to hang him, and such long arms that if his ankles itch he can scratch them without stooping."

In Somerset, Sheridan worked in a general store and later as head clerk and bookkeeper at a dry goods store. Fortunately, a regular customer was Representative Thomas Ritchey, who agreed to appoint the darkly handsome lad to West Point. Second Lieutenant Sheridan graduated in 1853, thirty-fourth in a class of fifty-two cadets. He was first assigned to Fort Duncan in Eagle Pass, Texas, and then Fort Reading in Anderson, California.

Sheridan's formative experience of war against an Indigenous population came during six years in the Oregon and Washington Territories as an officer in the Fourth U.S. Infantry Regiment and its participation in the Yakima and Rogue River Wars. He suffered his first wound in battle in March 1857 at Middle Cascade in Oregon when a bullet grazed his nose.

That experience in the Northwest territories was not all fighting—it included a live-in companion, Sidnayoh, a young woman whom his colleagues called Frances. The daughter of a Klickitat chief, she was in every way except legally Sheridan's wife.*

In March 1861, Phil Sheridan was finally promoted to first lieutenant, and perhaps to make up for the delay, he was elevated to captain just two months later, after the Civil War had begun. Rapid ascension would mark Sheridan's war years. Still in his early thirties, he was already a major general when Grant transferred Sheridan from command of an infantry division in the West to lead the Cavalry Corps of the Army of the Potomac.

In 1864, Sheridan defeated Confederate forces under General Jubal Early in the Shenandoah Valley. His destruction of the economic infrastructure of the valley, called "The Burning" by residents, was one of the first uses of scorched-earth tactics in the war. The following year, his cavalry doggedly pursued General Robert E. Lee and was instrumental in forcing his surrender at Appomattox Court House.

General Grant then devoted some attention to the situation in

---

* When Sheridan was reassigned to duty elsewhere, Sidnayoh did not go with him. From then on, he never acknowledged her existence. The woman who became his legal wife, Irene, in 1875, was a much better match in military circles, given that she was the daughter of the U.S. Army's Quartermaster General Daniel Rucker.

neighboring Mexico, where forty thousand French soldiers were propping up the puppet regime of Austrian Archduke Maximilian. He gave Sheridan permission to gather a large Texas force. Sheridan assembled fifty thousand men in three corps who quickly occupied Texas coastal cities and then spread inland while also patrolling the southern border.

The army's presence, U.S. political pressure, and the growing resistance of Benito Juárez induced the French to abandon their claims against Mexico. Subsequently, Mexico's republican army captured, tried, and executed Maximilian. Sheridan later admitted in his memoirs that he had supplied arms and ammunition to Juárez's forces that "we left at convenient places on our side of the river to fall into their hands."

Despite his mostly successful tenure there, Sheridan was not popular in Texas, and he did not have much appreciation for the state either. He once quipped, "If I owned Texas and Hell, I would rent Texas and live in Hell."

By 1875, Sheridan's base was in Chicago, from where he administered the Division of the Missouri. It was the largest and most turbulent military region in the United States. It extended from the Windy City west to the Rocky Mountains and the Canadian border south to northern Texas. The Great Plains took up some of that vast territory. It was estimated that the overall population of the various tribes in the district totaled 175,000 people. And, of course, thanks to the Oregon Trail, other trails, and the railroads, the white population under Sheridan's purview was increasing daily—as were their pleas for protection from hostiles.

To patrol and try to keep the peace—such as it was—between the Indian and wasichu societies in the district of one million square miles was a military that was an emaciated version of its former self. During the Civil War, over two million men had served in the Union military branches. Within a few years of the South's surrender, there were twenty-five thousand enlisted men in the U.S. Army. And they were not necessarily the cream of the crop.

According to James Donovan in *A Terrible Glory*, "Undeterred, undermanned, underpaid, undersupplied, undertrained, and underfed (a decade after Appomattox, Civil War–era hardtack was still being issued to frontier troops), the army Sheridan served faced a warrior culture that trained males from early childhood to fight, ride, and survive better than anyone else in the world. These people knew every hill and valley and water source in their wide land and eluded their pursuers with ease."

If defiant warriors would not come out and fight the soldiers in the open field, the soldiers would have to go and find them—and, when they did, burn their villages. By late 1875, the treaty that Red Cloud had signed seven years earlier at Fort Laramie seemed almost quaint, an unrealized dream for the Sioux and their allies. Protect Paha Sapa? Leave hunting grounds unspoiled? Provide Indians with gifts and food? Of course not, guffawed the expansionist politicians in Washington, DC, and investors in New York.

Though possessing more sympathy than his subordinates for the Indigenous tribes, President Grant had to find a way to accommodate the Manifest Destiny proponents while not ratcheting up public outcry over efforts to "exterminate" Indians. With being overrun by whites inevitable and the two societies too different and suspicious of each other to live side by side, the most humane solution was to create more reservations for Native communities.

But many headmen and their followers were not keen on being cornered in such nontraditional settings. They wanted to continue to roam and hunt at will, even while recognizing that they were hemmed in by white migration, railroad tracks, miners, entrepreneurs, and others for whom confining rebels on reservations was not an end but a beginning.

The holdover Civil War hierarchy of Grant, Sherman, and Sheridan convened. They concocted a plan to force the tribes onto their respective reservations. Clearly, combat with some resistors could not be avoided. The three men agreed that they needed a true fighting man in the field.

8

THE CUSTER CLAN

That man was George Armstrong Custer, who was far from being a hired thug. According to the eminent western historian Robert Utley in *Custer: Cavalier in Buckskin,* the young officer was a "complex man, enigmatic and full of contradictions. For the final decade of his life, the frontier years of 1866–76, he projected traits that made one set of contemporaries idolize him and another detest him. Hardly anyone regarded him with indifference."

Like his superiors Grant and Sherman, Custer was an Ohio native, born on a farm in New Rumley on December 5, 1839. His parents had met and married as widower and widow, and there were older siblings in the blended family. George was the first child Emanuel and Maria Custer had together. They would go on to have four more—Nevin, Thomas, Boston, and Margaret.

With his mother having her hands full and his father the busy farmer, much of the raising of the young stepsiblings was done by Maria's daughter Lydia Ann Kirkpatrick. "Autie"—the youngster's attempt at saying

Armstrong—who was fourteen years younger, would have a lifelong devotion to her. In fact, after Lydia married David Reed of Monroe, Michigan, Autie lived with them and attended school in the small town on Lake Erie. In the summers, he was back at the Custer farm to help with routine chores.

It was clear that the energetic and outgoing Autie was not cut out to be a farmer. He and his brothers Tom and Boston "grew up brimming with boyish exuberance," writes Utley. "Full of energy, good humor, and laughter, they engaged in strenuous athletics and even more strenuous horseplay. They inflicted the most ingenious and harrowing pranks on their father, who gave as good as he took."*

Though not as ardent a student as he was an athlete, Autie got through the Stebbins Academy and then the McNeely Normal School. In 1856, at only sixteen, Autie was considered qualified to teach grammar school. He had also added the pursuit of young women to his activities, and by several accounts, he was successful.

He was even less likely to be a teacher than a farmer. He may have considered other avenues, but a firm step was composing a letter to his congressman, John Bingham, asking to be appointed to the U.S. Military Academy. Given his pedestrian academic record, Autie was far from the ideal candidate, yet Bingham did provide the appointment.

Thus, a military career awaited—if the teenage Custer could make it through West Point. This proved to be much more difficult than anticipated.

---

* The other young Custer boy, Nevin, was often in poor health and exempt from being an instigator or target of pranks.

9

"GALLANT BOY"

During his four years at the U.S. Military Academy, Cadet Custer collected 726 "skins," or demerits, for a wide variety of infractions. Accumulating one hundred in a six-month period resulted in being kicked out, and Custer managed, barely, to avoid that. And he also managed to see West Point through—again, barely, graduating thirty-fourth in a class of thirty-four.

This dubious distinction would soon not matter. For George Armstrong Custer, war was his much-preferred classroom. And there, he would be at the top of his class.

He received a commission as a second lieutenant in the Second Regiment of the U.S. Cavalry upon his graduation in June 1861. With the Civil War two months old, it appeared there would be almost limitless opportunities for achievement and glory in battle. Sadly for some, the war would include former classmates clashing with each other because some of the newly minted army officers chose to fight for the Confederate States of America.

The first action Custer saw was literally that—he saw instead of participated. The Second Regiment stood idly by, without orders, as the Battle of Manassas unfolded in July. The result was an ignominious defeat for the Union army, leading to a humiliating retreat in the rain that night back to the Potomac River.

There was little more than frustration for cavalry officers wearing blue early in the war. While on the other side daring leaders like Jeb Stuart and Jubal Early were beginning to demonstrate how effective horse soldiers could be, Union generals used Custer and other cavalrymen as little more than messengers, with the occasional scouting mission thrown in. Even less promising was when the Fifth Cavalry, the former Second Cavalry, was assigned to do nothing more than be one of the units protecting Washington, DC, from attack.

Then, what would become known as "Custer's Luck" intervened. In the spring of 1862, as the Peninsula Campaign was getting underway, he was plucked from the dawdling cavalry regiment and put on the staff of General William Smith. As an aide-de-camp to "Baldy," as the general was known, and promoted to captain, Custer came into frequent contact with General George McClellan, who commanded the Army of the Potomac.

Soon, General Smith was down one aide-de-camp. "Little Mac" had taken a liking to the young captain with the long light-brown hair, and he invited Custer to join his staff. The position allowed him to range far and wide during the campaign. Perhaps too zealously for a staff officer, Custer got close to the action so he could report observations to McClellan. The cautious commander would have been appalled to know that his twenty-two-year-old staffer was often in the middle of fighting, going so far as to rally retreating troops and lead charges against the Confederates.

What he did know about the captain's perambulations during the Peninsula Campaign allowed McClellan to write that Custer "was a reckless, gallant boy, undeterred by fatigue, unconscious of fear; but his head was always clear in danger and he always brought me clear and intelligible reports of what he saw. I became much attached to him."

Having the top commander's favor was a plus for any young officer, but Custer was a cavalryman craving action, not being a mere messenger. Yet the "attached" advantage was taken away too when the overly cautious McClellan, whose only significant (and dubious) victory had been the bloody battle in Antietam, Maryland, in September 1862, was relieved of command by a frustrated President Lincoln that November. The new commander of the Army of the Potomac was General Ambrose Burnside, and he brought his own staff with him.

Perhaps Custer's career as a field officer was already over. With an inactive winter approaching, the distressed captain rode to Monroe, Michigan, to contemplate his future.

10

THE BEAUTIFUL BACON GIRL

During the winter of 1862–63, George Custer saw action on a different front. A prominent citizen in Monroe was Judge Daniel Bacon, and he had a daughter, twenty-year-old Elizabeth. She was both beautiful and intelligent, and the combination made her especially desirable. What chance did a furloughed staff officer with a meager captain's salary have?

Next to none. She disapproved of Custer's drinking and swearing and the attention paid to him by other available Monroe women. The biggest obstacle to the officer's ardent admiration for Libbie was that her father was staunchly opposed. It would be a totally unsuitable match for his well-born, privileged, and only daughter.

But Custer had faced more imposing odds. He vowed to drink and curse no more.* He wooed Libbie, and she had to allow that a major advantage the captain had was she found him handsome and charismatic—no wonder other women flocked around him. But if her father was opposed . . .

* Except for the rare swearing lapse, Custer kept to his vow.

The courtship was put on hold in April when Custer was ordered back to the Army of the Potomac. Maybe he could jump-start his career, especially if there was as much or more action than the previous fighting season. At first, though, the ambitious captain went backward, being demoted to a first lieutenant.

But soon, good news trumped the bad. There was a series of shake-ups in the high command of the Army of Potomac. The post-McClellan tenure of General Ambrose Burnside had been short-lived thanks to an embarrassing defeat at the Battle of Fredericksburg the previous December. His replacement was General Joseph Hooker. "Fighting Joe" would not live up to his nickname, but Hooker did two things that improved Custer's situation: He figured out how to employ the cavalry's lightning-strike abilities, and he appointed Custer to the staff of General Alfred Pleasonton.*

The thirty-nine-year-old Pleasonton was not afraid to fight, especially with cavalry leading the charge. That attitude appealed to Custer, whose loyalty shifted from the sidelined McClellan to the new division commander. Also appealing was that in June, when Pleasonton was promoted from brigadier to major general, Custer regained his captain's commission. The general immediately saw Custer as a younger kindred spirit. It was time to attack and turn the tide of war.

This was still true when Hooker was himself replaced following the failure at Chancellorsville.† General George Meade was the next

---

* Pleasonton's father, Stephen, had achieved some fame during the War of 1812. As a U.S. State Department staffer, he had saved crucial documents in the National Archives from destruction by British soldiers sacking Washington, DC, including the original Declaration of Independence and the U.S. Constitution.

† The Union Army lost the battle but may have won the war at Chancellorsville, when Confederate General "Stonewall" Jackson was mistakenly shot and killed by his own troops.

commander of the Army of the Potomac. "Old Snapping Turtle" barely had time to relocate his tent when General Robert E. Lee's forces were found entering Gettysburg, Pennsylvania.

An officer eager to take on the Rebs was General George Armstrong Custer.

General? This was more than "Custer's Luck"; it was an absolute fantasy become bizarre reality. Pleasonton had sent up the chain of command the required paperwork to elevate Custer and two other captains in rank so that they could lead larger fighting units. As Lee's Confederate forces furtively curved up toward Pennsylvania, a letter arrived at Pleasonton's headquarters addressed "Brigadier General George A. Custer, U.S. Volunteers."

However it happened, the envelope's contents confirmed that the incredible news was true: At age twenty-three, Custer had become the youngest general in the Union army.

This inexplicable promotion might have been sorted out and even rescinded over time, but then came the Battle of Gettysburg. Probably the two most famous actions in that fierce three-day engagement were Joshua Chamberlain and the Twentieth Maine's stubborn defense of Little Round Top on the second day and Pickett's Charge on the third day. Often overlooked, even with his subsequent legendary status in American history, was the pivotal role Custer also played on the decisive third day.

11

"COME ON, YOU WOLVERINES!"

General Pleasanton did not question the sudden promotion—he was only too happy to hand the "Boy General" command of the Second Brigade of the Third Division, which included the First, Fifth, Sixth, and Seventh Regiments of Michigan Cavalry. The members of the brigade had barely learned the name of their new commander by the time Lee's and Meade's armies met at Gettysburg on July 1, 1863.

After two days of almost relentless fighting, on the afternoon of the third day an improvising General Robert E. Lee took two actions. One was to place 12,500 troops under the command of General George Pickett, with orders to smash the Union center on Cemetery Ridge, splitting the Army of the Potomac. The other was to have the vaunted Confederate cavalry under General James Ewell Brown (Jeb) Stuart circle completely around the Union army to the east of Gettysburg and attack from the rear.

As we know, the action called Pickett's Charge came close, but not close enough. More than half of the men launched at Cemetery Ridge were killed, wounded, or captured. But the offstage clash involving Custer and Jeb Stuart was pivotal too.

Three Union brigades readied themselves to repulse the cavalry assault, with one of them commanded by Custer. The newly minted general had seen combat before, but he had never led so many soldiers at such a crucial juncture in a battle. When Stuart attacked, the men from Michigan held fast. But they soon ran low on ammunition and were in danger of being overrun.

The overall Union commander on the scene, General David Gregg, brought up the Seventh Michigan to bolster the Fifth's position. Suddenly, Custer leaped from one unit to another. On horseback, he cried out, "Come on, you Wolverines!" He charged at the Confederates with a host of inspired horsemen behind him.

There would be several charges that afternoon spearheaded by Custer, some involving hand-to-hand fighting with Stuart's forces. For the first time in the war, Union cavalry defeated their Confederate counterparts. That and the failure of Pickett's rebels resulted in Lee's overall defeat. During the night, in a rainstorm, the Army of Northern Virginia began its retreat to Virginia.

"On July 3, 1863, George Armstrong Custer came of age," declares Robert Utley. "In one spectacular burst he emerged a general in fact as well as name. Nor was Gettysburg a splashy anomaly. In the Union cavalry's harassment of Lee's retreat from Pennsylvania and in the subsequent maneuvers of the two armies in Virginia, Custer displayed superior leadership time and again."

Soon there was another conquest to attend to. In September 1863, after suffering a minor wound, Custer was given leave to return to Monroe. He scored another victory as Judge Bacon withdrew his opposition to the heroic general with the long locks. Custer had to go back to war—which included defeating Stuart again at Brandy Station—but eventually, in February 1864, Custer and Libbie were married. After a brief honeymoon, it was back to war once more.

12

CLOSE TO CATASTROPHE

Considering how much fighting he was involved in, it is something of a miracle that Custer survived the war. Indeed, he thrived on combat, always leading from the front and emerging unscathed. In one particularly pivotal battle, at Yellow Tavern in May 1864, Custer's cavalry not only defeated Jeb Stuart again, but the legendary rebel leader was also killed.

Another significant event for Custer was bureaucratic. After a series of successes in the West, Ulysses Grant was elevated to lieutenant general and given command of all Union armies. After installing himself above Meade with the Army of the Potomac, he installed Philip Sheridan as head of the Union cavalry. He quickly cottoned to Custer, recognizing his courage and energetic leadership. When Grant ordered Sheridan to take forty thousand men and rid the Shenandoah Valley of Confederates, the cavalry leader brought Custer with him. Their chief adversary would be General Jubal Early.

It was one victory after another for Sheridan's army. At the Battle of Winchester in September 1864, an all-day battle was decided when

Custer, brandishing his saber, led a charge of five hundred men and the Confederate defensive line crumpled. A week later, at Fisher's Hill, Sheridan's forces triumphed again. Soon after, Custer was awarded command of the Third Division. The troops welcomed him by wearing red neckties, which had become one of Custer's trademarks.

Sheridan's army advanced through the Shenandoah Valley, brushing aside Early's battered Confederates. At the Battle of Tom's Brook, another charge led by Custer and his swinging saber crushed the rebel cavalry and sent the remnants fleeing for miles.

The streak of victories culminated with the Battle of Cedar Creek—though the Union force initially had to avert catastrophe, which it did thanks to Custer. Sheridan had left his army to meet with Grant and others in Washington, DC. On October 19, in heavy fog, Early attacked before dawn and completely surprised many of the sleeping Union soldiers. His smaller army battered segments of the Union army from multiple sides. The bluecoats would have been completely overwhelmed if Custer had not pushed his division into the breach and offered some stability in the center of the line.

At about 10:00 A.M., Early, delighted with the results thus far, paused his attack to reorganize his forces. A half hour later, with very fortunate timing, General Sheridan, who had been on a train returning from Washington, arrived at the battlefield, having ridden in a rush from the train station. His dramatic appearance bolstered and revitalized his retreating army. That afternoon, Sheridan led a counterattack, making use of his superior cavalry force under Custer. Early's army was routed and fled south.

As a result of this snatching defeat from the jaws of victory outcome of the battle, the Confederate army was never again able to maneuver down the Shenandoah Valley to threaten Washington, DC, or northern states. Additionally, the verdant valley had been a key producer of supplies for the Confederate army, and Early could no longer protect it.

In gratitude, Sheridan designated Custer as the senior officer to lead a delegation to the capital. He was accompanied by thirteen soldiers, each carrying a captured Confederate battle flag. With his wife proudly observing the festivities, Custer presented the flags to Secretary of War Edwin Stanton, who in turn announced that the courageous cavalryman was now Major General George Custer.

13

"GALLANT HUSBAND"

The final defeat of Early's forces in the Shenandoah Valley came early the following March, when units of the Third Division attacked and overwhelmed what remained of the Confederate army. Sheridan and Custer were now free to join Grant for the final campaign against Lee's Army of Northern Virginia. By then, one of the Third Division's lieutenants was Tom Custer, about to turn twenty years old.

General Custer distinguished himself in several actions during the campaign. The most significant was at Sayler's Creek on April 6, 1865. Led by the Third Division, Union forces assaulted and captured nine thousand rebels, including seven generals. Also that day, Tom Custer earned the second of two Medals of Honor.

The first action took place on April 3. During fighting near the Namozine Church in Amelia County, Virginia, while Union troops were trying to dislodge a unit of rebels, George's younger brother rode up under fire and captured the Confederate flag. The action three days later was similar, but even more scintillating: During the Battle of Sayler's Creek,

Tom Custer leaped over southern breastworks, seized another Confederate flag, was shot in the face, killed the color-bearer, and returned to the Union lines with a flapping flag. His commanding officer was quite impressed (maybe even envious) and relieved that the facial wound was not serious.*

Subsequent actions involving General Custer put him in Lee's only remaining line of march as his troops camped at Appomattox Station on April 8. At dawn the next day, as the Third Division was preparing yet another attack, a man on a horse displaying a white towel approached. He carried a request from General Lee to meet with General Grant. According to Utley, "Fittingly, this emblem of war's end came to the young general who, by age twenty-five, had written a record of military exploits that few soldiers exhibit in a lifetime."

As a token of his appreciation for such selfless and successful service, at the Appomattox Court House, after the surrender ceremony concluded, Sheridan paid twenty dollars for the table on which Lee had signed the document. He had it sent, with a note praising her husband, to Libbie Custer: "Permit me to say, Madam," Sheridan concluded, "that there is scarcely an individual in our service who has contributed more to bring about this desirable result than your gallant husband."

A drawback to achieving so much at twenty-five is perhaps having peaked at twenty-five. After the surrender, Custer found himself a warrior without a war. But soon, the American West beckoned.

---

* There have been nineteen men who have received two Medals of Honor—five of them for the same action, and fourteen of them, like Tom Custer, for separate acts of valor.

14

FALL FROM GRACE

There was one more act of recognition. On May 23, 1865, the Army of the Potomac paraded down Pennsylvania Avenue, which included passing the White House. As the Third Division, its members sporting red neckties, neared the building and President Andrew Johnson's review, something spooked General Custer's horse. His blue hat was lifted off his head as the horse took off. The president and others on the reviewing stand were bemused as the young officer, his long golden hair like a comet's tail, raced past much of the army. The startling sight was a metaphor for Custer's career thus far.

By the following year, he would be merely a captain again, and he and Libbie would live in much-reduced circumstances. As did many other postwar officers, Custer could have left the military. The U.S. Army and its budget shrank drastically. At the top level were General of the Army Ulysses Grant and General William Sherman. At the lower levels, there was virtually no opportunity for promotion unless a superior officer died or retired. And no longer were there battle-related brevet promotions, which had inflated the upper ranks.

Those ranks became a bit complicated after the Civil War. Actually, they were already complicated. During the war, a Union officer could hold a full rank in the regular army, a full rank in the volunteers, and brevet, or temporary, ranks in both—four ranks at once. Medals, such as the Silver Star and Distinguished Service Cross, did not exist during the Civil War, so the reward for battlefield bravery or achievement was a brevet rank. After the war, most brevet promotions were rescinded. Thus, General Custer reverted to Captain Custer. However, an officer was entitled to be addressed by his wartime rank, and in Custer's case, those serving under him and other officers referred to him as "General."*

He explored options, including obtaining a Wall Street position in New York City. Politics was a possibility, but his skills in the field and courage under fire did not translate to backroom business battles. When his patron, Phil Sheridan, came through with a leap to lieutenant colonel, Custer, with Libbie in tow, was glad to take his new commission west, to the frontier. At Fort Riley in north-central Kansas, he assumed nominal command of the Seventh Cavalry.†

The unit's postwar experience was similar to that of other army regiments—fewer men, fewer officers, and fewer noncombatants (noncoms) as well as much less action than during wartime. This made for a

---

* Of course, officers who had fought for the South did not have rank complications after the war because the Confederate army ceased to exist.

† Because command of an army regiment required someone with the rank of colonel, the official commander of the Seventh was Andrew Jackson Smith. As an older officer aiming to retire soon—he graduated West Point a year before Custer was born—Smith was not about to lead troopers on horseback over even the smoothest terrain.

boring existence for the men in uniform, and for officers' wives too. Libbie was surrounded by young officers and scouts, some of them quite handsome. One in particular caught her eye—another long-haired legend in the making: James Butler Hickok.

Known along the frontier as Wild Bill, he served for a time as a scout for the Seventh Cavalry when it was stationed at Fort Riley. When Libbie encountered him there, she was obviously smitten: "Tall, lithe, and free in every motion, he rode and walked as if every muscle was perfection, and the careless swing of his body as he moved seemed perfectly in keeping with the man, the country, the time in which he lived," she gushed in her memoir *Following the Guidon*. "I do not recall anything finer in the way of physical perfection than Wild Bill when he swung himself lightly from his saddle, and with graceful, swaying step, squarely set his shoulders and well-poised head, approached our tent for orders."

His wife's lonely susceptibility to other men who quite rightly found Libbie attractive explains how it came to be that Custer was court-martialed and his career almost ended.

While in search of hostiles in July 1867, a weary Seventh Cavalry stopped outside Fort Wallace. The troopers expected some time to be taken for men and horses to rest and to take on fresh supplies. Instead, Custer led some of them—seventy-two men and four officers culled from the regiment—on a bizarre trek in the direction back to Fort Riley. The cavalry commander justified the journey with only an apparently overwhelming desire to see Libbie—possibly with some jealousy mixed in.

What ensued was a forced march of 150 miles in the midsummer heat. That was bad enough for the seventy-six men having to endure it, but an avoidable death occurred too. Custer sent a sergeant and six men in search of a missing mare. They were ambushed by Indians and one of the men was killed. Custer did not pause to wait for the survivors of the detail to catch up.

Arriving at Fort Harker, Custer barely offered an excuse to his commander, a startled Colonel Smith, before boarding the train to Fort Riley. When Smith thought more clearly about Custer's sudden appearance and then disappearance, he issued orders for the young officer's arrest. Among the charges was being absent without leave from his command and abandoning the detail that had been attacked.

On October 11, at Fort Leavenworth, Custer was court-martialed and found guilty. The verdict was approved by a disappointed General Sheridan, who now headed the Department of the Missouri. The sentence handed down was suspension from duty and pay for one year.

Finally feeling defeated, Custer "may well have been plunged into what a later generation would call an identity crisis," notes Robert Utley. "With the glory days behind and the future unclear but apparently unpromising, he had to sort out and come to grips with who he was and who he wanted to be. The civilian world looked enticing, especially in offering the possibility of wealth and the certainty of a married life untroubled by long separations."

In a scenario eerily to be repeated nine years later, Lieutenant Colonel Custer was called back to service before his punishment concluded because the frontier army needed him. Certainly, the Seventh Cavalry did.

15

ASHES ON HIS BOOT

During Custer's absence, the grizzled Colonel Smith had allowed discipline to diminish. This was true of most frontier units. Many officers felt exiled, and their authority eroded. Soldiers at frontier forts endured long stretches of time subjected to extremes in weather, isolation, and fear of the unknown surrounding them. There were very few entertainments, including female companionship. And all this for $13 a month.

Unsurprisingly, desertions were rampant, as was alcohol abuse, immobilizing some officers as well as troopers. A particularly sad example was Robert Wycliffe Cooper, a major in the Seventh Cavalry. During the war he received battle honors for his service at Shiloh, Corinth, Richmond, Chickamauga, Morgan's Raid into Kentucky, the Battle of Resaca, and Wilson's Raid on Montgomery. But the frontier was a far different and more difficult setting. In 1867, Cooper killed himself while in a fit of delirium tremens.

Given the poor condition of the troops, it was no wonder that campaigns conducted by General John Hancock (another hero of Gettysburg) and other commanders had been ineffective. The Plains tribes, though dwindling in numbers, still roamed free, only reluctantly—and when it suited them—remaining on newly established reservations. The beleaguered army needed an officer with much more fight in him.

In the summer of 1868, Custer was back home, in Monroe, uncharacteristically bedeviled by inertia, when a telegram arrived from Sheridan: "Generals Sherman, Sully and myself, and nearly all the officers of your regiment, have asked for you, and I hope the application will be successful. Can you come at once?"

Custer could, and when he returned to the frontier, he intended to whip the Seventh Cavalry back into shape. Among the officers he put to work on restoring the regiment to fighting trim were the Ireland-born Captain Myles Keogh; the Canada-born Lieutenant William Cooke; Louis Hamilton, a captain at only twenty-two; Lieutenant Donald McIntosh, who was half Scotch, half Native; Lieutenant Thomas Weir; Captain Tom Custer; Captain Frederick Benteen, who though not a Custer admirer at least had experience fighting Indians on the frontier; and the battle-scarred Major Joel Elliott, who twice had survived serious wounds during the war.

The transition took some time, but when the Seventh arrived in the Washita River Valley that November, it was a formidable fighting force—as the unfortunate Black Kettle and his Cheyenne families found out.

The Washita River "battle" gave new life to Custer's career. Journalists as well as his own superior officers portrayed him as the fightingest Indian fighter on the frontier. This was good PR for the overall 1868–69 campaign against the western tribes. But there were issues connected to the Washita attack that would linger for Custer.

One was the fate of Major Joel Elliott. When last seen, he was leading a detachment of nineteen troopers across the river to find any Cheyenne fleeing that way. Firing was heard from that direction. When the regiment and its captives moved out, there was still no sign of Elliott's ad hoc command. Custer and his other officers had no idea that the detachment had been wiped out by Cheyenne and Arapaho warriors.

Where did those additional warriors come from? As would be repeated less than eight years later, Custer had gone into battle not knowing the size of the overall Indian encampment. Ironically, Black Kettle had positioned his village upstream from a much larger collection of Indians because he figured if the army was going to attack anyone, it would be the more defiant and enticing grouping, not his small and peaceful band.

By the time the soldiers of the Seventh Cavalry realized there were more Indians than anticipated, the twenty troopers in the Elliott detachment were dead. Warriors from three larger villages—Kiowa as well as Cheyenne and Arapaho—hearing the commotion in the small Cheyenne camp, had put on war paint, grabbed their weapons, and galloped upstream. Like Black Kettle, Elliott and his men were in the wrong place at the wrong time, being the only troopers caught and killed by the much larger force of warriors.

Not one to retreat with his tail between his legs, Custer employed a tactic he would use again at Little Bighorn. When it dawned on him that his regiment could possibly be outnumbered and even outgunned, he attacked. With the band apprehensively playing "Ain't I Glad to Get Out of the Wilderness" and with the sun soon to set, the regiment with colors flying marched downstream.

The tactic worked. The Indians, fearing for the safety of their families, peeled off the hills and rushed toward the villages. As darkness descended on the valley, Custer ordered a countermarch. Reeling in their colors and with the band silenced, the Seventh Cavalry swung around and headed back upstream. A forced, all-night march put the regiment far out of harm's way.

On December 2, Custer led his men into Camp Supply. He proclaimed victory over a hostile force and turned over the captive women and children—supposedly, with the exception of Monahsetah. In his book *My Life on the Plains*, published in 1874, Custer described her as "a woman of rare beauty."

The Seventh Cavalry was sent out several more times during the next four months to demonstrate that there could be an effective winter campaign against the tribes. There was indeed a campaign, but it was not terribly effective. The Cheyenne, the primary target, proved elusive, and the weather conditions were daunting. Finally, on March 28, the ragged and worn-out regiment returned to Camp Supply and stayed there.

Two weeks earlier, Custer had rashly decided to meet with his adversaries and thereby created one more issue that would reverberate all the way to June 1876. The Seventh Cavalry had been tracking evidence of Cheyenne lodges on the move into Texas, and when Custer and his troopers arrived at Sweetwater Creek, they found not one but two villages consisting of over 250 lodges.

Even the aggressive cavalry commander knew his men were too weary to mount a successful attack against so many Cheyenne. But it also made no sense, having come this far and after such exhausting effort, to simply turn around and slink away. So, Custer decided he would visit the combined village with only his adjutant, Lieutenant Cooke, accompanying him.

Puzzled warriors escorted them to the lodge of the overall Cheyenne head man, Medicine Arrows. He invited the officers to sit by the fire and participate in a pipe ritual. After passing the pipe around, Medicine Arrows deferred to his chief medicine man, who tapped the remaining ashes onto the toe of Custer's boot. The medicine man told Custer that the Cheyenne would keep the peace promised that day, but if Custer and his soldiers betrayed the Cheyenne, they would all die.

Even if Custer did not understand every word, the message was clear. He should have listened.

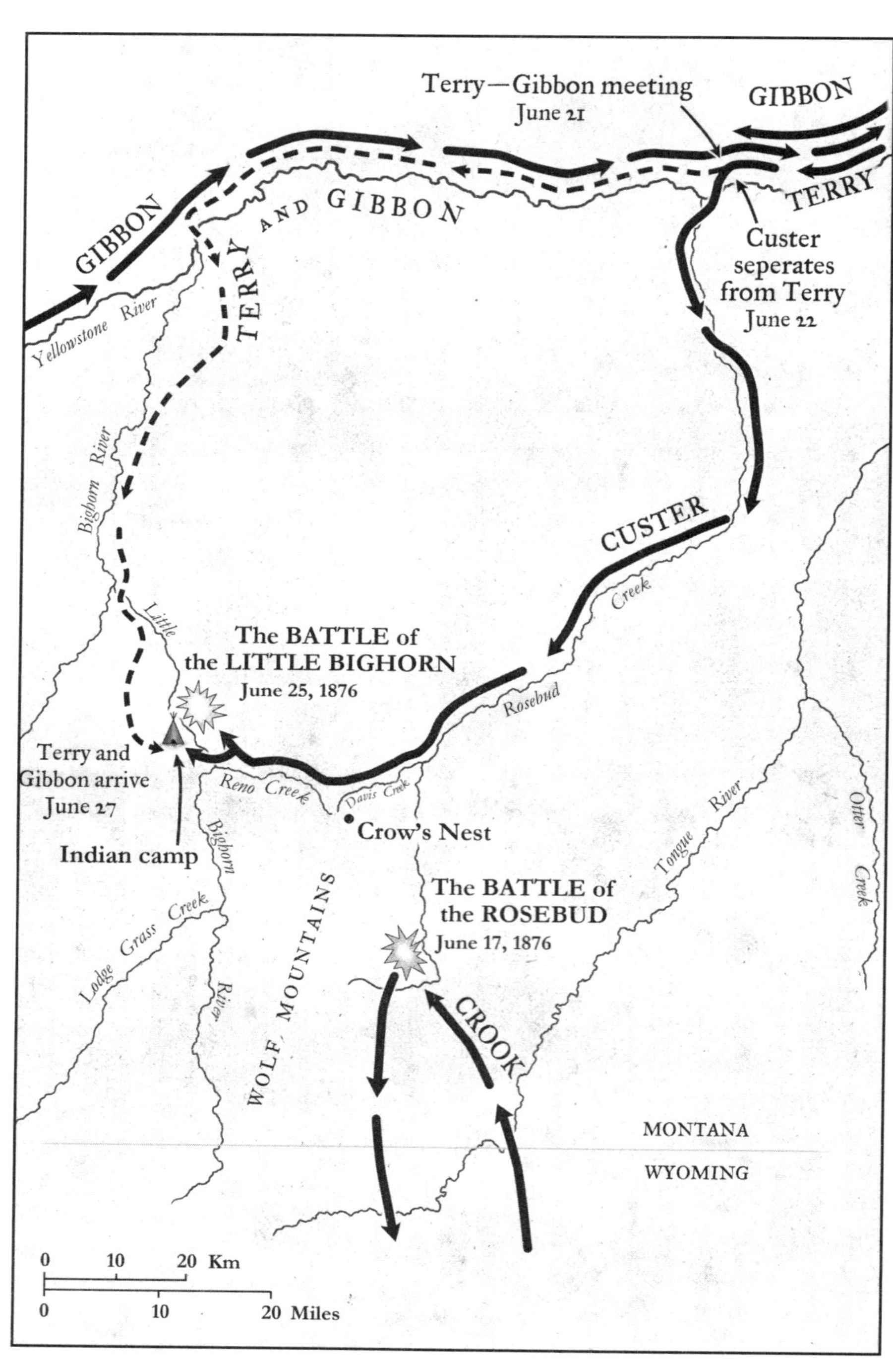
Terry—Gibbon meeting
June 21
GIBBON
TERRY
Custer
seperates
from Terry
June 22
GIBBON
TERRY AND GIBBON
Yellowstone River
Bighorn River
CUSTER
Creek
Rosebud
Little
The BATTLE of
the LITTLE BIGHORN
June 25, 1876
Terry and
Gibbon arrive
June 27
Indian camp
Reno Creek
Davis Creek
Crow's Nest
Bighorn
River
Lodge Grass Creek
WOLF MOUNTAINS
The BATTLE of
the ROSEBUD
June 17, 1876
CROOK
Tongue River
Otter Creek
MONTANA
WYOMING
0 10 20 Km
0 10 20 Miles

ACT II

THE DEFENDERS

If we must die, we die defending our rights.

—**SITTING BULL**

16

SITTING BULL'S WAR

With Red Cloud having retired to preside over the Oglala reservation in northwest Nebraska, the leadership of the Lakota Sioux fell to a Hunkpapa—who was ready for the role.

According to Stephen Ambrose, "Sitting Bull was an extraordinary man for any race at any time, and such a man is of necessity complex. He was all that the whites thought he was, and much more. He was an orator, a philosopher, an adviser, a propagandist for his cause, a lay preacher, a teacher, a husband and father, a healer of the sick, a psychiatrist, a political leader, and a man. In somewhat the same way [as Red Cloud's War], the struggle that began in 1872 and lasted until 1877 is sometimes called Sitting Bull's War."

According to family oral tradition, Sitting Bull was born in 1831 along the Yellowstone River, south of present-day Miles City, Montana, to Jumping Bull and Her-Holy-Door. He was named Jumping Badger at birth and nicknamed "Slow" because of his careful and unhurried nature.

When Jumping Badger was fourteen years old, he accompanied a group of Lakota warriors, who included his father and his uncle Four Horns, on a raid to take horses from a camp of Crow warriors. He displayed bravery by riding forward and counting coup on one of the surprised Crow, which was witnessed by the other mounted Lakota.

Counting coup was not the most practical warfare against whites, but it was the gold standard of fighting behavior among the Sioux. "Unlike whites, the Indians did not fight to kill, but to win prestige," explains Ambrose. "The highest honors went to the man who touched a live enemy with a bow, spear, or hand. Killing an enemy from a distance with an arrow or bullet carried almost no prestige with it because in the Native view it took no great bravery to fire a weapon at a distant enemy. Although the Indians would never have admitted it, their system of honors—common to all Plains tribes—had the salutary effect of holding down the losses. And since the plains were underpopulated and every able-bodied man was required for the hunt, holding down losses was crucial."

Upon returning to camp from the raid, Jumping Bull gave a celebratory feast at which he conferred a new name on his son. In the Lakota language, it roughly translates to "Buffalo Bull Who Sits Down." At this ceremony before the entire band, the newly christened Sitting Bull was presented with an eagle feather to wear in his hair, a warrior's horse, and a hardened buffalo hide shield to mark his passage into manhood as a Lakota warrior.

He did not use his status to advocate war against the whites to slow down the migrant intrusion. Initially, he felt the opposite: Sitting Bull urged his people to leave the Oregon Trail and withdraw to the ways of their ancestors. "I don't want to have anything to do with people who make one carry water on their shoulders and haul manure. The whites may get me at last, but I will have a good time till then. You are fools to make yourselves slaves to a piece of fat bacon, some hardtack, and a little sugar and coffee."

But subsequent events were beyond his control. Sitting Bull's first

experience of fighting white soldiers came as a consequence of the Dakota War of 1862, even though the Hunkpapa were not directly involved. Several bands of eastern Dakota killed at least three hundred and possibly as many as eight hundred settlers and soldiers in south-central Minnesota in response to poor treatment by the government and in an effort to drive the whites away.

Though in the midst of the Civil War, the U.S. Army retaliated in 1863 and 1864, even against Indians who had not been involved in the violence. In 1864, a force of about 2,200 soldiers under Brigadier General Alfred Sully attacked a Sioux village. The defenders of that village were led by Sitting Bull, Gall, and Inkpaduta.* The Lakota and Dakota were driven out, but skirmishing continued into August at the Battle of the Badlands.

The long-game strategy employed by Sitting Bull and other Sioux leaders was to have more of a running skirmish than an all-out fight, to harass the soldiers, impede their advance, and deprive them and their horses of water. That strategy came close to working after the end of the skirmishes as General Sully and his men struggled across parched desert to reach the Yellowstone River, some fifty miles distant. The men were on short rations and only a pint of coffee each, made with alkaline water, per day. The livestock of the expedition died of thirst in large numbers.

On August 12, 1864, the soldiers reached the Yellowstone and found there two steamboats loaded with supplies. However, because of the lack

* Though today he is one of the least-known Great Plains leaders, Inkpaduta was a courageous and durable warrior and headman. Born in 1797, he became a leader of the Santee Sioux Indians at the battles of Big Mound, Dead Buffalo Lake, and Whitestone Hill, the latter in North Dakota in 1863. The following year, however, after the Battle of Killdeer Mountain, Inkpaduta was forced to flee to Canada. He would return, and though in his late seventies with failing eyesight, he fought in the Battle of the Little Bighorn. He passed away in Canada in 1881 at age eighty-four.

of grass for horses and low water, Sully marched downstream. He found on his arrival at Fort Union at the junction of the Yellowstone and Missouri Rivers that the Sioux had stampeded and stolen all but two of the horses belonging to the fort. Lacking mounts and with an army of worn-out men, Sully abandoned his plan to continue the expedition against the Sioux.

That September, Sitting Bull and about a hundred Hunkpapa encountered a small civilian party near what is now Marmarth, North Dakota. They had been left behind by a wagon train escorted by a cavalry contingent to try to repair an overturned wagon. As he led the attack, Sitting Bull was shot in the left hip. The bullet exited through the small of his back and the wound was not as serious as it could have been.

But the wasichu had drawn blood. Sitting Bull would not forget.

17

SOLDIERS FALLING FROM THE SKY

Sitting Bull's participation in Red Cloud's War was often obscured by the leadership of the Oglala headman and the exploits of the young and dynamic Crazy Horse. But the Hunkpapa led numerous war parties against the army outposts at Fort Berthold, Fort Stevenson, and Fort Buford.

Sitting Bull rejoiced when the U.S. government asked for peace and the three forts on the Bozeman Trail were burned, but he did not agree to sign the Treaty of Fort Laramie. He told the Jesuit missionary Pierre Jean De Smet, "I wish all to know that I do not propose to sell any part of my country."* He continued his hit-and-run attacks on forts in the upper Missouri area and refused to live on a reservation.

In 1871, when the Northern Pacific Railway conducted a survey for

* Father De Smet is one of the more remarkable figures in the history of the American frontier. His missionary work among dozens of tribes, from the 1830s almost to his death at seventy-two in 1873, covered an estimated 180,000 miles as he roamed throughout the western United States and Canada. One

a route across the northern plains directly through Hunkpapa lands, it encountered stiff resistance from warriors led by Sitting Bull. The same railway surveyors returned the following year accompanied by federal troops. Sitting Bull and the Hunkpapa attacked the survey party, which was forced to turn back.

The railroad company's bankruptcy and the subsequent Panic of 1873 resulted in a decline in the pressure to pierce Sioux sovereignty. However, a turning point for Sitting Bull and other Lakota leaders of his generation was President Ulysses Grant's edict in November 1875 that all Indian bands outside the Great Sioux Reservation had to move onto the reservation.* The following February 1, the Interior Department certified as hostile those Indians who continued to live off the reservation. This certification allowed the military to pursue Sitting Bull and other hostiles. The Lakota coalition, which included Cheyenne and with Sitting Bull as the ostensible head, became the primary target of the federal government's pacification program.

Sitting Bull's position as leader of the coalition was itself certified in the summer of 1875, when the Northern Cheyenne, Hunkpapa, Oglala, Sans Arc, and Miniconjou camped together for a Sun Dance. This sacred ceremony includes dances and songs passed down through many generations, the use of a traditional drum, a fire, praying and the passing of a pipe, fasting from food and water before participating in the dance, the ceremonial piercing of skin, and trials of physical endurance.

The Sun Dance was a grueling ordeal for the dancers, a physical and spiritual test that they offered in sacrifice for their people. Young men

---

of the affectionate nicknames bestowed on De Smet by Indians was the "Great Black Skirt."

* The Great Sioux Reservation—designated by the U.S. government, not the Sioux—was much of the western half of what is now South Dakota.

danced around a pole to which they were fastened by rawhide thongs pegged through the skin of their chests. Piercing was accomplished using skewers or needles through a small fold of skin on the upper chest or back. Leather was then used to attach a buffalo skull or other heavy weight to the skewers. A dancer would dance while bearing the weight until he collapsed or the skin was torn loose. At most such ceremonies, family members and friends prayed in support of the dancers.

Sioux men believed that only by subjecting the body to excruciating physical suffering could they release the spirit imprisoned in the flesh and come to understand the true meaning of life. This was no mere quest for spiritual enlightenment. It was the key to gaining a physical edge, to avoiding bad luck and illness, and to ensuring success during the hunt and in battle. Warriors felt that completing the Sun Dance ceremony made them much harder to kill.

It was at this gathering that Sitting Bull had a major revelation. At the climactic moment, he intoned, "The Great Spirit has given our enemies to us. We are to destroy them. We do not know who they are. They may be soldiers."

Reports of this revelation spread. Many members of various Sioux bands and other tribes, such as the Northern Cheyenne, came to Sitting Bull's camp. His reputation for "strong medicine" developed as he continued to evade the wasichu soldiers.

Thus, when the U.S. Army began to enforce Grant's edict, with increasing frequency warriors and their families arrived to gather around Sitting Bull's lodge. He took an active role in encouraging this "unity camp." He sent scouts to the reservations to recruit warriors and told the Hunkpapa to share supplies with those who joined them. An example of his generosity was Sitting Bull's provision for Wooden Leg's Northern Cheyenne tribe. They had been impoverished by a March 1876 attack by army troopers and fled to Sitting Bull's camp for food and shelter.

Over the course of the first half of the year, Sitting Bull's camp continually expanded as more bands joined him for safety in numbers. His leadership had attracted warriors and families, creating an extensive village of several thousand people. In mid-June, an epic Sun Dance performed by Sitting Bull inspired awe and the belief that war with the wasichu was inevitable.

Because of his religious devotion and belief in a connection with his ancestors, Sitting Bull, though at forty-five much older than many of the other participants, took part in the ceremony on June 6 at the large camp in the Rosebud River Valley. He offered one hundred pieces of flesh from his arms as a sacrifice. Despite the loss of blood coupled with the requisite fasting, Sitting Bull danced throughout the night until he finally fainted.

When he awoke, he had startling news to tell his family and followers. He had a vision of soldiers attacking an Indian village, but they and their horses were upside down in the camp, with their feet toward the sky. As word spread, the Sioux and their allies interpreted this vision as a strong sign that they would be victorious should soldiers attack them. It was an advantage to know what direction the soldiers would come from: east, Sitting Bull declared, according to his vision.

"The effect of the Sun Dance," writes Joseph Marshall III in *The Journey of Crazy Horse*, "the most holy of Lakota ceremonies, was to rekindle a sense of unity and remind the agency Lakota that the true path of the Lakota way was still very much alive and viable. The growing encampment buzzed for days with speculation on the meaning of Sitting Bull's vision. Interpretations varied but the unmistakable message was definitely victory over the Long Knives," as army cavalry was called because of their officers' sabers.

18

KILLDEER MOUNTAIN

The warrior who would be most associated with Sitting Bull was Crazy Horse. But of equal importance to the Hunkpapa medicine man was Gall.

Born in present-day South Dakota, the young Lakota, like Red Cloud a generation earlier, overcame the challenges of growing up fatherless. He received his name after a neighbor killed an animal and Gall ate the gallbladder without flinching at the vile taste of the bile.

By his early twenties, Gall, also a Hunkpapa, was already an accomplished warrior. He particularly distinguished himself and forged a bond with Sitting Bull in the Battle of Killdeer Mountain. This pivotal clash is often overlooked, although it was to be the largest operation the U.S. Army mounted against the Sioux. It was in retribution for the Dakota War of 1862. It lasted for five brutal weeks; in the aftermath, the Dakota people were banished to reservations in the Dakotas and Nebraska, and Minnesota officials confiscated and sold all their remaining land in the state.*

* The war also resulted in the largest mass execution in U.S. history, with the

The following year saw large military expeditions—such as General Sully's—into Dakota Territory to protect the frontier of white settlement in Minnesota and the Dakotas, thereby pushing most of the Sioux to the western side of the Missouri River. Settlers were not completely safe, however, as evidenced by four of them being killed by Sioux raiders in the spring of 1864.

Another motive for a new military campaign against the Sioux was to safeguard lines of communication with recently discovered goldfields in Idaho and Montana. The lifeline for the American gold miners was steamboats plying the Missouri River through the heart of Sioux territory. During the winter of 1863–64, Major General John Pope mandated the construction of several forts along the river and in the eastern Dakotas to secure the communication routes to the goldfields and eliminate the Sioux threat to the settlers east of the river.*

General Pope chose as his field commander Alfred Sully. Though a brevet brigadier general, his military record was spotty. In service back east during the Civil War, Sully had been removed from command by then-General John Gibbon for failure to suppress a mutiny by a New York infantry regiment. Though cleared by a court of inquiry of any wrongdoing, Sully was shipped out to command the District of Iowa, which included the North Dakota Territory, in the Department of the Northwest.

Departing from Sioux City, Iowa, General Sully's First Brigade followed the Missouri River. The Second Brigade would march overland from Fort Ridgely in Minnesota. On the march up the Missouri, the

---

hanging of thirty-eight Dakota men in Mankato, Minnesota, the day after Christmas.

* Pope himself had been banished, sent packing west after leading the Union Army to a stunning defeat in the Second Battle of Bull Run in August 1862.

Sioux killed one soldier and wounded another. The three Sioux warriors were caught, killed, and, for good measure, decapitated. Additional soldiers and civilians on steamboats chugged up the Missouri River to support Sully's expedition.

The two columns of soldiers united on June 29, 1864. A week later, Sully established Fort Rice on the Missouri River in North Dakota as a base of operations, supplied by steamboat. His scouts—consisting of Winnebago, friendly Sioux, and mixed-bloods—informed him of a large encampment of Sioux 130 miles northwest near the Little Missouri River. On July 19, Sully and his combined force left Fort Rice to search for the Sioux encampment. The cumbersome column was further burdened by a wagon train of two hundred miners and their families headed for the goldfields, whom Sully reluctantly agreed to escort.

Scouts reported as many as 1,800 tepees in the Sioux village, which led Sully to calculate, incorrectly, that he might be facing as many as 5,000 warriors. (The Sioux later claimed they had 1,600 warriors in the battle.) The Indian encampment consisted mostly of Lakota plus Yanktonai, Teton, and a handful of Santee. The Sioux were armed only with bows and arrows and a few short-range muskets and shotguns. Many of the Sioux, especially the Tetons, had not been hostile to the United States before this encounter.

Having left some soldiers behind to guard Fort Rice, Sully had 2,200 men under his command. He also had eight howitzers. On July 26, his scouts skirmished with thirty Sioux warriors near present-day Richardton, North Dakota. Recognizing that the Sioux were now aware of his presence, Sully advanced rapidly. On the morning of the twenty-eighth, a mixed-blood Santee scout informed Sully that the large Sioux encampment was just ten miles ahead.

Killdeer Mountain was at the edge of the Dakota Badlands, cut up by deep, impassable ravines and featuring high, rugged hills. Realizing that a cavalry charge would be difficult in the broken terrain, Sully had his men dismount and form into a square, one mile per side. His horses and artillery were sheltered inside the square. The soldiers advanced on foot while the Sioux on horseback formed up in groups on Sully's flanks and on hilltops.

For a while, the only fighting was verbal—the two sides exchanged insults at long distance. One warrior, a Hunkpapa named Lone Dog, rode within rifle range of the soldiers, taunting them. Sully ordered him shot by sharpshooters. With those first shots fired at Lone Dog (who was unharmed), the soldiers advanced with a skirmish line, and the Sioux darted at the flanks of the army, seeking weak spots. Artillery fire discouraged the Sioux from congregating in large numbers. A thrust at Sully's rear was broken up by an artillery shell that felled several of the warriors. Sully's square of soldiers advanced steadily.

The Sioux quickly realized that they could not hope to turn the soldiers back, and they shifted their focus to packing up their tepees and equipment and protecting the flight of their women and children.

Attempting to slow Sully's advance, the Sioux mounted charges on his right and left flank. Major Alfred B. Brackett and his Minnesota Battalion on the right mounted their horses and launched a countercharge, supported by artillery. He scattered the Sioux forces after close-quarters fighting with sabers and pistols.

The warriors had indeed slowed Sully enough that the sun was setting before the soldiers could get to the now-abandoned village. The general halted his men for the night but ordered an artillery bombardment of the village. In the morning, Sully entered and surveyed the deserted encampment; then he detailed seven hundred men to destroy all that had been left behind. This included tepees, large supplies of dried buffalo meat, and up to three thousand dogs, which were shot. A few Sioux, including children, who had not been evacuated were killed by the Winnebago scouts.

The physically powerful Gall and his fellow Hunkpapa Sitting Bull had fought tirelessly during the Battle of Killdeer Mountain before melting away in the darkness. The two would become so close that as Sitting Bull rose through the Lakota ranks, Gall was his favorite protégé and probable successor, more so than the independent and mercurial Crazy Horse.

That Gall survived the battle was less surprising than the outcome of another encounter. Near Fort Berthold in late 1865, he was surrounded, bayoneted, and left for dead by soldiers led to his camp by the Arikara scout Bloody Knife. This was revenge for the abuse the younger Gall had heaped on the mixed-bloods in their Hunkpapa village. Bloody Knife was kept from shooting Gall's prostrate body by the commanding officer, and somehow Gall survived.

In the summer of 1872, Gall was side by side with Sitting Bull in the attacks against the military escort of Northern Pacific Railway survey parties across southeastern Montana. The following summer, Gall again helped lead resistance to a second Northern Pacific survey. As a result of the U.S. government's ultimatum in December 1875 to live on a reservation or else, Gall led his band from Standing Rock Agency to join Sitting Bull's nontreaty Lakota.

19

HE WAS CALLED "CURLY."

The precise year of Crazy Horse's birth has never been pinned down. Encouraging Bear, an Oglala medicine man and spiritual adviser to Crazy Horse, reported that Crazy Horse was born "in the year in which the band to which he belonged, the Oglala, stole One Hundred Horses, and in the fall of the year," a reference to the annual Lakota winter count. Among the Oglala winter counts, the stealing of one hundred horses is noted as occurring in 1840–41.

Crazy Horse was born to parents from two different tribes of the Lakota. His father, also named Crazy Horse, was an Oglala born around 1810. His mother, Rattling Blanket Woman, born around 1814, was a Miniconjou. Their baby was originally named Among the Trees, meaning he was one with nature. His mother died when he was four years old, and by then he was known by another name.

"This boy was different from other Oglala babies," writes Stephen Ambrose in *Crazy Horse and Custer*. "He had light, curly hair and a light complexion. The Indians called him various nicknames, all connected to his distinguishing physical characteristics. Sometimes he was 'Curly Hair,' sometimes the 'Light-Haired Boy'; as he grew older he usually was called 'Curly.'"

Crazy Horse, the father, was a respected figure because he was a combination healer and interpreter of dreams. His status was enhanced when the widower married two sisters of Spotted Tail, an admired warrior who in later years would rival Red Cloud as leader of the Lakota Sioux.

Life changed dramatically in the 1840s, when the Oregon Trail became flooded with wasichu wagons. Before then, there had not been serious clashes between the migrants and Indians. There were the occasional raids to steal a few cows and horses, but mostly the Indians approached the wagon trains to trade for coffee and sugar. The wagons were allowed to pass as long as they kept moving.

"Almost every day young braves would nip off a horse here, a cow there, or sneak into a camp at night and take an iron cooking pot or even a rifle," writes Ambrose. "It was great fun, of course, and profitable; best of all, the emigrants did not pursue the thieves as the Crows or Pawnees would have done, and the tiny infantry garrison at Fort Laramie was much too small to do anything about it. Or so the Sioux believed."

For many Sioux warriors—which the child Curly was destined to be—this harassment of the hapless wasichu was less fun than actual fighting, which was reserved for jousting with enemy tribes. Real war involved capturing horses, defending hunting grounds, and, by participating in such activities, gaining glory and respect. For a Sioux warrior, counting coup against a hostile group of Crow or Pawnee meant much more than stealing a pot.

For a victimized white family, the thievery was real and frightening enough, especially if it entailed a glimpse of the perpetrator. A mature Sioux warrior on a fast, well-trained pony was an imposing sight. He carried a bow and arrow (and eventually a rifle), a knife, a shield, sometimes a lance, and a rawhide sack in which he carried extra moccasins, ceremonial items, a pipe and tobacco, a bonnet or coup feathers (if he had earned them), and edibles like pemmican and jerky. Most men wore shirts and leggings made of deerskin.

However, being imposing could not overcome the rapidly rising number of migrants. In 1841, the probable year of Crazy Horse's birth, there was a trickle of travelers across the rough-hewn Platte River Road. Four years later, with the arduous but available Oregon Trail, there were over five thousand whites wagoning west. Beginning in 1847, the Mormons alone accounted for thousands of migrants to their new home in Utah. In 1849, as many as thirty thousand people passed through Lakota territory.

Also that year came a catastrophe that made the increasing presence of white settlers and soldiers a more pressing issue: Both the Sioux and Cheyenne were ravaged by cholera. A year later, there was a smallpox epidemic. With no immunity to or treatments for these white men's diseases, the plains inhabitants were especially vulnerable.*

Ironically, diseases saved wasichu lives on the Oregon Trail. Explains Joseph Marshall III, "Beneath dark, angry scowls dozens and dozens of warriors watched the lines of plodding wagons, keeping their hands on their weapons. The white men and their bullets they could confront, but the sicknesses that caused strong men to take to their deathbeds in a matter of days was another matter. So, for the most part, the wagons and their occupants plodded along unmolested, not because

---

* Infectious diseases were the primary killer among Native American communities. Infections ranging from smallpox, bubonic plague, chickenpox, cholera, the common cold, diphtheria, influenza, malaria, measles, scarlet fever, some sexually transmitted diseases, typhoid, typhus, tuberculosis, leptospirosis, and pertussis produced illness and extensive deaths. It is estimated that 95 percent of the Indigenous populations in the Americas were killed by infectious diseases during the decades following European colonization, amounting to an estimated twenty million people.

of words on a paper or the power of the 'great father' but because of the fear of sickness."

Because of the agonizing deaths he saw around him, the young Crazy Horse was already turning against the whites. Then there was an event Crazy Horse witnessed early in his teenage years that truly embittered him.

20

THE STOLEN STRINGY COW

In the summer of 1854, Crazy Horse was living with his father and younger stepbrother, Little Hawk, in an Oglala camp. Also present was Conquering Bear, who had been designated a chief by the white commissioners who had pushed through the Treaty of Fort Laramie three years earlier. Crazy Horse and his best friend, Hump, were kept busy hunting.

One day in August, tied to the back of a wagon heading west was a skinny old cow. A Miniconjou hunter, High Forehead, saw some easy pickings—he cut the rope, and as he hauled it away, the Mormon wagon and its terrified occupants hurried to Fort Laramie. The cow was butchered and the meager meat distributed among the Oglala residents. Who would miss a stringy old animal like that?

A twenty-four-year-old second lieutenant did. The day after the cow was killed, John Grattan of the Sixth Infantry Regiment led an armed detachment into the Sioux camp to take custody of High Forehead and bring him back to Fort Laramie. In the detachment were a sergeant, a corporal, twenty-seven privates, and Lucien Auguste, a French Indian interpreter. They dragged with them two artillery pieces. Another white man, James Bordeaux, who owned a nearby trading post and was married to a Brule Sioux, was curious about the contingent's purpose and joined in.

By the time the soldiers reached the encampment, Auguste was drunk. Grattan took away his bottle, but that did not make him any less intoxicated. Worse, Auguste was not much of an interpreter—he spoke only some Dakota Sioux and had little grasp of dialects. And worse than that, as the detachment entered the camp, Auguste began to taunt the Sioux, calling their warriors women and saying the soldiers were there not to talk but to kill them all.

Lieutenant Grattan might have been a fool to undertake this mission, but he was not stupid. It was estimated that the large camp consisted of almost 5,000 Sioux residents, and of those, as many as 1,200 were warriors. It dawned on Grattan that he was greatly outnumbered, so a fight was not his first option—make an arrest and get out of there, no one hurt. The soldiers made their way to the lodge of High Forehead, who was ordered to surrender. He refused.

Grattan next approached Conquering Bear, saying the Sioux should arrest the guilty party and turn him over. Conquering Bear also refused. But he tried to negotiate, offering a horse as compensation for the cow. Auguste failed to fully or accurately translate Conquering Bear and Grattan's back-and-forth dialogue.

Realizing this, Conquering Bear asked Bordeaux to act as interpreter. This helped, but the conversation did not get any more conciliatory.

As Grattan pressed Conquering Bear, numerous Sioux warriors moved into positions around the soldiers. Realizing a clash was almost certain, Bordeaux turned tail and headed back to the trading post, where he told the whites there to arm themselves. Meanwhile, Grattan gave up trying to overcome Conquering Bear's stubbornness. As he returned to his column, a nervous soldier fired his gun, wounding a Sioux. The fight was on.

The warriors started shooting arrows, and Conquering Bear tried to stop them. But he was mortally wounded and would die nine days later. The Sioux warriors, led by Spotted Tail, quickly killed Grattan, eleven of his men, and the intoxicated interpreter, Auguste. A group of eighteen soldiers retreated, trying to reach some rocks for defense, but they were cut off and overwhelmed by warriors led by the Oglala warrior Red Cloud. (One of Grattan's soldiers survived the immediate situation but later died of his wounds.)

Conquering Bear was the only Lakota fatality. The Sioux spared Bordeaux back at the trading post, both because he was married to a Sioux woman and because he had a friendly relationship with the tribes.

A consequence of this violent event further embittered Crazy Horse and others of his generation of Lakota. President Franklin Pierce vowed to avenge Grattan and his soldiers. General William Harney was instructed by the War Department to "whip the Indians."*

His expedition set out in the summer of 1855. On September 1, it came across a Sioux encampment along the Platte River in a place known as Blue Waters. Harney sent a regiment on an overnight flanking maneuver led by Lieutenant Philip St. George Cooke. Harney moved up in the morning to drive the Sioux against Cooke's position. He first attempted to parlay with the Sioux chief, Little Thunder, but his demands to hand over the men responsible for the Grattan attack were rebuffed. During the parlay, several Sioux braves discovered Cooke's men. After learning of this, Harney ordered an attack.

Some of the Sioux took refuge in caves along the river. Harney had

---

* The president picked the right man to pursue people of color. In June 1834, while he was a major stationed in St. Louis, Harney was charged with beating an enslaved woman, Hannah, to death because she had lost a set of keys. He was tried for murder but acquitted. In addition to this, Harney owned a group of muscular male slaves whom he enjoyed provoking into fistfights with soldiers.

his men fire into the caves, where they killed many women and children. A large group of mounted warriors rode toward an escape route but were pursued on horseback by troopers. They had a running fight for about five miles, which lasted several hours.*

Once the shooting had stopped, Harney's men had killed eighty-six Sioux—about half of them women and children—and taken seventy prisoners. His soldiers also mutilated some of the dead, hacking off and taking body parts as souvenirs. Afterward, the soldiers made a wide sweep of the surrounding area but encountered no further resistance. The Sioux called Harney the "Butcher" for the battle at Blue Water, the "Hornet" for invading their territory, and the "Big Chief Who Swears" for the treaty he forced on them.

According to Ambrose, "This was an unmitigated disaster, on a scale undreamed of by the Sioux." That is what Crazy Horse found when he returned from a hunting trip. "What he witnessed no Sioux had ever seen before—a Sioux camp completely destroyed. [He] had been brought up to believe that the loss of one or two warriors on a raiding party was a shocking business, the loss of three or four a tribal disaster. Now he saw dozens of dead warriors stretched out before him, Sioux women dead too, their dresses thrown over their heads."

Word of the massacre spread quickly among the Lakota and their allies, further militarizing emerging warriors like Crazy Horse and Hump.

---

* One of the officers, Captain Henry Heth, got so far ahead of his men that he was presumed killed in action. His death was reported in newspapers around the country. After he reappeared, he took satisfaction in the obituaries his friends had written. As a Confederate general in July 1863, Heth would be blamed for accidentally starting the Battle of Gettysburg by sending half his division into the town before the rest of the Army of Northern Virginia was fully prepared. Later in the day, Confederate troops succeeded in routing two Union corps, but at a heavy cost in casualties.

21

LIFE-CHANGING VISIONS

It was good to have a father who interpreted dreams when Crazy Horse began to have trance visions. Now named Worm, the father's other routine tasks included curing fevers, treating broken limbs and snake bites, and helping families prepare for funerals. Unlike most Lakota Sioux peers, Worm did not hunt or go to war.

In his oldest son's most vivid and powerful trance vision, a warrior on his horse rode out of a lake, and the horse seemed to float and dance. The warrior wore simple clothing, no face paint, his hair down with just a feather in it, and a small brown stone behind his ear. Bullets and arrows flew around him as he charged forward, but neither he nor his horse was hit.

A thunderstorm came over the warrior, and his people grabbed hold of his arms, trying to hold him back. The warrior broke their hold, and then lightning struck him, leaving a lightning symbol on his cheek and white marks like hailstones appearing on his body. The warrior told Crazy Horse that as long as he dressed modestly, his tribesmen did not touch him, and he did not take any scalps or war trophies, he would not be harmed in battle. As the vision ended, he heard a red-tailed hawk shrieking off in the distance.

Worm later interpreted the vision and said that the warrior was going to be Crazy Horse. The lightning bolt on his cheek and the hailstones on his body were to become his war paint. Crazy Horse was to follow the warrior's example to dress simply and to do as the warrior's prophecy said so he would be safe when fighting. For the most part, the vision proved to be true, and Crazy Horse was not harmed in battle.

Worm then took his son to what is today Sylvan Lake, South Dakota, where they both sat to do a vision quest. A red-tailed hawk led them to their respective spots in the hills—as the trees are tall in the Black Hills, they could not always see where they were going. Crazy Horse sat between two humps at the top of a hill north and to the east of the lake, while Worm sat south of Black Elk Peak.

Crazy Horse's next vision first took him south, where, in Lakota spirituality, one goes upon death. He was brought back and was taken west in the direction of the thunder beings. He was given a medicine bundle to protect him for life. One of his animal protectors would be the white owl, which would give extended life. He was also shown his "face paint" for battle, to consist of a yellow lightning bolt down the left side of his face and hailstones of white powder. Crazy Horse put no makeup on his forehead and did not wear a war bonnet.

From that day forward, that would be his appearance in battle. It certainly made him a distinctive warrior and presumably target, but the "medicine" proved true that bullets could not kill him.

"Every Lakota boy of the time grew up on a horse, and Crazy Horse was no exception," states Joseph Marshall III in *The Journey of Crazy Horse*. "Many who rode with him into battle remembered that he used two horses for combat, a bay and a sorrel. He favored the bay, a gelding. Because geldings had more endurance than mares or stallions. Crazy

Horse liked to rest and refresh his horse by riding him to the top of a hill to catch a breeze or stand in the wind."

Crazy Horse was known to have a personality characterized by aloofness, shyness, modesty, and lonesomeness. He was generous to the poor, the elderly, and children. In *Black Elk Speaks*, author John Neihardt, who had interviewed some of the few remaining Sioux and Cheyenne who knew him, writes that Crazy Horse "was a queer man and would go about the village without noticing people or saying anything. In his own teepee he would joke, and when he was on the warpath with a small party, he would joke to make his warriors feel good. But around the village, he hardly ever noticed anybody, except little children. All the Lakotas like to dance and sing, but he never joined a dance, and they say nobody ever heard him sing. But everybody liked him, and they would do anything he wanted or go anywhere he said."

Like his peers, Crazy Horse learned from his surroundings. "There were signs everywhere on the Plains," writes Ambrose. "If the wild horse herd was strung out and walking steadily along, it was headed for water; if the horses were scattered and grazing they were coming from water. Plains Indians knew the medicinal properties of more than two thousand plants, they understood weather patterns, and so on. All this information was passed on from one generation to the next."

Through the late 1850s and early 1860s, Crazy Horse's reputation as a warrior grew, as did his fame among the Lakota, who gave accounts of him in their oral histories. His first kill was a Shoshone warrior who had murdered a Lakota woman washing buffalo meat along the Powder River.* Crazy Horse fought in numerous battles between the Lakota and

---

* Actually, the first kill in battle had come when Crazy Horse was in a war party led by Spotted Tail against the Omaha. As attackers appeared, he shot an ar-

their traditional enemies, including the Crow, Pawnee, Blackfeet, and Arikara.

In 1864, after the Sand Creek Massacre in Colorado, Oglala and Miniconjou bands allied with the Cheyenne against the U.S. military. Crazy Horse was present at the Battle of Platte Bridge and the following year at the Battle of Red Buttes. Also in 1865, because of his fighting ability and his generosity to the tribe, Crazy Horse was named a "Shirt Wearer," or war leader, by the Oglala.

Having this high honor, his fall from grace was all the more shocking. In the fall of 1870, Crazy Horse invited Black Buffalo Woman to accompany him on a buffalo hunt in the Slim Buttes area of present-day northwestern South Dakota. She was the wife of No Water, who had a reputation for drinking alcohol to excess. It was a Lakota custom to allow a woman to divorce her husband at any time. She did so by moving in with relatives or with another man or by placing the husband's belongings outside their lodge. Although some gifts might be required to smooth over hurt feelings, the rejected husband was expected to accept his wife's decision.

No Water did not. He was away from camp when Crazy Horse and Black Buffalo Woman left for the buffalo hunt. He tracked them down, and when he found them in a tepee, he called Crazy Horse's name from outside. When Crazy Horse answered, No Water stuck a pistol into the tepee and fired. The bullet struck Crazy Horse in the face, but it was not a mortal wound. No Water did not remain to find out: He rode his horse until it died and then continued to flee on foot until he reached the safety of his own village.

Several elders convinced Crazy Horse and No Water that no more

---

row. When he went to scalp his kill, he discovered that the dead Omaha was a young woman.

blood should be shed. As compensation for the shooting, No Water gave Crazy Horse three horses. Because Crazy Horse was with a married woman, he was stripped of his title as Shirt Wearer.

Sent to help Crazy Horse heal was Black Shawl, an Oglala and relative of Spotted Tail. The two soon married, and Black Shawl gave birth to Crazy Horse's only child, a daughter named They Are Afraid of Her.*

* Black Shawl would live to 1927, when she died during an influenza outbreak.

22

FRESH FIREPOWER

During Red Cloud's War, after the Fetterman Massacre in December 1866—which the Lakota and Cheyenne called the Battle of the Hundred in the Hand—Crazy Horse led warriors in the Wagon Box Fight the following year, also near Fort Phil Kearny. The outcome of this battle was quite different and probably influenced Red Cloud's thinking about wasichu military power even before his trip to Washington, DC.

On the morning of August 2, Captain James Powell's force was divided. Fourteen soldiers were detailed to escort the wood train to and from the fort while thirteen soldiers guarded the woodcutting camp, about one mile from the wagon box corral. The plan of attack on the woodcutters and soldiers was tried-and-true, similar to the plan used the previous December: A small group of warriors led by Crazy Horse would entice the soldiers to chase them, leading the men into an ambush by a larger hidden force.

The plan broke down when a number of fighters attacked an outlying camp of four woodcutters and four soldiers, killing three of the latter.

The other soldier and the woodcutters escaped and warned the soldiers near the corral. The pursuing force halted at the woodcutters' camp to loot and seize the large number of horses and mules there, which gave the men taking refuge in the corral time to prepare for the attack. There were twenty-six soldiers and six civilians in the corral.

The first assault came from mounted warriors from the southwest, but the raiders encountered heavy fire from the soldiers using new breech-loading Springfield Model 1866 rifles and lever-action Henry rifles. Most likely, the Lakota had never encountered such advanced weapons. The soldiers and civilians also had a defensive wall of wagon boxes to protect them.

The warriors withdrew, regrouped, and launched several further attacks on foot. They killed Powell's second in command, Lieutenant John Jenness, and two soldiers. The battle lasted from about 7:30 A.M. until 1:30 P.M.—the defenders had plenty of ammunition.

The garrison at Fort Phil Kearny learned of the fight from its observation station on Pilot Hill. About 11:30 A.M., Major Benjamin Smith led 103 soldiers out of the fort to the wood camp to rescue the men in the corral. Smith took with him ten wagons, driven by armed civilians, and a mountain howitzer. He proceeded carefully and, when he neared the wagon box corral, began firing his cannon at long range. The attackers were forced to withdraw.

Smith advanced without opposition to the corral, collected its sun-blistered occupants, and returned quickly to Fort Phil Kearny. Additional civilian survivors who had hidden in the woods during the battle made it back to the fort that night.

For the remainder of 1867, the Lakota and their allies concentrated on small-scale, hit-and-run raids against parties along the Bozeman Trail. When the war ended the next year, Crazy Horse and Red Cloud grew apart. The former field general did not agree with the Lakota leader's move toward peace and life on a reservation. For Crazy Horse, it was time for new leadership. It was time for him to seek out Sitting Bull.

23

PROUD TO BE FREE

By June 1876, Crazy Horse was not only to Sitting Bull what he had been to Red Cloud, but his mysteriousness and battle skills had many of the Sioux and Cheyenne in awe of him. If there was to be a big fight against the approaching wasichu army, no doubt Crazy Horse would be in the middle of it. Or more likely, at the front.

Sitting Bull and Crazy Horse had "struck up a fast friendship," writes Stephen Ambrose. "They drew together because of their mutual vow to resist any change in their way of life, whatever the cost, for as long as possible. To the Sioux, and increasingly to the whites, they symbolized a policy of bitter Indian resistance to white encroachment on Sioux lands. Most of all, Sitting Bull and Crazy Horse were proud to be Sioux and prouder still to be free."

It was clear that Sitting Bull's camp on the Greasy Grass—the Sioux name for the Little Bighorn River—consisted of hundreds of lodges, perhaps close to one thousand. Many men, some with families in tow, had journeyed there from their own, smaller camps or reservations to be part of a great hunt for buffalo and other game. Others were looking for a good fight, one that would stop the invasion of wasichu for good. It was a mostly festive time for the allied tribes.

Sitting Bull may have had to bite his tongue about those who had traveled to Montana from the various reservations. He had once said, "All agency Indians I have seen are worthless. They are neither red warriors nor white farmers. They are neither wolf nor dog. If the Great Spirit had desired me to be a white man, he would have made me so in the first place. It is not necessary for eagles to be crows. Now we are poor but we are free."

Sitting Bull was at the peak of his power, and the large and mostly unified encampment reflected that. According to Robert Utley:

> Above all the tribal leaders towered a single chief of commanding influence—Sitting Bull. In earlier battles, especially the fighting against General Sully in 1864–65, he had made an outstanding record. Since then, he had broadened his influence into spiritual and political realms.
>
> Rocklike dedication to traditional Indian values and unwavering opposition to all relations with the white people ran deep in his makeup and fortified his dominance. All the Teton and Cheyenne roamers, while honoring immediate tribal allegiances, looked beyond them to the forceful personality, superior intellect, and persona magnetism of Sitting Bull. In the eyes of Indians and whites alike, the Powder River bands came more and more to be identified as Sitting Bull's people.

In the third week of June, the Little Bighorn River was clear and swollen from snow that was still melting in the upper mountains. The rushing water was cold but otherwise perfect for drinking and washing, and even swimming for the hardier villagers. That resource would be tested because Sitting Bull's followers now numbered as many as 8,000 men, women, and children, with at least 1,500 being of fighting age. And there were thousands of ponies needing grass and water.

Sitting Bull's lodge was on the southern edge of the Hunkpapa camp, a place of honor. Before the Sioux had encountered and mastered horses, a lodge was only as large as the load of possessions that could be transported by dogs, typically about fifteen feet across. With horses allowing for heavier loads, lodges could be larger. The lodge of a revered headman like Sitting Bull and his extended family was anywhere from eighteen to twenty-two feet across.*

"Most of the greatest leaders and bravest warriors of the Sioux and Northern Cheyenne were there," reports James Donovan. "Many of the older fighters were veterans of more than a decade of constant battling and skirmishing with the whites and their soldiers. All but the very youngest had gained combat experience fighting traditional enemies such as the Crows and other tribes on the northern plains."

In other words, it could be argued that no previous wasichu military force had encountered an Indian force so capable, prepared, and eager for battle. And that included Red Cloud's army. President Grant had not planned for that.

Among those "greatest leaders and bravest warriors," in addition to Sitting Bull, were Gall, Rain-in-the-Face, and Crow King. Gall was always ready to fight the wasichu. Crow King, another Hunkpapa and also known as Medicine Bag That Burns, headed a band of eighty warriors. There was, of course, Crazy Horse. And the elderly and much-respected Inkpaduta and his small but determined group of Yanktonai followers had joined with Sitting Bull.

Next to the river, which varied from thirty to fifty feet wide and five

* Adding to Sitting Bull's enjoyment of his surroundings was that a few days earlier, Seen by Her Nation, one of his wives, had given birth to twin boys.

feet deep in the middle, the Lakota Sioux had created five large circles of lodges, and the Cheyenne had constructed a sixth one. Other tribes were represented, too, in much smaller though attached enclaves. There were Assiniboine, who in the past had aligned against the Lakota Sioux and their allies. Gros Ventre warriors had thrown in with Sitting Bull. Somewhat reluctant members of the village were five Arapaho warriors. They had been pursuing a war party of Shoshone, and when they showed up at Sitting Bull's encampment, they were thought to be advance scouts for the white soldiers and almost killed.

Fortunately, a Cheyenne chief, Two Moons, questioned and then vouched for them. The Arapaho were told, however, they could not leave the village. Just because they were not enemy scouts did not mean they might not choose to warn the wasichu army of such a large congregation of Indians.

Even so, being surprised by such an army was possible because the huge village's location was a liability. West of it was mostly flat for a mile, and the foraging of the ponies made the land flatter still. Opposite that were cliffs as high as three hundred feet carved by ravines and coulees. An approach from the east might not be detected until the white soldiers were close enough to open fire.

But Sitting Bull was not troubled by this seeming disadvantage. He knew the enemy was coming from the east—his vision had told him so.

Still, there would be some surprise. The morning of June 25, 1876, at the large village of unified Native allies—anywhere from two to three miles long—was "reminiscent of a thousand similar mornings," writes Gregory F. Michno in *Lakota Noon*. "The east-facing lodge openings admitted arrows of light from the red-orange sun making its appearance over the bluffs. A few wandering dogs yipped here and there, rummaging for scraps of food. Ponies grazed on the luxuriant grasses, watched over by a few sleepy boys. Early risers began to cook their breakfasts. The curling smoke drifted lazily above the tipis, caught by a slight northerly breeze and carried up the valley. A haze enveloped the bottomlands, the start of another hot day."

But this day, a Sunday, would not be just another hot day on the northern plains: The legendary "Long Hair" and his Long Knives were coming.

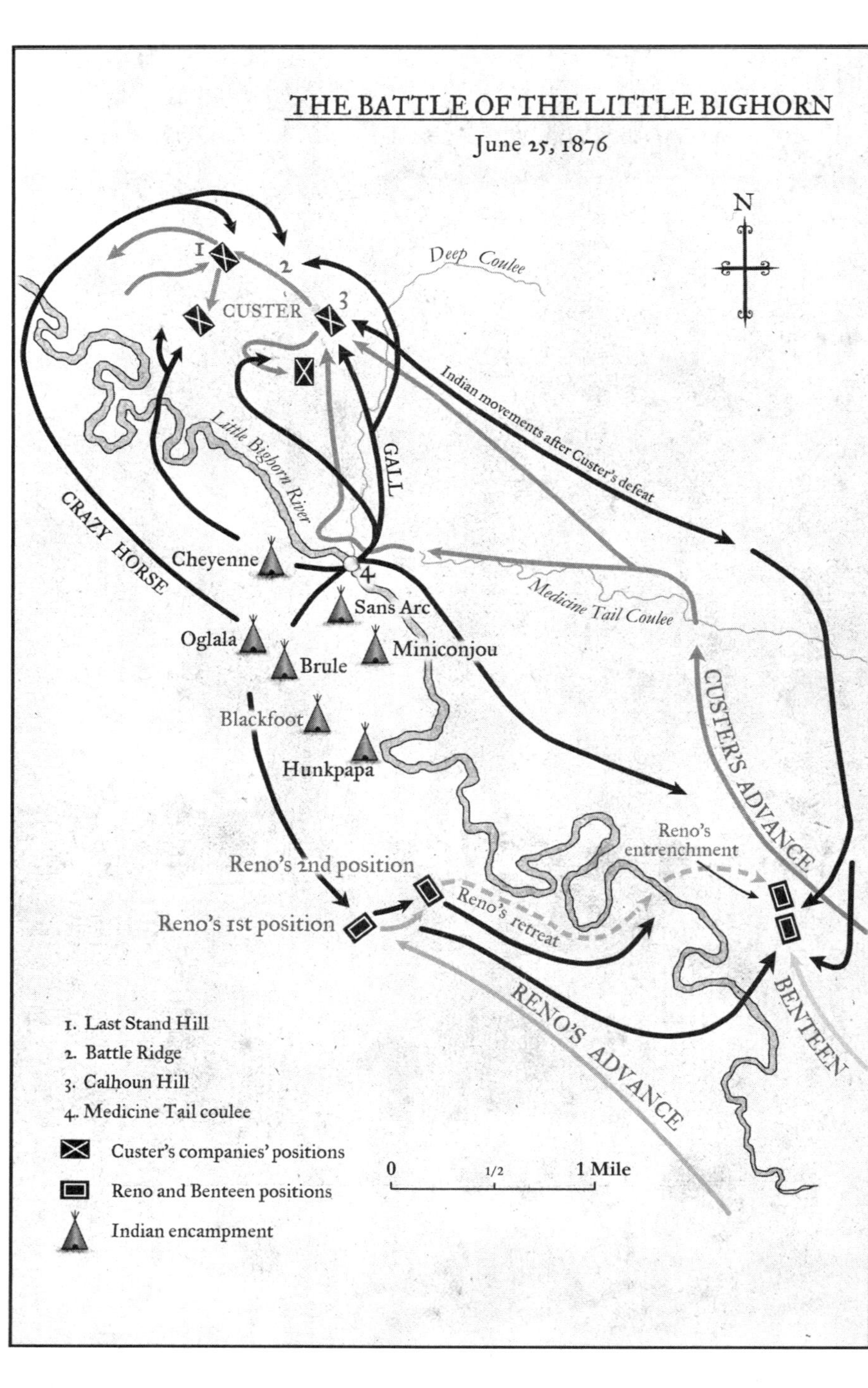
THE BATTLE OF THE LITTLE BIGHORN
June 25, 1876
N
Deep Coulee
1
2
CUSTER
3
Indian movements after Custer's defeat
Little Bighorn River
GALL
CRAZY HORSE
Cheyenne
4
Medicine Tail Coulee
Sans Arc
Oglala
Miniconjou
Brule
Blackfoot
Hunkpapa
CUSTER'S ADVANCE
Reno's entrenchment
Reno's 2nd position
Reno's retreat
Reno's 1st position
BENTEEN
RENO'S ADVANCE
1. Last Stand Hill
2. Battle Ridge
3. Calhoun Hill
4. Medicine Tail coulee
Custer's companies' positions
Reno and Benteen positions
Indian encampment
0
1/2
1 Mile

ACT III

THE EXPEDITIONS

It's not how many times you get knocked down that count, it's how many times you get back up.

—**GEORGE ARMSTRONG CUSTER**

24

A REUNITED REGIMENT

By 1872, the incessant approach and then intrusion of railroad tracks alarmed the Sioux and their increasing array of allies. Where would they end? How many more wasichus would the steaming iron horses bring? Were the Black Hills still safe, as the treaty four years earlier had promised?

No. When defiant Sioux and Cheyenne war parties harassed enough surveyors and construction crews and their army escorts, the Grant administration ordered a crackdown. The responsibility for that was given to the Department of Dakota and its commander, General Winfield Hancock. From the department's headquarters in St. Paul, he oversaw Minnesota, Montana, and the Dakota Territory. The latter included much of the Black Hills. It was Hancock who had warned his superior, General Sheridan, that the Yellowstone Valley was unsafe: "It is evident that more troops will be needed if the railroad is to continue its advances north and west."

Also, writes James Donovan in *A Terrible Glory*: "The U.S. government soon found out that it was one thing to assign tribes to reservations and quite another to keep them there—especially when the food rations and supplies promised them by treaty were delayed, stolen, inedible, or simply never delivered. What had been presented as a policy designed to prevent bloodshed soon became yet another rationale for it."

In March 1873, the Seventh Cavalry was pulled back together. This was not an easy task. The regiment had become scattered around the South, with some companies even pulling Reconstruction guard duty. New orders were issued, and the reconstituted Seventh gathered in Memphis. The commander of record would be Colonel Samuel Sturgis. An 1846 graduate of West Point, he had seen action in the Mexican War and in the Civil War, attaining the rank of brevet major general.* Like many nonessential career officers, Sturgis had been riding a desk since. He would continue to do that now, establishing his headquarters also in St. Paul.

This left Lieutenant Colonel Custer to resume his role as field commander. He relished this after years of relative inactivity and flirting with occupations outside the military. He took technical, if not official, command after the Seventh Cavalry units completed their journey by train and horse to Yankton and then Fort Rice in the northern half of the Dakota Territory.

The Custer "team" was reunited, with a couple of new additions. His second in command would be a familiar if not friendly face, Marcus Reno. The major disliked Custer—a big reason was blaming Custer for Joel Elliott's death in the Washita Valley—and had never been part of the

---

* Fellow 1846 graduates that year included John Gibbon, George McClellan, A. P. Hill, Thomas "Stonewall" Jackson, and George Pickett. Sturgis, South Dakota, which hosts the famous motorcycle gathering every August, was named after the Seventh Cavalry commander.

lieutenant colonel's inner circle. Custer had little respect for Reno's abilities, but he had at least acquired plenty of combat experience.

Marcus Albert Reno had been born in November 1834 in Carrollton, Illinois, one of seven children whose mother died when Marcus was thirteen. Two years later, seeking a way out of a crowded and unhappy household—his father had just died—Marcus had the gumption to write to the secretary of war, Charles Conrad, asking how to enter the U.S. Military Academy. Perhaps 1851 was a lean year for West Point admissions because when Conrad's response finally arrived, after Reno had turned seventeen, it was an appointment to the academy.

Reno graduated—despite excessive demerits, many awarded for drinking—twentieth in a class of thirty-eight and was assigned to the First U.S. Dragoons in Carlisle, Pennsylvania. Next stop was Fort Walla Walla in Washington Territory. With the outbreak of the Civil War, the First Dragoons were renamed the First Cavalry Regiment and transferred through Panama to Washington, DC, arriving in January 1862. Reno's war career would be a busy one.

As a captain, he fought in the Battle of Antietam.* He was injured during the Battle of Kelly's Ford when his horse was shot and fell on him, causing a hernia. Easing the pain was being awarded the brevet rank of major for gallant and meritorious conduct. After convalescing, Reno returned to fight in July 1863 at the Battle of Williamsport. Among the battles he participated in the following year were Cold Harbor, Darbytown Road, Winchester, Kearneysville, and Cedar Creek. For service in the latter, he was breveted lieutenant colonel.

In January 1865, Reno was transferred to the Twelfth Pennsylvania Volunteer Cavalry and commanded a brigade in pursuit of John Mosby's

---

* Whether wearing blue or gray, surviving the Battle of Antietam in Maryland was an accomplishment for any participant. It remains the deadliest day in U.S. military history, with close to twenty-three thousand combined casualties.

guerrillas. By the time the war ended, Reno had risen as high as brevet brigadier general. But like almost all Union officers, that height could not be maintained. He was soon a captain, which had to feel something like starting over without the advantages of war.

According to Nathaniel Philbrick in *The Last Stand*, "Dark-haired and dark-eyed—the Arikara scouts called him 'the man with the dark face'—Reno was the quintessential outsider. Whether or not it was because he'd lost both his parents by fifteen, something always seemed to be smoldering inside him, and his reticent, stubborn manner won him few friends."

He had climbed back one notch to major when he suffered a tragedy. In the midst of war, in 1863, Reno married the nineteen-year-old Mary Hannah Ross. The following year, a son, Ross, was born. It had been an especially difficult pregnancy and birth, and Mary's health never recovered. She was barely thirty when she died.

A crushed Reno was able to gain a leave of absence from the army, and he took his son on a tour of Europe. Upon his return, he made the unhappy and somewhat contentious decision to have his late wife's family become Ross's legal guardian. Reno certainly could not take the boy with him to his western posting, and he was not about to give up the military life—the only life he knew.

"The sudden loss of his wife, the estrangement of his in-laws, and the surrender to her family of his only son contributed to an increase in his drinking and a darkening of his already dour personality," notes James Donovan. "He had nothing left except his army career."

Custer and Reno were not pleased to see each other, but both had to follow orders.

25

BENTEEN'S BATTLES

Also returning to the fold was Captain Frederick Benteen. Though born in Petersburg, Virginia, in August 1834, and the family later relocating to Missouri, Benteen had no sympathy for the South. This cost him the enmity of his father, Theodore Benteen, an ardent secessionist. To him, it was an unforgivable act when his son joined the Union army on September 1, 1861, as a first lieutenant in the First Missouri Volunteer Cavalry Regiment.

Benteen found plenty more battles away from home. They included Wilson's Creek, Pea Ridge, Vicksburg, and Westport. In February 1864, Benteen was promoted to lieutenant colonel and commander of the Tenth Missouri Cavalry. He survived more fighting, and when the Civil War ended, he chose to remain in the U.S. Army, serving with several units—including as commander of the 138th Infantry Regiment, U.S. Colored Troops—until January 1867, when he was assigned to the Seventh U.S. Cavalry Regiment.

There was not an auspicious beginning. After arriving, Captain

Benteen made a customary courtesy call to the quarters of Lieutenant Colonel Custer and his wife. Benteen said later that he regarded Custer as a braggart from their first meeting. A much happier experience came in March, when Benteen's wife gave birth to their son in Atlanta.

Despite what became a mutual dislike, Custer and Benteen were active in the field against the Indian tribes. One notable action was in August 1868, when Benteen, commanding thirty troopers, encountered a Cheyenne raiding party along the banks of Elk Horn Creek near Fort Zarah, at the junction of the Santa Fe Trail, Walnut Creek, and the Smoky Hill Military Road in Kansas. He charged into a force of what appeared to be about fifty warriors. After they scattered, to Benteen's surprise, he next discovered more than two hundred Cheyenne raiding a ranch. He and his troopers pursued the Cheyenne without rest until dark.

During the Washita River Valley attack that November, Benteen led H Troop under Major Elliott's command. He came very close to being a casualty. He encountered the fourteen-year-old son of Black Kettle, who held a pistol. Benteen yelled he would spare the boy's life if he dropped the gun and made the peace sign. In reply, the boy aimed his revolver at Benteen and fired. The bullet missed, so the boy fired again, and the bullet passed through the sleeve of Benteen's coat. The boy fired a third time, although Benteen was making friendly overtures. This bullet hit Benteen's horse, killing it, and pitching Benteen into the snow. When the Indian boy raised his pistol to fire once more, Benteen finally shot him dead.

After the battle, Benteen joined Reno in believing that Custer had abandoned Elliott. He went a step further and wrote to a friend, criticizing Custer. The letter was passed to *The St. Louis Democrat*, which ran it in the newspaper without Benteen's permission or name. On its publication, Custer called the regiment's officers together and threatened to "horsewhip" the author. Benteen admitted authorship, albeit with a hand on his pistol. Custer did not attempt a whipping but dismissed the matter with a curt "Mister Benteen, I will see you later."

For Marcus Reno and Frederick Benteen, it was at best a mixed blessing to be reunited with the Seventh Cavalry and its field commander. For Custer, it, too, was a mixed blessing. A teetotaler, he had to tolerate Reno's drinking. And Benteen being Benteen, he was often critical and churlish. But both were battle-tested officers with frontier experience. In the postwar army, such men were not easily found.

A lot more pleased to be serving directly under Custer again was Captain Thomas Weir. Also an Ohio native, he had fought with Custer during the Civil War except for the seven months he had spent in a Confederate prison camp. Similar feelings about the reunion were felt by Captain George Yates. He, too, had fought with Custer during the war, having first met the young commander in Monroe, Michigan.

And there was Tom Custer. After the 1868–69 campaign against the Cheyenne concluded and the Seventh Cavalry was idle, his unit was assigned to keep the peace in South Carolina, where Reconstruction anger was red-hot. Tom Custer was back with his brother for both the Yellowstone and Black Hills Expeditions in 1873 and 1874. It was in the latter year that he arrested Rain-in-the-Face, who vowed revenge.

New to the team was, like Tom, a member of the Custer family, though by marriage. Margaret Custer, George's younger sister, had married James Calhoun in March 1872. He had been born in Cincinnati into a prestigious and wealthy Scottish American merchant family that included his brother Frederick. When the Civil War broke out, he was traveling in Europe with Frederick. They stayed put, planning on waiting out the war, but after three years, when it hadn't ended, both Calhoun brothers returned and joined the Union army. A year later, when the Civil War was finally over, "Jimmi" Calhoun had risen to the rank of sergeant.

He also chose to remain in the army, and in July 1867, he was commissioned a second lieutenant. Three years later, he met Margaret Custer, and the two married. His new brother-in-law brought him into the Seventh Cavalry as a first lieutenant. Calhoun was nicknamed the

"Adonis" of the regiment because of his handsome features. More important, he was welcomed into the "Custer Clan," offering complete loyalty to his commanding officer.

Margaret Calhoun and Libbie Custer traveled with their spouses to Fort Rice. However, there may have been some poor domestic reconnaissance because upon arrival, it was clear there was no room for wives in the rudimentary frontier structure. The women would spend that summer back in Michigan while the campaign against the Sioux and their allies got underway.

While the Seventh Cavalry was in the field, new accommodations were created. The regiment would soon be based at Fort Abraham Lincoln on the west bank of the Missouri River just south of Bismarck, a Northern Pacific railhead. Meanwhile, that summer, the regiment was tasked with guarding a team of railroad surveyors working their way west from the Missouri River into Montana. Everyone, including the Indians, knew the tracks would soon follow.

26

SCORCHING SKIRMISHES

Also that summer, Winfield Hancock was replaced as head of the Department of Dakota by Alfred Terry. This was a familiar role for Terry, as he had been the commanding officer when the department was created in 1866. He was something of an anomaly in that after the Civil War, he had not been excised from the ranks or demoted but remained a general. Terry was a lawyer and a good organizer and was easily noticed in a group because of his full, robust beard.*

Most relevant was that Major General Terry already had at least some experience in the west fighting Indians. He had led troops during Red Cloud's War and had been one of the negotiators of the Treaty of Fort Laramie in 1868.

One of General Terry's first acts as department head was to remove the Seventh Cavalry from its listless guard duty and give it a mission—

---

* When not on duty, Terry, who never married, lived in St. Paul with his mother and four sisters.

what became known as the Yellowstone Expedition. In June 1873, after resupplying at Fort Rice, Custer and ten of his twelve companies set off. There were close to 1,500 men on the expedition, counting the drivers of three hundred mule-drawn wagons and the cowpunchers who drove the seven hundred head of cattle destined to provide meals. And, of course, the regimental band.

They were to meet up with the vanguard of the expedition, a group of surveyors escorted by four companies of infantry. The overall commander was David Sloane Stanley. Yet another Ohio native, the forty-five-year-old Stanley had been a Union army general during the war. He took part in numerous battles, and at a critical moment in the Battle of Franklin in November 1864, he saved part of George D. Wagner's division from destruction. For this action, Stanley received the Medal of Honor.*

The expedition had a rough start. It rained during fourteen of the first seventeen days, in some instances with three or four heavy rainfalls in twenty-four hours. After taking a day to cross the infantry units and wagons over the Heart River, Colonel Stanley received a report that the surveying party had "been overtaken by a most furious hail-storm . . . in which men had barely escaped with their lives, and the animals stampeding on the march had broken up their wagons to such an extent as to completely cripple both engineers and escort."

Stanley sent the remainder of the Seventh Cavalry and the mechanic outfit ahead to the surveyors to help repair the damage while the infantry stayed with the heavy wagon train.

By July 1, the expedition had crossed over the Muddy River, which

* The Stanleys were a multi-generation military family. David Stanley's son-in-law, Willard Holbrook—married to his daughter, Anna Huntington Stanley, an American Impressionist artist—also served as a major general in the U.S. Army. His only son, David Stanley, and five of his grandsons would later graduate from West Point. Additionally, his son was the principal founder of the Army Navy Country Club in Arlington, Virginia.

was flooded approximately sixty feet wide, via a makeshift pontoon bridge of overturned wagon beds. At this time, Stanley sent forty-seven wagons back to Fort Rice for additional supplies. Four days later, the infantry escorting the wagons had caught up with the surveying party as well as the Seventh Cavalry. The combined expedition pushed on, crossing the flooded Little Missouri River and entering Montana Territory, finally reaching the Yellowstone River on July 13.

After two more weeks of dusty and sweaty traveling—and swearing—the expedition reached the mouth of Glendive Creek, where the steamboat *Key West* had created a supply depot. Stanley left two cavalry companies and an infantry company to guard it and had the rest of the expedition ferried across the Yellowstone River. They then pushed on, and on the night of August 1 came the first evidence of the presence of Indians. The camp guards fired at several figures, and the next morning, the trail of ten Natives was plainly seen going up the valley.

Still, from that point on, the supply of the expedition's cattle was not diminished quickly because the venture turned out to be more of a hunting outing than a military or exploratory campaign. Custer prided himself on being a top marksman—as he frequently reminded Libbie in letters—and every day he led groups of men (and his hounds) on hunting forays to find deer, elk, and other game plentiful in the fields and forests of Montana.

There were two notable members of the Yellowstone Expedition whose company Custer enjoyed. Tom Rosser was an engineer with the Northern Pacific Railway who had been a good friend at West Point and then a worthy adversary as a Confederate cavalry general during the war. The other was Frederick Grant. Two years after graduating from West Point, the president's oldest son was appointed a lieutenant colonel and temporarily assigned to the expedition.*

---

* Among the positions Grant would hold after leaving the army in 1881 was commissioner of the New York City Police Department.

Custer did not completely overlook hunting for hostiles too. There were occasional skirmishes as bands loyal to Sitting Bull were encountered. One such skirmish, in early August, came close to costing Custer his life.

A group of warriors suddenly appeared at the mouth of the Tongue River where the Seventh Cavalry had camped. The warriors made for the regiment's large gathering of resting horses. They were chased away, but that was not enough for Custer. Chafing for action, he leaped on his horse.

He led twenty troopers, including his brother Tom and brother-in-law Jimmi Calhoun, on a chase after the raiders. For two miles up a valley they rode, until Custer, in as much of a lather as his horse, and his orderly had well outpaced the other men. That was when the warriors sprang their trap.

Six of them rode out from a stand of timber. As the troopers formed into a skirmish line, Custer and his orderly spun around and retraced their steps. They reached the rescuers just as the Sioux attacked. Three rifle volleys persuaded them to back off, but the warriors did not leave entirely. Through the boiling-hot afternoon, the two sides exchanged fire—almost literally, as the warriors set fire to the grass, but the breeze was too weak to push the flames toward the troopers. Just as the cavalry was coming dangerously close to running out of ammunition, the rest of the regiment arrived and routed the raiders.

There was more fighting to come. On the morning of August 11, another scorcher, part of the Seventh Cavalry was encamped along the north side of the Yellowstone River at what was later known as Pease Bottom (near present-day Custer). In the early morning hours, warriors from the village of Sitting Bull started firing at the camp from across the river, and by dawn, skirmishing had broken out in several locations.

Warriors then crossed the river above and below the camp and attacked Custer's troops. They managed to fight off this advance and counterattacked with a charge, breaking the warrior positions and driving the Sioux eight or more miles from the battlefield. At about the same time, the rest of the regiment appeared in the distance, ending the skirmish. The Seventh sustained four men killed and three wounded. It was estimated that forty Sioux were casualties.

27

CRAZY HORSE AND CUSTER

As military campaigns go, the Yellowstone Expedition did not do much except almost get its field commander killed. And there may have been a close call that the participants did not know about. "He was sleeping, then, when Crazy Horse first saw him," writes Stephen Ambrose. He contends that one afternoon, during a halt near the mouth of the Tongue River, Custer had stretched out for a nap, using his saddle as a pillow, unaware his party of eighty-five soldiers was being observed.

"Along with other warriors," reports Ambrose, "Crazy Horse had crawled to the crest of a nearby bluff, from which point they could look down on Custer's position."

The Sioux decided this was a good time to try to steal the soldiers' horses. They were turned back, and that was when Crazy Horse's plan B was attempted: Try once more to lure the troopers into a trap. He positioned his three hundred or so warriors near a heavy growth of timber and showed himself and several other warriors to the alarmed soldiers.

Custer had sprung up from the ground, put the saddle back on his horse, and led a detachment of cavalry rushing at the half dozen decoys. He was impetuous, but not stupid: Nearing the timber, Custer halted. Up ahead, the Sioux had also stopped and turned to face the troopers.

According to Ambrose,

> For a brief instant the two parties stared at each other, there beside the Yellowstone. Did Crazy Horse and Custer see each other? Certainly Custer stood out; even without his red shirt he would have caught Crazy Horse's eye, as he was obviously the leader of the whites, a big man among them. Crazy Horse would have been less likely to catch Custer's eye—with his single feather in his hair and unpainted body, he paled beside his resplendent fellow warriors. Still, Custer had heard of Crazy Horse, knew of his skills as a decoy, and had Fetterman very much in mind.
>
> Whether they saw each other or not, it was a dramatic instant, each side wondering what to do next.

It was very unlikely that either man was aware of the bond they shared of seeking redemption. For Crazy Horse, it was to overcome the humiliation of having been stripped of his Shirt-Wearer status. For Custer, it was the shame of having been court-martialed and almost losing his career. Possibly, one would find redemption at the other's expense.

The warriors hidden behind the timber emerged to try an attack. But it was too little, too late. The rest of the heavily armed cavalry showed up in support of their commander. When they charged, the warriors broke into smaller groups and fled. Custer once again concluded that where Indians are concerned, attack, attack, and then attack again—they will always break and run.

To the Lakota and Cheyenne, though, the Yellowstone Expedition was significant. Once again, it was clear the promises in previous treaties were meaningless. More iron horses would steam into their hunting grounds, and more troops would protect those planning and laying the tracks. The wasichus might even be motivated enough to violate the sacred Black Hills.

Indeed they would, and the motivation would be gold. As the Seventh Cavalry was being welcomed back at Fort Abraham Lincoln at the conclusion of the arduous Yellowstone Expedition, to the east the Panic of 1873 was beginning—mostly caused by the Northern Pacific Railway going broke. With the United States still reeling from bankruptcies and financial malaise into the next year, the West and its seemingly unlimited resources offered hope. In the summer of 1874, that hope would be realized.

28

PRECIOUS METAL

George and Libbie Custer and their extended family—by blood or otherwise—waited out the winter of 1873–74 at Fort Abraham Lincoln. The couple occupied a two-story house with a veranda. But in February, they were homeless. The house caught fire and was destroyed, and most of their possessions burned with it. Fortunately, there were no human casualties. Troopers rallied around, and in short order the debris was cleared away and a new house was constructed. The Custers would call this one home for the next two years.

The northern plains winter was predictably brutal, featuring frequent blizzards and subzero temperatures. But it was warm enough inside the fort. The Custers in their old and new houses presided over dances and other entertainments. With weather conditions keeping soldiers sheltered within the fort, the part of the regiment doing the most work that winter was the band. There were mixed emotions when spring finally arrived and a more stringent military life replaced the carefree social life.

Spring setting in on the northern plains also meant the resumption of two connected activities—new advances by the railroads and raids by agitated warriors. The latter sometimes resulted in the deaths of ranchers and incautious travelers and caused aggravation for the Seventh Cavalry.

In April, for example, there was a raid on mules herded together within view of Fort Abraham Lincoln. Custer mustered his troopers, and they chased the Indians vigorously enough that the mules they had culled were left behind as they escaped—a frustrating exercise for the regiment. A few weeks later, the Seventh again took to the field, this time to intercept a Sioux war party that was rumored to be on its way to attack the Mandan and Arikara. The Indian allies were protected, but the Sioux slipped away with no casualties.

General Philip Sheridan, headquartered in Chicago, determined there needed to be a new fort that would be more strategically located as part of the effort to subdue the Sioux. He would have it built in the Black Hills . . . and named after himself. The job of leading an exploratory mission was given to the Seventh Cavalry.

Did not the Treaty of 1868 that ended Red Cloud's War prohibit such an excursion? Yes. But it was now six years later, and Red Cloud and Spotted Tail were securely ensconced on their respective reservations. Their making-war days were over. Sitting Bull and Crazy Horse and their more militant followers were the ones who now needed to be tamed.

And in the process, the military could take possession of the Black Hills.

To many people—especially the influential and deep-pocketed ones back east—it made sense that the verdant and beautiful region, chock-full of game, would also contain valuable minerals, especially gold. *The Bismarck Tribune* claimed that the Black Hills was "a region of fabulous wealth, where the rills repose on beds of gold and the rocks are studded with precious metal." What a mistake that it had been allowed to remain in Lakota hands.

29

FRIVOLOUS FUN

As coveted as the Black Hills were, at first the army kept its own hands off. Its only aggressive activity in the region was to remove the miners slipping in to dig in the rocks and pan in the streams. To its credit, for months the Grant administration attempted to keep the Black Hills free of white intruders. Increasingly, though, it faced waning public support for protecting the region, and the trickle of miners became a gully washer.

Perhaps the best way to ward off this potentially big problem was to send an expedition to explore the area; when no riches were revealed, the pressure to seize Sioux land would dissipate. But what if riches were discovered? Well, then, there would be irrefutable proof that the Sioux had to be pushed out. In addition to the mandate of Manifest Destiny, the depressed nation needed gold.

The Yellowstone Expedition had gone well enough the year before, so on July 2, 1874, Lieutenant Colonel Custer led the Seventh Cavalry out of Fort Abraham Lincoln and turned south. The new foray dwarfed the Yellowstone Expedition. In addition to the regiment, the Black Hills

Expedition included geologists, topographers to map the area, journalists, and, again, Lieutenant Colonel Frederick Grant.

The expedition also included a contingent of Indian scouts. The most prominent, who would become a Custer favorite, was Bloody Knife. Now around thirty-five years old, he had been born to a Hunkpapa Sioux father and an Arikara mother. Because of this mixed parentage, he had been abused and discriminated against by the other Sioux in his village. A particular antagonist was Gall, who had nothing but contempt for the mixed-blood.

When Bloody Knife was a teenager, he left his village with his mother to live with the Arikara tribe. This offered some relief from the cruelty—until his brothers were killed during a Sioux raid led by Gall in 1862. Bloody Knife found employment as a courier and hunter for the American Fur Company and then served as a scout and interpreter for General Alfred Sully before being hired and favored by Custer.

Summer was in full swing in the northern plains, and under a blazing sun the Seventh Cavalry traveled southwest for two weeks, covering the 225 miles to the Upper Missouri River. When the troopers entered the Black Hills, they received a glimpse of what all the fuss was about. They saw the area teeming with game, they breathed in the cool fresh air, and they marveled at the deep woods and flower-filled meadows.

But the regiment could not relax in such welcoming surroundings. It had, of course, just pierced Paha Sapa, which was sacred to the Lakota Sioux. They could expect an attack at any moment. However, during the first two weeks, as the expedition meandered around the Black Hills, nothing happened other than occasional sightings of observing warriors. Then, in Castle Creek Valley, the cavalry stumbled upon five lodges.

It was explained to Custer that the startled and scared twenty-seven people in the small village had journeyed up from the Red Cloud Agency to hunt. No danger here. Custer and the headman, One Stab, smoked a peace pipe, and his people were given coffee, bacon, and sugar.

Then there was danger—from the Arikara scouts. Here was an opportunity to annihilate a village—albeit a tiny one—of their hated enemy and take twenty-seven scalps. When the agency Sioux saw the scouts painting and dressing for battle, they fled, vanishing into the wooded hills. Maybe not as frightened, or as agile, One Stab stayed behind and was given a job as a guide.

Once again, a Custer expedition turned into a hunting party, though the target was not Lakota Sioux, who clung to being observers and not provoking any skirmishes. Tom Custer had been joined on the staff by his twenty-five-year-old brother Boston. The three brothers spent much of their time hunting antelope, bison, bighorn sheep, and even bears.* At other times, they and members of the regiment entertained themselves with baseball games and band concerts and looking for physical features to name, leading to the landmarks Terry Peak and Custer Peak.

There was even a scientific component to the frivolity. Lieutenant Colonel Custer collected porcupines, toads, snakes, and even fossils and crammed them into one of the expedition's ambulances. Many of the animals somehow survived the journey and in September were delivered to the Central Park Zoo in New York.

The outing might have continued to be little more than a lark for the Seventh Cavalry and the three fun-loving brothers except for a discovery made on the second-to-last day of July. Then, everything changed for the sacred homeland of the Lakota.

---

* Even a grizzly was no match for Custer. The bear was brought down by the bullets of the commander, Bloody Knife, and William Ludlow, one of the expedition's engineers. In a letter to Libbie, Custer took full credit for the kill.

38

THIEVES' ROAD

It was the miner with the seaworthy name of Horatio Nelson Ross who got the first glimpse of gold.

He and William McKay were panning in French Creek when Ross noticed a few shiny flakes. This by itself was not a big find, but for the next two days, the two men kept at it until late in the day of August 1, when there was enough gold collected to inspire further investigation. Custer put troopers and civilians to work as prospectors. Not taking any chances, almost two dozen members of the expedition created the Custer Park Mining Company.

Custer wrote of this promising find and gave the message to Charles Reynolds to ride the almost one hundred miles to deliver to Fort Laramie in Wyoming. The Kentucky-born Reynolds was the regiment's chief white scout. The son of a physician was college educated, which did not mean much when his schooling was done, and he became a rider for the Pony Express. During the Civil War, Reynolds served in the Tenth Kansas Infantry Regiment.

He became known as "Lonesome Charley" because he drifted from state to state and job to job and kept his life's details private—also, he made clear that he was to be left alone. In 1867, Reynolds had a quarrel with an army officer at Fort McPherson, and when it was done, the officer was missing an arm. Two years later, needing an experienced guide and buffalo hunter, Lieutenant Colonel Custer hired him.

After more exploring and frolicking, the expedition was ready to leave the Black Hills. The men emerged from them on August 14 and camped at Bear Butte. There, the commander penned a full report on the beauty of the Black Hills and their potential. Conveniently overlooked was the presence of the Sioux, probably because they had been so circumspect during the expedition's travels.*

Two weeks later, somewhat wilted from the late-summer heat, the Seventh Cavalry and its civilian entourage entered Fort Abraham Lincoln. When Custer submitted his report, a passage confirmed the thrilling news Lonesome Charley had brought: gold. The excitement spread fast, spurred by gushing newspaper headlines. Miners and prospectors and all manner of riffraff made for the Black Hills. Little or no thought was given to the fact that this Shangri-La of riches was in the Great Sioux Reservation.

Custer had acquired a new nickname from the Sioux and Cheyenne during the long expedition: Long Hair was now also "Thief." And the route he had taken would be known as the Thieves' Road.

War was inevitable.

A visit by Reynolds to the Standing Rock Agency in December would touch off an incident that would, in a way, conclude eighteen months later. At the Sioux Reservation in the northern half of Dakota Territory, the

---

* Also overlooked, or forgotten, was the expedition's original mission, which was to find a suitable location for a fort. Fort Meade (not Fort Sheridan) was eventually constructed in 1878.

scout overheard Rain-in-the-Face brag that two years earlier, he had killed three white men at the Yellowstone River. When informed of this, Lieutenant Colonel Custer dispatched his brother Tom and Captain George Yates to arrest the Hunkpapa warrior.

Accompanied by troopers, the officers worked their way through snow and subzero temperatures to the Standing Rock Agency. Tom Custer arrested Rain-in-the-Face, and he was hauled to Fort Abraham Lincoln. He remained in the guardhouse for months while George Custer interrogated him and finally elicited a confession about the murder of the three men. In mid-April, while Custer mulled the punishment to be meted out, Rain-in-the-Face escaped. He had felt humiliated being a captive at the fort, and he vowed to kill the white chief with the long yellow hair.

31

NOT FOR SALE

The year following the discovery of gold, there were over a thousand miners in the Black Hills. The Grant administration had pretty much given up on border patrol of the Great Sioux Reservation. And, increasingly, the political view became that if the Lakota land could not be protected, it might as well be exploited as much as possible. As usual, the wasichus wanted more. And memories were short about the 1868 treaty that protected Paha Sapa.

General Philip Sheridan placed oversight of the Black Hills with the Department of the Platte, headed by General George Crook, who had more experience against hostiles than Terry. Another Ohio native, Crook attended West Point, though he graduated in 1852 near the bottom of his class. He was assigned to the Fourth U.S. Infantry as a second lieutenant and served in California and Oregon, alternately protecting or fighting several tribes. He commanded the Pitt River Expedition of 1857 and, in one of several engagements, was severely wounded by an arrow.

During his nine years of service out west, Crook extended his prowess in hunting and wilderness skills, often accompanying and being instructed by Indians whose languages he learned. These skills led one of his aides to liken him to Daniel Boone, and more importantly, they provided a strong foundation for his abilities to understand, navigate, and use Civil War landscapes to Union advantage.

When the war broke out, Crook accepted a commission as colonel of the Thirty-Sixth Ohio Infantry. A survivor of Antietam, he also fought at the Battle of Chickamauga and was in pursuit of "Fighting Joe" Wheeler during the Chattanooga Campaign.* An important alliance was made in 1864, when Crook served with distinction during the Shenandoah Valley campaign led by General Sheridan.

After the war, Crook was placed in command of the Arizona Territory. His use of Apache scouts during the Tonto Basin campaign in the Yavapai War brought him much success in forcing Apache bands onto reservations. Crook's victories during that war included the Battle of Salt River Canyon—also known as the Skeleton Cave Massacre—and the Battle of Turret Peak. By the time Sheridan brought him back under his command to head the Department of the Platte, Crook was a brigadier general.

A military option to take the coveted Black Hills was not initially explored because the Department of the Interior believed the area could be bought. A visit to Washington, DC, by both Red Cloud and Spotted Tail contradicted that belief. The sacred site was not for sale at any price.

Trying a different tack, William Boyd Allison, U.S. senator from Iowa, formed a commission that traveled to Nebraska. There, in September, near

---

* Joseph Wheeler indeed enjoyed fighting. After the war, the former Confederate cavalry general served as a congressman from Alabama, and as a U.S. Army officer, he fought in the Spanish-American War in 1898. The Georgia native died eight years later in, of all places, Brooklyn and became one of the few former Confederate officers to be buried at Arlington National Cemetery.

the Red Cloud Agency, the commissioners met with five thousand Lakota Sioux.

On the first day of deliberations, a war party of Sioux, Northern Cheyenne, and Arapaho donned their finest garments, painted their faces, and adorned their hair with feathers. They rested rifles on their thighs as they rode, except when they raised their weapons to fire salutes. They also chanted war songs. The long line of charging Indians finally halted one hundred yards from the tent shielding the commissioners from the sun. The warriors fired a final round, fortunately again into the air, turned, and rode away. The quivering commissioners breathed sighs of relief.

But after a week of less-dramatic discussions, no agreement about purchasing the Black Hills could be reached. If anything, the Lakota were even unhappier. And angry. And divided between war and peace.

The older, peace-preferring headmen held sway, and there was next to no fighting during the rest of 1875. But there were backstage deliberations. While General Alfred Terry had some empathy for the Lakota, his colleague Crook and superior, Sheridan, were leaning toward a military solution. Whites and Indians simply could not coexist in the Black Hills. If you can't join them, beat them. The top military brass repaired to a planning board.

According to Robert Utley: "The program that Generals Sheridan and Crook pushed through to presidential approval reflected the desperation to which the Grant administration had been brought. On the one hand, the Treaty of 1868 imposed an unarguable legal mandate on the government to preserve the integrity of the Indian lands. On the other hand, an overpowering public opinion demanded that the government step aside and allow enterprising citizens to tap the mineral riches locked up by a handful of natives who could never use them. That dilemma led the United States to manufacture a war."

For Custer, war could not come soon enough. But when it began, he was on the sidelines.

32

CHARISMATIC COUPLE

George Armstrong Custer might embellish military reports as well as the articles he sent to the newspapers describing his latest adventures. He could withhold information, even from superiors—especially from superiors. But he was mostly an honest man. And that got him in hot water with the U.S. president.

In the fall of 1875, an investigation by *The New York Herald*—whose publisher, James Gordon Bennett Jr., was a friend of Custer's—revealed corruption within the Grant administration involving stealing and selling supplies promised by treaties to Indian reservations. While Congress moved to hold hearings on the allegations, and with all quiet on the northern plains, Custer was on leave. He and Libbie spent some of that winter living in a boardinghouse in New York. There, they went to the theater, attended parties, and looked into business opportunities.*

* A close friend was the actor Lawrence Barretts, and Custer saw him perform in *Julius Caesar* forty times.

The Civil War general and frontier hero and his lady were fawned over at every appearance.

One business opportunity was especially enticing. The Redpath Lyceum Bureau put speakers on tour, and it wanted to add Custer to its stable of loquacious luminaries. The offer was that after the anticipated summer campaign was concluded, Custer would tour the nation for several months, giving lectures five nights a week for $200 per lecture—a whopping $1,000 a week. Custer could really cash in on his expanding fame—if, however, he was not running for president.

Custer was a Democrat, and he was courted by fellow Democrats. While the expected nominee in 1876 was Samuel Tilden, the governor of New York, to run against whoever the Republicans put up to succeed Grant, the prospect of replacing one military hero with another had to be considered. If Custer were to return from the summer campaign covered in glory, he would be as unbeatable politically as he was militarily.* Custer kept that in mind when his leave concluded and the couple boarded a train to return west.

Back under the command of General Crook, Custer was apprised of the plan concocted by Crook with Generals Terry and Sheridan. The Grant administration was giving up even the pretense of trying to protect the Black Hills from white intrusion. Further, members of the northern plains tribes were to be required to reside on their respective reservations full-time. Those who refused would be hunted down. When Custer arrived in St. Paul on February 15, 1876, rebellious Lakota and Cheyenne

* True, by the end of June, Tilden had been officially nominated by the Democrats. But party leaders would have found a way to accommodate a national hero in the wake of his latest victories out west. And as it turned out, in the election of 1876, Tilden lost, to Rutherford B. Hayes of Ohio—a Civil War hero who had risen to brevet major general. While a major in the Twenty-Third Regiment of Ohio Volunteer Infantry, Hayes had under his command Private William McKinley, who became the last U.S. president to have served in the war.

bands were two weeks beyond the deadline set for them to be settled in their new and for many unfamiliar homes.

Many of the Indians did not have a choice. Because of ineptitude as well as corruption within the Department of the Interior, not enough food and other supplies promised to the reservations were received, and the residents were threatened with starvation before the long winter ended. Hunting for buffalo, even in the harshest weather conditions, was a necessity. And there was the notion of freedom: As far as the Indians knew, the Treaty of 1868 allowed for bands to roam off the reservations, and the wasichus could not arbitrarily disallow that.

They could and did. When it was reported to Zacharia Chandler, the secretary of the interior, that many Lakota, Cheyenne, Arapaho, and Kiowa were not staying put on the reservations, he washed his hands of the matter by turning it over to the War Department. Its secretary, William Belknap, let Sheridan know that he and his team were free to plan a new campaign. All were in agreement: George Armstrong Custer would be at the forefront of it.

And then, abruptly, he was out of the campaign completely.

33

AN ANGRY PRESIDENT

In Washington, DC, the House Committee on Expenditures in the War Department undertook its own investigation and also discovered that indeed the Native American reservation system was riddled with corruption. Lieutenant Colonel Custer was about to become collateral damage.

In 1870, President Grant had granted to the secretary of war the sole power to appoint and license sutlers with ownership rights to highly lucrative "traderships" at U.S. military forts on the western frontier. The burly Belknap—who had served and been wounded in action under Grant—appointed a New York contractor, Caleb P. Marsh, to the trader post at Fort Sill, which was already held by John Evans. An illicit partnership contract authorized by Belknap was drawn up that allowed Evans to keep the tradership at Fort Sill, provided that he make payments to Marsh, who in turn split those payments with Belknap's wife.

The committee's hearings revealed an even more convoluted scheme: Profits from the Fort Sill tradership and similar activities at other posts along the frontier were split among Marsh, Evans, Belknap, his current wife, and, generously, his ex-wife. The primary victims were the Indians on the reservations because every dollar being pocketed by Belknap and his conspirators was a dollar not spent on food, blankets, clothing, and other necessities. Hence, the anger and desperation during the long winters.

During the committee's investigation, Custer was called to Washington to testify in general about malfeasance in the Grant administration. He did and should have left it at that; however, he further infuriated the president by accusing his brother, Orvil Grant, of being involved in the trader post rings. The testimony earned national headlines because Custer, though a high-profile figure, was still a lieutenant colonel, challenging both the president and the secretary of war.

In retaliation, a boiling-mad President Grant had Custer suspended from duty. The frontier campaign would have to get along without him.

General Sheridan did not think that was possible, and George Crook and Alfred Terry were not keen on taking the lead. But even Sheridan, who not only occupied a powerful military position but had strong ties to Ulysses Grant dating back to the war, could not oppose an angry president. Perhaps a personal appearance to kiss the ring and beg forgiveness?

Custer twice attempted to visit Grant at the White House but was rebuffed. On May 1, Custer tried again. Most likely, he was prepared to apologize if doing so would get his command back. But he did not get the chance. After five hours of dawdling in a waiting room, Custer left.

34

SOLDIERS IN THE SKY

Seemingly out of options and his career on pause—at best—Custer boarded a train for Chicago. There, he changed trains for one that would take him to St. Paul and then on to reunite with an anxious Libbie. And who knew what after that. Custer could not possibly bide time at Fort Abraham Lincoln and witness the campaign getting underway with Marcus Reno at the head of the Seventh Cavalry.

On May 6, Custer arrived in St. Paul and went directly to Terry to tearfully plead for help. The general agreed. Yes, there was some compassion, but as Robert Utley notes, Terry "had never campaigned against Indians, and none of his other subordinates could boast more than a pale shadow of Custer's experience. Terry needed Custer at his side." Or at the end of a long leash.

Drawing on the expert experience he had as an attorney, Terry crafted a carefully worded plea to President Grant that Custer would sign. It concluded with "Custer" making a masterful military argument to the former general of the army: "I appeal to you as a soldier to spare me the humiliation of seeing my regiment march to meet the enemy and I not to share its dangers."

In an accompanying message, Terry wrote, "Lieutenant Colonel Custer's services would be very valuable with his regiment." And he prevailed on General Sheridan to send to Grant his endorsement of the Custer/Terry missive.

"He might attempt to cast himself as the noble truthsayer victimized by an implacable tyrant, but as was now obvious to Terry, no one had done more to undermine Custer's career than Custer himself," writes Nathaniel Philbrick. "He was an impulsive blabbermouth, but he was also the most experienced Indian fighter in the Dakota Territory, and Terry, fifty years old and very content with his office job in St. Paul, needed him."

This mini-campaign worked. The president lifted the suspension. Grant's heart might have been softened by Custer's poignant appeal, but more probable was the president had pondered how he and the eventual Republican ticket would be pummeled by the press if the campaign against the Indians failed. The risk was not worth the continuing detention of a lieutenant colonel, no matter how insubordinate he was.

And so, on May 14, at Fort Abraham Lincoln, the full Seventh Cavalry collected themselves and their supply wagons and prepared to set off. Among the troopers and civilian workers was Mark Kellogg, a reporter for *The Bismarck Tribune* who also contributed news from the frontier to the Associated Press and *The New York Tribune*.*

According to Evan S. Connell in *Son of the Morning Star*, "Kellogg is an indistinct figure. Until his death nobody paid much attention to him. He was about forty years old, youthful in appearance except that he wore spectacles and his hair was turning gray, a widower who smoked

---

* The purple prose–loving Mark Kellogg would have the unhappy distinction of being the first correspondent for the Associated Press to die in the line of duty.

Bull Durham and enjoyed playing chess. Dying with Custer gave him a thimbleful of immortality."

In a dispatch written that day, Kellogg described the buckskin-wearing cavalry commander—Colonel Sturgis, of course, would not be saddling up—as "flitting to and fro, in his quick eager way."

Kellogg concluded: "The General is full of perfect readiness for a fray with the hostile red devils, and woe to the body of scalp-lifters that comes within reach of himself and brave companions in arms."

There was more flitting and froing for three days back at the fort because of threatening midspring storms. Finally, the weather became more amenable to traveling, and the regiment was ready to ride. As the mounted band played "Garry Owen," the Seventh Cavalry, with Custer leading, paraded through and then out of Fort Abraham Lincoln, colorful guidons and flags flapping in the early morning breeze. In the regiment's wake were 150 wagons, their worn white canvas tops quivering as the wheels creaked up the hill.

Finally, the Campaign of 1876, intended to end the defiant independence of nonreservation Natives, had begun. Many in the fort believed the pageantry of the Seventh Cavalry's departure would soon be bookended by a glorious return.

However, Libbie Custer had doubts right away. She and her sister-in-law, Maggie Calhoun, had been invited to accompany the regiment to its first camp that night on the Heart River and then return to Fort Abraham Lincoln. While riding alongside her husband, Libbie turned back to look at the almost two-mile-long column. The morning sun was getting rid of the damp mist that had obscured the blue sky.

And Libbie saw a mirage: Because of a rare meteorological phenomenon, a mirror image of the Seventh Cavalry was seen in the sky—as if they were already in heaven or poised to fall from the sky.

ACT IV

THE SEARCHERS

I would be willing, yes glad, to see a battle every day of my life.

—GEORGE ARMSTRONG CUSTER

35

SURRENDER OR DIE

At the end of that long first day of travel, the regiment camped on the Heart River. There, Custer might have surveyed the soldiers and scouts under his command. Most of his more senior officers—for example, Major Marcus Reno and Captains Frederick Benteen, Thomas Weir, and Tom Custer—had served with the man they still called "General" for years.

Also, many of the men were seasoned troopers and hailed from other countries, primarily from Germany and Ireland. As isolated and uncomfortable as life on the frontier could be, the army offered them the opportunity to explore their adopted country and get paid to do so. It was a job, and they made the best of it. There were risks, but those risks broke up the boredom.

And perhaps that made the hardships of a frontier campaign a bit tolerable. As Nathaniel Philbrick puts it, "The smells associated with this column of approximately twelve hundred men and sixteen hundred horses and mules were pungent and inescapable—an eye-watering combination of horsehair and sweaty human reek. The stench was particularly bad at night, when all of them were contained within a half-mile-wide parallelogram of carefully arranged tents, picketed horses, and freshly dug latrines. If it was too wet to light a fire, the men lived on hardtack and cold sowbelly doused with vinegar and salt. Since wet boots shrank as they dried, it was necessary to wear them at night."

Civilian interpreters and Indian scouts were valuable to the regiment. There was loyal Lonesome Charley Reynolds, of course. Also: "I now have some Crow scouts with me, as they are familiar with the country," Custer informed Libbie in a letter dated June 21. "They are magnificent-looking men, so much handsomer and Indian-like than any we have ever seen, and so jolly and sportive; nothing of the gloomy, silent red-man about them."

And on this mission was Mitch Boyer. Born in 1837, his father was a French Canadian who worked for the American Fur Company, and his mother was a Santee Sioux. Mitch—his Sioux name was Kar-pash—grew up with two half brothers, John and Antoine Boyer, and triplet sisters.*

After the Civil War, he was working as an interpreter at Fort Phil Kearny, where he married a Crow woman named Magpie Out-of-Doors. They had two children, and one of the other benefits of marriage was that Boyer became fluent in the Crow language. It was because of this that Custer requested that Boyer become part of the Seventh Cavalry. Also, Boyer knew the area better than most men.

While camped that first night, Custer may have also reviewed with Terry the plan for the campaign. It was mostly General Sheridan's idea, and a simple one. The Seventh Cavalry was making its way south and west. A second force would march east from Fort Ellis in Montana. This column was commanded by Colonel John Gibbon. At forty-seven, he was

---

* John Boyer's only claim to fame was being the first man legally executed in Wyoming Territory. In 1871, after being convicted of a double homicide, he was hanged at Fort Laramie.

a bit long in the tooth to be a field commander, but his age also meant he was an officer with a long battlefield résumé.

Early in the Civil War, Gibbon was made chief of artillery for Major General Irvin McDowell, and a year later, he was promoted to brigadier general and placed in command of the "Iron Brigade" consisting of men from Wisconsin, Indiana, and Michigan. He made his mark on this illustrious unit, instilling rigid discipline and drilling them into some of the more tenacious fighters in the Army of the Potomac. Gibbon led them at the Battle of Second Manassas and at the Battle of South Mountain, where General Joseph Hooker gave the Iron Brigade its famous nickname.

The brigade suffered heavy losses fighting in the bloody cornfield at Antietam, where Gibbon himself personally manned an artillery piece. Late in 1862, Gibbon was promoted to command of the Second Division, I Corps, which he led at Fredericksburg, where he was wounded. Returning to duty several months later, Gibbon commanded the Second Division of the Hancock's II Corps at Gettysburg and even directed the corps itself for brief periods during the battle. On July 3, Gibbon's men, stationed along Cemetery Ridge, played a significant role in the repulse of Pickett's Charge, and Gibbon was wounded for a second time. During his convalescence, he attended the dedication of the new national cemetery on November 19 and heard Abraham Lincoln deliver the Gettysburg Address.

By the time of the opening of the Overland Campaign of 1864, Gibbon was back in command of his division and led his men in the Wilderness, Spotsylvania, Cold Harbor, and Petersburg battles. The apparently unkillable Gibbon was promoted to major general and in January 1865 was given command of the XXIV Corps in the Army of the James. At the conclusion of the Appomattox campaign that spring, Gibbon served as one of the surrender commissioners when the Army of Northern Virginia finally succumbed to defeat.

According to General Terry, Colonel Gibbon's task was to take his combined force of infantry and cavalry to the north bank of the Yellowstone River. At the very least, if an attack sent Sitting Bull's warriors and families running north, Gibbon would prevent them from getting too far, certainly not escaping into Canada. They would have no choice but to surrender or die.

The third column would be commanded by George Crook. The general with the prominent beard had once, like Custer, almost ridden into death. While campaigning in eastern Oregon during the winter of 1866–67, Crook's scouts located a Paiute village near the eastern edge of Steens Mountain. After covering all the escape routes, Crook ordered an attack on the village. His intention was to view the raid from afar, but his horse got spooked and galloped ahead, and inadvertently the bouncing commander led his own charge. The horse carried Crook through the village and a crossfire. Miraculously, he exited the other end of the village without a scratch.

Now, in June 1876, "a campaign of converging columns was taking shape," notes Robert Utley. However, "It did not involve any concert of action." Worse: "Neither Terry nor Crook knew where the Indians were. None of the generals or their staffs proved adept at analyzing and digesting the intelligence placed before them" by Reynolds, Boyer, and the Indian scouts. And: "Gibbon knew exactly where they were, although he shared his knowledge with no one."

That could be a drawback. Certainly, so, too, would be the annihilation of one of the three columns. On the seventeenth, Crook found himself in at least as much danger as he had been in Oregon.

36

CRAZY HORSE AT THE ROSEBUD

The Cheyenne would call it the Battle Where the Girl Saved Her Brother. Less prosaic white writers would call it the Battle of the Rosebud. By any name, it was almost a disaster, one that canceled George Crook's participation in General Sheridan's overall plan and may have doomed the Seventh Cavalry.

The column that had departed from Fort Fetterman (near present-day Douglas, Wyoming) under Crook was called the Bighorn and Yellowstone Expedition. It consisted of 993 cavalry and mule-mounted men, 197 civilian packers and teamsters, 65 Montana miners, three scouts, and five journalists.* Crook's much-valued chief scout was Frank Grouard.

He had been born in September in French Polynesia. His father was a Mormon missionary who married a Native woman. When he returned to

* One of the teamsters, disguised as a man, was twenty-four-year-old Martha Jane Canary, who would become more familiar to American West aficionados as Calamity Jane.

the U.S., the family lived in Utah. At about age nineteen, Frank Grouard was captured by Crow Indians, stripped of all possessions, and left in the forest. Sioux hunters found him, and Sitting Bull himself adopted him as a brother. Grouard married a Sioux woman and learned to speak the language fluently.

For seven years, Grouard lived in the camps of Sitting Bull and Crazy Horse. Around age twenty-six, he decided to return to white civilization. Soon after, he took the job as a chief scout for Crook. His knowledge of the Sioux was appreciated by the general, and the scout was well paid. However, Grouard was probably unaware that when Sitting Bull learned that he would be the scout for General Crook, the Hunkpapa vowed to kill his former brother in battle.

Crook's column first encountered Indians on June 9. The expedition had camped the night before at the Tongue River. Lakota scouts had been monitoring the army's progress, and the next morning an attack began. It was, however, a long-distance one, firing from afar. Still, even though only two men were wounded, Crook decided not to advance farther until Grouard returned with reinforcements.

On the fourteenth, he did, leading quite a contingent—175 Crow and 86 Shoshoni. The large force of well-armed warriors welcomed the opportunity to strike a blow against their old enemies, although they warned Crook that the Lakota and Cheyenne were as "numerous as grass." To the newcomers, that just meant more to kill and more coups to count.

Two days later, with the Crow and Shoshoni in the lead, Crook's column advanced northward beyond the Tongue to the headwaters of Rosebud Creek. Each soldier carried four days' rations and one hundred rounds of ammunition. Crook's intention to make a quick and quiet march was spoiled when the Crow and Shoshoni encountered a buffalo herd and began shooting them.

Crook was further hampered by two misperceptions. He expected to soon find a large Indian village on Rosebud Creek to attack, but the

Indian village was farther to the west, on Ash Creek. Second, he underestimated the determination of the hostiles: He expected them to employ their usual hit-and-run tactics, not stand and fight.

A mostly Sioux and Cheyenne force of almost one thousand men set out from their village before midnight on June 16 to seek the soldiers on the Rosebud. They were led by Sitting Bull himself. He had not necessarily endorsed the attack. His dream had suggested that the army soldiers would come to him. But the younger warriors seethed with anger at this latest and boldest invasion. Realizing they could not be restrained, Sitting Bull had agreed to go along.

His presence, however, was mostly inspirational. At forty-five, he was old to be charging wasichu soldiers, and he was still not fully recovered from the ordeal of the Sun Dance. Again, Crazy Horse, idolized by the eager warriors, would be the field general. He would be assisted by One Bull, the adopted son of Sitting Bull.

For Crazy Horse, fighting the whites had become personal. His close friend Hump had been killed six years earlier. Though it was in a battle with the Shoshoni, Crazy Horse still lashed out at every enemy over the loss. Worse, They Are Afraid of Her, his daughter with Black Shawl, had died at age three from cholera—one of the diseases brought to the northern plains by the wasichu. He had mourned for days beside her burial scaffold. He would never stop mourning his daughter.

Crazy Horse wanted vengeance, and the cumbersome General Crook column offered an opportunity for it.

The large Sioux and Cheyenne war party rode the rest of the night and then let their horses eat and recuperate for a couple of hours while the men applied their war paint. Soon after they resumed the ride, at about 8:30 A.M., they spotted Crook's scouts.

Meanwhile, the column had marched northward along the south fork of Rosebud Creek. The soldiers, particularly the mule-riding infantry, were still fatigued from the previous day's thirty-five-mile march and then reveille at 3:00 A.M. At eight o'clock that morning, Crook stopped to rest his men and animals. Although deep in hostile territory, the general made no special dispositions for defense. The Crow and Shoshoni scouts remained alert while the soldiers played cards and even napped.

Soon, the soldiers began to hear gunfire coming from the bluffs to the north, where the Crow and Shoshoni were positioned. They thought the Indian scouts were back to shooting buffalo. But as the intensity of fire increased, two Crow rushed into the army camp, shouting, "Lakota, Lakota!"

The Sioux and Cheyenne had hotly engaged Crook's scouts on the high ground north of the main body. Heavily outnumbered, the Crow and Shoshoni fell back toward the camp, but their fighting withdrawal gave a startled Crook time to organize his forces.

Given the size of the Lakota and Cheyenne army and the advantage of surprise it had, plus the weariness of the troops, Crook's command could have been destroyed. It was instead saved by the fierce fighting of the Crow and Shoshoni, who stood up to the assault. Of course, their priority was not the soldiers and civilians—the scouts wanted to kill their longtime enemies. But the result was the same.

37

STAYING PUT

The battle that ensued would last for six hours and consist of disconnected actions, charges, and countercharges by the combatants. Crook and his men may have been unaware that their adversaries' field general was the near-legendary Crazy Horse. The Sioux and Cheyenne were divided into several groups, as were the soldiers as the battle progressed. The soldiers could fend off assaults by the Indians and force them to retreat but could not catch and destroy them.

According to the eighteen-year-old Cheyenne warrior Wooden Leg, "There were charges back and forth. Our Indians fought and ran away, fought and ran away. The soldiers and their Indian scouts did the same. Sometimes we charged them, sometimes they charged us."

Crook initially directed his forces to seize the high ground north and south of the Rosebud Creek. He ordered one of his senior officers, Captain Stewart Van Vliet, with two companies of the Third Cavalry, to occupy the high bluffs south of the creek to guard against an Indian attack from that direction. In the north, the commands of Major Alexander

Chambers, with two companies of the Fourth Infantry and three companies of the Ninth Infantry, and Captain Henry Noyes, with three troops of the Second Cavalry, formed a dismounted skirmish line and advanced toward the enemy. Their progress was slow due to flanking fire from Indians occupying the high ground to the northeast.

To accelerate the advance, Crook ordered Captain Anson Mills, commanding members of the Third Cavalry, to charge the Indians.* Mills's mounted assault unnerved the warriors enough that they withdrew along the ridgeline. Mills quickly re-formed his men and led another charge, driving the Indians northwest again to the next hill.

Mills was preparing to drive the Indians from that hill, too, when he received orders from Crook to cease the advance and assume a defensive posture. Chambers and Noyes led their forces forward in support and within minutes joined Mills on top of the ridge. The bulk of Crook's command, joined by the packers and miners, occupied a hill that would unimaginatively be called Crook's Hill. Establishing his headquarters there at approximately 9:30 A.M., Crook considered his next move.

During Mills's advance the event had occurred that would earn the Cheyenne name for the battle. The horse of a Cheyenne warrior, Comes in Sight, was shot out from under him. While fleeing on foot from chasing soldiers, his sister Buffalo Calf Road Woman rode to his rescue. Comes in Sight jumped onto her horse, and the two successfully escaped.

Captain Mills was impressed with the swarming Indians at his front. He would later report: "They were the best cavalry soldiers on earth. In charging up toward us they exposed little of their person, hanging on with one arm around the neck and one leg over the horse, firing and lancing

---

* Anson Mills, who would live to ninety, founded El Paso, Texas, and became wealthy from inventing and manufacturing a woven cartridge belt for the U.S. and British armies.

from underneath the horses' necks, so that there was no part of the Indian at which we could aim."

A sidebar to the battle was the humiliation of Jack Red Cloud. The son of the Oglala headman was knocked off his horse and surrounded by Crow scouts, who recognized him. They tore his war bonnet off, whipped and taunted him, and took his rifle, all the while laughing with glee. A Sioux warrior appeared and pulled Jack Red Cloud onto his horse, and the two fled. The embarrassment was too great to bear—the once-defiant son of the great Oglala headman returned to the Red Cloud Agency in Nebraska and stayed there.*

Crook decided to have his cavalry charge, and the attack secured key terrain; however, it did little damage to the Sioux and Cheyenne warriors. Assaults scattered them, but they did not quit the field as Crook kept expecting. They fell back a bit and kept firing from a distance, attacking several times in small parties. When counterattacked by the soldiers, the warriors sped away on their swift ponies.

It finally dawned on Crook that his charges were ineffective. The general's previous experience in Arizona had him believing incorrectly that the unusual aggressiveness of the Sioux and Cheyenne was propelled by needing to defend their families in a nearby village. He ordered Captains Mills and Noyes to withdraw their cavalry from the high ground on Crook's Hill and swing eastward to follow the Rosebud north to find the suspected village. He recalled Van Vliet's force from the south side of the Rosebud to reinforce him on Crook's Hill.

While Mills and Noyes made their way up the Rosebud, searching for a village that did not exist, they found the force led by Lieutenant Colonel William Royall, Crook's second in command, in a tight spot. Royall had

---

* Upon his father's death in 1909, Jack Red Cloud became the headman of the Oglala. He would fulfill the role for only nine years, until his own death in 1918 at age sixty.

pursued the Indians attacking Crook's camp with six companies of cavalry, unwisely advancing rapidly along the ridgeline to the northwest to a point about one mile away from Crook. Seizing this opportunity, Crazy Horse shifted his warriors' main effort away from Crook and concentrated their attacks on Royall, and he was in danger of being cut off from Crook and overwhelmed.

Royall's situation continued to worsen, and he tried to withdraw his entire command across Kollmar Creek, but the hostiles' fire was too heavy. Next, he began to withdraw southeast along the ridgeline. A large group of Sioux and Cheyenne broke off from the fight against Crook's main forces and charged boldly down the valley, advancing all the way to the Rosebud. Just as the outmatched soldiers began to panic, the Crow and Shoshoni arrived and drove the Sioux and Cheyenne back. The arrival of Mills and Noyes's horse soldiers also helped.

At approximately 12:30 P.M., Royall began another withdrawal. His cavalry remounted and prepared to ride through gunfire to reach the safety of Crook's main position. As the troopers began their dash, the Crow and Shoshoni scouts countercharged the pursuing Sioux and Cheyenne and relieved much of the pressure on Royall's men. Two companies of infantry provided covering fire from the northeast side of the ravine. Royall's command suffered most of the Army casualties during the battle.

Captain Mills and his men pursued the retreating force led by Crazy Horse but soon gave up the chase. The Battle of the Rosebud was over at about 2:30 P.M.

By the standards of the usual hit-and-run raids of the Plains Indians, the battle was a long and bloody engagement. The Sioux and Cheyenne fought with persistence and demonstrated a willingness to accept casualties rather than break off the encounter. The delaying action by Crook's Crow and Shoshoni allies during the early stages of the battle saved his command from a devastating surprise attack. Indeed, the repeated intervention of the scouts throughout the battle was crucial to averting disaster for Crook. Instead of expressing relief or gratitude, the general claimed victory by virtue of occupying the field at the end of the battle day.*

Concerned for his wounded and short on supplies, Crook retraced his steps and made camp on Goose Creek. He remained there immobile for seven weeks, awaiting reinforcements. He had his wounded piled into wagons and transported 175 miles to Fort Fetterman. When it became apparent that there was no fight left in the commanding officer, the force of Crow and Shoshone warrior-scouts quit and headed for home. A parting shot was to call Crook "Squaw Chief."

He was, effectively, absent from the rest of the campaign. Most egregious, Crook made no move to search for the two other columns or even try to pass along any knowledge he had gleaned from the Battle of the Rosebud.

* After Crook's departure, some Lakota and Cheyenne warriors returned to the battlefield and piled up rocks at the location of key events in the battle. Some of the rock piles they built can be seen there today.

38

THE STEAMBOAT

Unaware of Crook's brush with catastrophe, the two other columns under Colonel Gibbon and General Terry pushed on to carry out Sheridan's plan. During the next week, they would be searching almost as much for each other as for Sitting Bull's village.

General Terry was startled by the result of a reconnaissance led by Major Reno—or lack thereof. While a disgruntled Custer and the rest of the Seventh Cavalry were camped at the mouth of the Tongue River, Reno, as ordered by Terry, had taken troopers into the valleys of the Tongue and the Powder Rivers.

According to James Donovan, "Custer had expected to lead the scouting expedition, as he had led every other during the march from Fort Lincoln. But Custer had tested Terry's patience more than once on the march, and Terry may have wanted to show him who was in command. This was what Reno had been waiting for: an independent command and a chance to show what he could do."

Unfortunately, he did. Reno and his men—including the scout Mitch

Boyer—mostly wandered around under the watchful eyes of Sioux and Cheyenne scouts. During the meandering journey of almost 250 horse-wearying miles, they had found two large Indian villages that had been abandoned. This was actually useful intelligence—while it did not tell the army where Sitting Bull and his followers were, it showed where they weren't, which was where Terry had expected to find them. The plan would have to be reworked.

But first, Reno had to be upbraided. Instead of praising him for a rare display of initiative, Reno was reprimanded for knowingly exceeding his orders by roaming way too far and wide. Custer took his second in command to task, too, for risking being detected by Sitting Bull's warriors, which could have robbed the regiment of a surprise attack—or any attack at all, if the big village packed up and left the area.

Custer took his resentment a startling step further. He wrote and sent a dispatch that was published, without attribution, in *The New York Herald*. It began: "Reno, after an absence of ten days, returned, when it was found, to the disgust and disappointment of every member of the expedition, from the commanding General down to the lowest private, that Reno, instead of simply failing to accomplish any good results, has so misconducted his force as to embarrass, if not seriously and permanently mar, all hopes of future success of the expedition."

Custer concluded: "A court-martial is strongly hinted at, and if one is not ordered it will not be because it is not richly deserved."

Fortunately, Terry did not have access to *The Herald*. The general convened a meeting of his commanders on the afternoon of June 21. The location of the conference on that first day of summer was aboard the *Far West*, moored at the south bank of the Yellowstone at the mouth of the Rosebud River.

It is not known if Sitting Bull was aware of the steamboat, but in any case, it represented a big transportation advantage the army employed. The boat could steam up and down the Yellowstone, bringing supplies much faster and relatively risk-free compared to cavalry horses and especially infantry. It was another example of wasichu technology widening the gap between them and the northern plains tribes.

The *Far West* had been built in Pittsburgh in 1870 for the Coulson Packet Company. It was 190 feet long with a beam of 33 feet and had three decks, a cupola-like pilothouse, and two tall smokestacks. A big advantage the boat had was it drew only 30 inches of water fully loaded with two hundred tons of freight, which made travel through shallow sections of rivers possible. Between its first and second decks were two high-pressure steam engines powered by three boilers that consumed as many as thirty cords of wood a day. The engines drove a single 30-foot-wide stern wheel. The *Far West* also had two steam capstans, one on each side of the bow, being the first boat built with more than one.

The captain was Grant Prince Marsh, who was in the midst of what would be a legendary career thanks to many exploits during the decades of piloting boats on the Missouri and Yellowstone Rivers. Born in 1834, Marsh began as a cabin boy on the Missouri and eventually became a captain at an opportune time. After the discovery of gold in the Montana Territory in the early 1860s, the Missouri River became the major artery for freight and passengers traveling to Fort Benton near the head of navigation on the upper river. The last three hundred miles ran through a vast unsettled prairie and the remote Missouri Breaks.

As a riverboat pilot in this wilderness, Marsh contended with migrating buffalo herds, hostile tribes, and severe weather, including violent windstorms, along with numerous water hazards from rapids, snags, and sandbars. In 1875, he made the farthest upriver ascent of the Yellowstone, arriving at a point just above present-day Billings, Montana.

The new plan concocted in the cabin of the steamboat was not much different from the first plan. General Terry was not going to stray from the strategy formulated by Sheridan, even though the latter was nowhere near Montana.

Terry determined that Custer, coming from the east, would search out and find Sitting Bull's main camp and attack it. Gibbon and his Montana column of 440 men would be to the west and north of where the Indian village was expected to be—somewhere on the Little Bighorn River—and would block efforts at escape.* The Sioux and Cheyenne—especially the women, children, and elderly—would be trapped, and the warriors would have to surrender. Such an outcome, particularly if Sitting Bull was killed or captured, could well end any significant resistance—maybe even forever.

Though not nearly the glory hound Custer was, Terry had to be envisioning the headlines that would declare a historic victory. With Crook effectively out of commission, Terry was the only general in the field—even if he was on a boat. Let the reconfigured campaign begin.

* Much to Custer's relief, Terry enjoyed the nicer accommodations on the *Far West* enough that he made it his command headquarters rather than remain on land.

39

"SON OF THE MORNING STAR"

At noon on June 22, with an unusual cold wind coming out of the north to greet the first full day of summer, Terry ordered the Seventh Cavalry—composed of 31 officers, 578 enlisted men, and 45 scouts and guides—to begin a reconnaissance in force along the Rosebud. The general probably did not admit that this was what Custer would have done if given the assignment that had gone to Reno. However, he did allow Custer the prerogative to "depart" from orders if he saw "sufficient reason."

With the expectation of this search finally finding a large number of hostiles, Custer was offered the use of a Gatling gun.* But he declined, believing they would slow his rate of travel. He was passing up another

* The deadly but cumbersome weapon was a rapid-firing, multiple-barrel firearm invented in 1861, a forerunner of the modern electric motor–driven rotary cannon. Its creator was the North Carolina native Richard Gatling, who had a remarkable if overlooked career. Among his other inventions were a screw propeller for steamboats (at age twenty-one), a rice-sowing machine, a wheat drill, and improvements to toilets and bicycles. Also, in 1850, Gatling graduated from

weapon that demonstrated the technology gap. The rotating barrels of the Gatling gun could fire 350 rounds per minute. But Custer knew that hauling the weapon slowed everyone down, and he was in a hurry.

As they said goodbye to each other and promised to rendezvous when attacking fleeing Sioux and Cheyenne, Colonel Gibbon called, "Now, Custer, don't be greedy, but wait for us."

The former Boy General laughed and said, "No, I will not."

Custer's column set off lacking two crucial pieces of information.* One was Crook's whereabouts and what, if anything, his column was doing to put pressure on the combined strength of the Sioux and Cheyenne. The other was the different way the northern plains tribes were fighting. This was when Crook's experience in the Battle of the Rosebud would have been valuable. But Crook, more concerned with licking his wounds than communicating, would send out a report too late for its details to make a difference.

Custer need not have bothered about what worried him most—that Crook's absence and silence indicated he was busy engaging the enemy and would have all the subsequent laurels to himself. Or possibly worse: Crook was letting the Sioux and Cheyenne slip away, and there would be no decisive battle at all.

"The lack of concern over Indian strength reflected the usual military assumption that the Indians would scatter and run if given the chance," explains Robert Utley. "If only they could be caught, Custer often boasted, the Seventh could whip any force of Indians on the Plains. Thus everyone worried not about how to defeat the Indians but how to catch them before they discovered the soldiers and fled in all directions."

Ohio Medical College. He was elected as the first president of the American Association of Inventors and Manufacturers in 1891, serving for six years.

* Also under Custer's command were two of his dogs, Tuck and Blucher, as well as Joe Bush, a dog that belonged to I Company.

While Gibbon's column was marching toward the mouth of the Little Bighorn, Custer's regiment was retracing Reno's steps. During the day of June 23, the Seventh Cavalry pushed on from the point where Reno had halted. Even without a newspaper, Reno had to be aware of his commander's condemnation, and reliving his reconnaissance foray had to be humiliating. Helping him suffer in silence was the flask tucked inside his tunic.

There were plenty of Arikara scouts, but Custer preferred the contingent of six Crow scouts: White Swan, Goes Ahead, Curly, Hairy Moccasin, White Man Runs Him, and their leader, Half Yellow Face. He liked, too, that their name for him was "Son of the Morning Star." Like the Arikara, the Crow wore a red band on their right arm. They were well aware that to many soldiers, one Indian looked like another, so the red band could prevent a scout being killed by friendly fire.

"Custer impressed the [Crow] scouts deeply," writes John S. Gray in *Custer's Last Campaign*. "Custer did have a better knack for handling Indian scouts than most officers; he treated them decently, made the effort to understand them, and recognized their unique skills and knowledge, all of which inspired their best efforts and loyalty."

The column soon encountered an abandoned Sun Dance lodge with a white man's scalp hanging from it. Whether or not they took this as an omen, Custer and his men continued, following a trail carved into the ground by dragged lodgepoles.

The next discovery made the Crow and Arikara scouts nervous: It became obvious from the marks left by lodgepoles and pony droppings that an increasing number of Indians were joining together on the trail. Plus, as determined by the droppings, this large number of Indians was only thirty miles ahead.

40

TRIBAL POWER

Indeed, a massive village was about that far away. In the previous weeks, Sitting Bull and his followers, housed in about four hundred lodges, had worked their way up the Rosebud. The size of the gathering as well as the pony herd forced the Sioux and Cheyenne to keep on the move after only a few days to another location to find buffalo and other game, fresh water for drinking and bathing, and firewood. In addition to hunting parties, Sitting Bull sent scouts out to watch for approaching soldiers. Thus, he was well aware of Colonel Gibbon's column to the north and west and, midmonth, Crook's column heading down the Rosebud.

The day after that battle, the village was on the move again, lumbering down Sundance Creek to the Little Bighorn, where the lodges were once again raised. Daily life resumed, and it featured a fresh and large influx of Indians. With the approach of summer, hundreds of them had left their reservations to join Sitting Bull's followers to begin a new season of hunting. They were not supposed to be doing this, according to the dictates of the Grant administration, but many of the reservation dwellers did not understand or care about the Great White Father's orders. It was time to hunt and renew ties with their northern plains cousins.

Six separate tribal circles were crowded into the narrow valley. Five of them belonged to the Sioux—Hunkpapa, Oglala, Miniconjou, Sans Arc, Blackfeet, Two Kettle, Brule, and a handful of Yanktonai and Santee. The sixth circle consisted of about 120 Cheyenne lodges.

"In the past few days a horde of summer roamers had expanded the Sioux and Cheyenne village from the four hundred lodges of the winter roamers to one thousand lodges," reports John S. Gray. "Furthermore, the Rosebud fight had fully warned the Indians that the army had marked them and their way of life for destruction; to them, the issue was nothing less than survival."

There was another reason for the swelling size of Sitting Bull's camp: The charismatic headman had sent out runners to agencies and reservations, boldly telling them to come north and fight the wasichu army. Plenty of coups would be counted as they defeated the soldiers and kept the land open to the Sioux and their victorious allies. Most older leaders, like Red Cloud and Spotted Tail, rejected the invitation. But a younger generation was ready to fight.

It was the markings of the multiplying number of lodgepoles and related signs that told the Seventh Cavalry's scouts that what was already expected to be a big village with many occupants was rapidly growing even bigger.

"Equally significant," writes Robert Utley, "the village contained a people basking proudly in the fullness of tribal power. Contrary to the assumptions and the mindset of the planners aboard the *Far West*, the Indians felt little inclination to avoid conflict. Their grievances united them in a determination to fight against those who would seize the Black Hills and send soldiers to force them out of unceded territory."

41

YET ANOTHER NEW PLAN

Late in the afternoon of June 24, Custer's Crow and Arikara scouts returned to the regiment with welcome news: The trail of Indian movements indicated that Sitting Bull's village was directly ahead, on the lower Little Bighorn River. But that meant Custer faced a dilemma. His orders from Terry told him to keep following the Rosebud, which would take the Seventh Cavalry away from the village. The dilemma was dashed in moments as Custer accepted—with relish—that as commander in the field, he would have to improvise.

That evening, Custer gathered his officers together and announced a new plan. The regiment would follow the Indian trail while it was dark to reduce the risk of detection. The next day, the twenty-fifth, would be one of rest, and then at sunrise of the next day, the Seventh Cavalry would attack the village. Sitting Bull and his warriors would be routed, and those who survived would be happy to seek the safety of reservations. This action would be another Washita River triumph.

The troopers were roused at midnight, and they set off in total darkness, the Crow scouts leading the way along the trail. After two hours of travel, the regiment made camp. Several of the Arikara and Crow scouts, accompanied by Charley Reynolds and Lieutenant Charles Varnum, advanced to an overlook east of the Little Bighorn River, a site that would be called the Crow's Nest. At sunrise the next day, the scouts reported they could see a massive pony herd and signs of the Indian village—hopefully, Sitting Bull's—roughly fifteen miles in the distance. However, the herd could not be seen by the weary eyes of the white men.

Still, trusting the scouts, Varnum sent two Arikara to locate Custer and inform him of where the village was believed to be. This they did by 8:00 A.M. Custer, with a small party, immediately leaped on a horse and followed the two scouts back to the Crow's Nest. Like his lieutenant, Custer was unable to make a sure sighting. He rode swiftly back to camp and borrowed a pair of German high-powered binoculars from Lieutenant Charles DeRudio, who had brought them along when he emigrated from Italy.

This time from the Crow's Nest, Custer could see a cluster of lodges perhaps a dozen miles away, and beyond them indications of another and larger Indian encampment. This was an exciting sight. But there was disturbing news as well: Earlier, the Crow and Arikara scouts had seen the Seventh Cavalry's cooking fires from ten miles away, disclosing the regiment's position. This information may have already been conveyed by Sioux and Cheyenne scouts to Sitting Bull.

For the Seventh Cavalry to remain where it was invited an attack. Or what was more likely, based on past experience, the Indians, having become aware of the nearness of soldiers, would pack up and flee, dispersing along the way to make pursuit even more difficult for the troopers.

Sticking to the latest plan of attacking Sitting Bull's main village on June 26 was scuttled when it was further reported to Custer that several soldiers had exchanged gunfire with Indians on the *other* side of the regiment's camp.*

This deflating news coupled with the cooking fires miscue convinced Custer that the Seventh Cavalry's presence had been exposed and there was nothing else to do but attack—that very day.

* Though it probably would not have made a difference, Custer did not know that the group consisted of Sioux warriors and families who had decided to return to their reservation. They kept going after the encounter with white soldiers, and no mention of Custer's regiment was conveyed to Sitting Bull.

42

"HEARTS OF THE WARRIORS"

At about noon on what was turning into a blistering hot Sunday, Lieutenant Colonel Custer had his twelve already weary companies divide into three battalions. Companies A, G, and M were commanded by Major Reno, who was finally being let out of the doghouse. Captain Benteen would lead Companies H, D, and K into battle. Under Custer's immediate command would be Companies C, E, F, I, and L, about 225 troopers. The remaining company, B, commanded by Captain Tom McDougall, would escort the slower packtrain carrying provisions and additional ammunition.

For Custer, the similarities to the Washita River Valley battle were gaining strength. Here, again, almost eight years later, with sufficient surprise, this day's fight would create the same scenario, with warriors routed and hostages taken. The only significant difference would be that action on the Little Bighorn would be on a much grander scale.

However, immediate action might have been put on hold if Custer had heeded the interpreter Mitch Boyer, who that day was wearing a piebald calf's vest. Boyer was being badgered by the Arikara and Crow scouts about the magnitude of the Indian encampment. Boyer told Custer, "General, I have been with these Indians for 30 years, and this is the largest village I have ever heard of."

And one of the Crow scouts, Half Yellow Face, warned Custer through Boyer, "You and I are going home today by a road we do not know."

But that was of lesser concern than the possibility that, aware of an approaching wasichu army, Sitting Bull might order his followers to pack up and flee immediately. Now that would be a disaster—trying to attack dividing bands of Indians on the move compared to a concentrated core of warriors and families. This was no time to hesitate. Custer wanted his three wings on the move toward the village of hostiles and to attack in full daylight.

And as before, Custer would be front and center. Because of the intensifying heat from the merciless sun directly overhead, he had removed his buckskin jacket but kept his buckskin pants, the bottoms of the legs tucked into boots. His shirt was dark blue, and shading a few inches of his face was a broad-brimmed white hat. The guns in the holsters on his belt were not army issue but English Webley pistols known as "bulldogs" because of their stubby shape.

Custer was ready, and he believed every man under his command was too. There would be plenty of glory for everyone.

Despite the distinct possibility of hundreds upon hundreds of lodges, as reported by the jittery regimental scouts, Custer surmised that there were less than a thousand warriors present. Indian agents had estimated no more than 800, based on the number of Lakota who had reportedly remained away from reservations and agencies rather than comply with U.S. government policies. This estimate was close enough until recently, when the new batches of Indians who had wintered on the reservations left to join Sitting Bull's ranks for the summer buffalo hunt. Thus, Custer unknowingly faced as many as 1,500 warriors, if not more.

As Custer and his column of troopers and scouts began their final approach toward the encampment in the Little Bighorn River Valley, the commanding officer's strategy was to swiftly go after the noncombatants at the encampments. His troopers would capture women, children, and the elderly to serve as hostages to convince the warriors to surrender. If Custer's column, supported eventually by the battalions of Benteen and Reno, could occupy the village before widespread resistance developed, the Sioux and Cheyenne warriors would understand that if they started to fight, they would be endangering their families.

Custer was adhering to what he had written about the Washita River Valley assault in his book *My Life on the Plains,* published two years earlier: "Indians contemplating a battle, either offensive or defensive, are always anxious to have their women and children removed from all danger. . . . For this reason I decided to locate our camp as close as convenient to the Cheyenne village, knowing that the close proximity of their women and children, and their necessary exposure in case of conflict, would operate as a powerful argument in favor of peace, when the question of peace or war came to be discussed."

Recalling that morning of June 25, Lieutenant Edward Godfrey, of Company K, riding in Benteen's battalion, wrote that Custer "expected to find the squaws and children fleeing to the bluffs on the north, for in no other way do I account for his wide detour. He must have counted upon Reno's success, and fully expected the 'scatteration' of the non-combatants with the pony herds. The probable attack upon the families and capture of the herds were in that event counted upon to strike consternation in the hearts of the warriors and were elements for success upon which General Custer fully counted."

43

HIGH NOON

A landmark along the Seventh Cavalry's march would be dubbed the Lone Tipi. It was where the Indian encampment had been eight days earlier during the Battle of the Rosebud. Upon relocating, the Indians had left a single tepee standing. In it was the body of a Sans Arc warrior, Old She-Bear, who had been wounded in the Rosebud fight and soon after had died. The body was surrounded by the warrior's possessions.

Enough planning and preparing—it was time for action. Custer ordered the lone tepee burned. He hoped it would be the first of many that afternoon.

Ignoring conventional military wisdom, Custer had already divided the regiment by sending Captain Benteen's battalion south. It was to remain to Custer's left as it searched for other Indian villages—what he had failed to do in the Washita Valley. Farther down, at Ash Creek, Benteen's troopers would curve to the right and rejoin Custer's column—unless they had found and attacked a village.

As the Seventh set off from the Sans Arc burial tepee, Custer further divided his command by having Major Reno and his battalion go first. Possibly, it could catch up to and kill or capture the band of Indians who may have recently fled.

Indeed, it seemed so: "Here are your Indians, General," shouted one of the interpreters, pointing from atop a hill, "running like devils." If they could be seen that easily, the cavalry could run them down.

In any case, Reno's battalion could be the first army force to attack whenever the enemy was met, if Benteen did not beat him to it. Custer, with the largest contingent in the middle, could maneuver left or right in support of Benteen or Reno, whichever column needed reinforcements. The most optimistic view was that the wings of the regiment would rendezvous with the main body near the village of Sitting Bull and launch a coordinated attack.

To make this crystal clear to Major Reno, in whom he had never had much confidence, Custer had Captain Myles Keogh and Lieutenant William Cooke ride ahead. When they pulled abreast of Reno, Cooke told him, "General Custer directs you to take as rapid a gait as you think prudent and charge the village afterwards, and you will be supported by the whole outfit."

In other words, don't dawdle: Search out and engage the enemy. "Bring them to battle," Cooke emphasized.

Reno's column crossed the Little Bighorn at the mouth of Reno Creek at around 3:00 P.M.* To the immediate consternation of the cavalry troopers, they saw that the Lakota and their northern Cheyenne allies were present "in force and not running away," Reno would later report.

To the advancing troopers' chagrin, it was clear that an attack would not be a surprise. As if to drive that realization home, the Crow scouts in

* It was not, of course, a fantastic coincidence that the body of water was called Reno Creek. It was Ash Creek on maps, but from the Little Bighorn battle forward, it would be known as Reno Creek.

the lead of the battalion observed two warriors on horseback coming toward them from the village. The two got close enough to see the large dust cloud produced by mounted soldiers. The alarmed duo hurried up a ridge and began to ride in circles—apparently, a warning to the village below.

Upon hearing of this from one of the scouts, Curly, Major Reno knew he now had no choice but to advance as rapidly as possible across the open prairie toward Sitting Bull's village.

Custer was not taking any chances with Reno's initiative. His own scouts had seen the two Indians riding up the ridge, and he had his adjutant, Lieutenant Cooke, return to Reno's battalion and order that it charge the village. Now.

The village inhabitants were thus far unaware of the danger. It could have been just another early summer day: "Some of the haze burned out of the Little Bighorn," writes Gregory F. Michno in *Lakota Noon*. "The horses would need watering. Children would go swimming in the river to escape the increasing heat. Some of the men would just be rolling out of their buffalo robes while the women began preparations to take down the lodges. A large herd of antelope was reported to the north. The village would head downriver in search of game and fresh grass.

"For the approaching soldiers, with their watches set on Chicago time, it may have been about three o'clock in the afternoon. For the Lakota, it was high noon."

44

CYPRESS LIMBS

For a time, the approach of Major Reno's column was shielded by the timber, a thick belt of trees and brush that ran along the western banks of the Little Bighorn River. This offered some solace as the column crossed the wide field, leaving Custer's main battalion well behind. At first, there were two forty-man companies abreast, and soon all three companies were charging abreast.

Less helpful was that the timber also obscured Reno's view of the Indian village until his force had passed a bend on his right front and was suddenly within arrow-shot of the outer band of lodges.

A lot of commotion could be seen, with Indian women and children scurrying for the temporary safety of the lodges and warriors running for their ponies. The warriors already mounted tried to improvise a defense. The first gambit was to ride to and fro so the ponies would kick up large clouds of dust, behind which nothing could be seen.

While Custer was certain about what Reno should be doing, he was less sure about his own battalion's next move. One option was to ride with speed to catch up with Reno's force to see if he had engaged Sitting Bull's warriors. However, he could not risk leaving Benteen's battalion adrift and the packtrain too far behind. If there was real fighting and it lasted long enough, he would need both. For once, Custer decided on a cautious tack: His battalion continued to follow Reno's trail, but at half-speed.

When Reno's column came into the open in front of the south end of the massive village, the major sent his Arikara and Crow scouts forward on his exposed left flank.

When crossing the river ahead of the column, Major Reno's Arikara scouts had found ten women and children bathing and washing clothes. The scouts slew them all. Among them were Gall's two wives and three of his children.

Realizing the full extent of the village's width, Reno quickly suspected what he would later call "a trap" and stopped a few hundred yards short of the encampment.

"There was still no support from Custer, though many men riding with Reno had seen his command on the bluffs on the east side of the river, a ways behind them," writes James Donovan. "Reno, likely inebriated to some extent, was becoming increasingly anxious."

That anxiety explains why instead of charging into the village as he had been ordered to do, Reno had his men halt and dismount. They did so and formed a skirmish line, according to standard army procedure. In this formation, every fourth trooper held the horses for the troopers in firing position, with five to ten yards separating each trooper, officers to their rear, and the soldiers with the horses behind the officers. Of course, this formation reduced Reno's firepower by 25 percent—not that it would ultimately make much difference.

To the Hunkpapa watching from the village, it appeared that they were not attacked because the wasichus were physically unable to do so. "It would be impossible to overstate the extent of their weariness, after days of marching with little or no sleep," writes Stephen Ambrose.

Sitting Bull later recalled, "They were brave men but they were too tired. When they rode up, their horses were tired and they were tired. When they got off their horses they could not stand firmly on their feet. They swayed to and fro like the limbs of cypresses in a great wind."

In a way, the village was attacked: Four horses did not follow Reno's order. Two of them, each carrying a private, charged ahead, disappearing into the dust clouds. They did not return, and it had to be assumed the troopers were killed, the first wasichu casualties of the day. The horse of the German-born Roman Rutten, also a private, was spooked, too, and galloped around in circles until it took off toward the timber.* A fourth horse followed the first two, but after gunshots were heard, it reemerged from the dust, and its unscathed rider rejoined the battalion.

It was nearing 3:30 on that blazing afternoon. Where was Custer? The "general" had revised his plan yet again. After watering their horses in Reno Creek, instead of resuming to ride in the major's wake, the five companies turned north, toward higher ground. From there, Custer had a better view down into the Bighorn Valley.

If Reno's attack was not faring well, the main body could hurry down and support it. Or, as expected, if the attack put the Sioux and Cheyenne into disarray and families tried to flee to the north, Custer's mounted troopers could race to stop them. True, that was ultimately the purpose of Colonel Gibbon's column, but with the attack on Sitting Bull happening a day earlier than planned, Custer could not be sure that Gibbon was already in position.

The fewer hostiles who broke out free from the big village, the better. That would mean more hostages to harvest during the attack.

* The no-doubt dizzy but fortunate Rutten survived the battle and remained with the Seventh Cavalry as a tailor, retiring after a thirty-four-year army career. He died in Leavenworth, Kansas, in 1925.

45

RUN TO THE RIVER

Marcus Reno feared that he could soon be encircled. There were many more warriors on ponies, kicking up clouds of dust. Then it seemed like hundreds of them emerged from the clouds, swarming out of the village.

The major saw that his men were firing their rifles effectively, but they might soon find that there were more attackers than bullets. Being cut off from Custer and Benteen meant a massacre. Already, warriors were trying to circle around the open left end of the skirmish line.

Still, the situation could have been worse. According to John S. Gray, "Reno's abrupt halt short of the village was clearly well-advised. At that moment he had no support at all, and there was no way his 140 soldiers could expect to survive a charge through a village of 1,000 lodges. Even the minority of warriors who poured out to attack him made bad enough odds."

For about twenty minutes, Reno's battalion kept firing until its commander, even in a sodden state, realized they would soon be overrun.

The major had his men retreat into the timber. When they stumbled into a clearing, the now-mounted column re-formed. Or tried to: Here, Reno could have organized a more orderly and lifesaving retreat. Instead, maddened by terror and alcohol, he shouted hoarsely, "Every man for himself!"

He took off out of the clearing. Many of his men spurred their horses and followed their commander, and those without mounts began running. When they exited the timber, they bolted for the Little Bighorn River. If they could get across, Custer's oversized battalion would save them.

But warriors on ponies who had skirted the timber or thrashed through it were close behind. Any wounded soldiers who could not remain in their saddles fell, to be killed by clubs and lances. The troopers without horses were easy prey. A rout was underway.

Most likely, Major Reno was not the only one in the battalion maddened by fear and whiskey. "Drinking before and during a battle was not unusual in the nineteenth century," notes Nathaniel Philbrick. "Several of the Cheyenne warriors who fought in the battle later claimed that many of Custer's soldiers had whiskey in their canteens."

It's one thing to be a tipsy private; it's another to be the commander of a battalion in battle: "Whiskey had a most deleterious effect on Reno," Philbrick continues, "making him appear hesitant and fearful at a time when his officers and men needed a strong, decisive leader."

Before reaching the river, Major Reno halted his lathered horse and tried to recover his senses. The veteran Arikara scout Bloody Knife rode up to him and began to report that his fellow scouts were buying valuable time so Reno could reorganize his battalion. But as the dazed officer was trying to grasp what Bloody Knife was telling him, the scout's head exploded.

46

A SISTER'S VENGEANCE

Given that the Sioux and Cheyenne had very few sharpshooters, it was most likely that a random bullet found the back of Bloody Knife's head. Bits of bone, blood, and brains splashed on Reno's face. The major became completely unnerved—he issued orders for the men who had collected around him to dismount and then mount again and dismount once more.

Then, full panic took control: Instead of managing an orderly retreat, Reno blurted out, "Any of you men who wish to make your escape, follow me!"

He spurred his horse and was on his way before many of his men could react. When they did, it was to follow their commanding officer as fast as possible. Because no rearguard was arranged, warriors began to chase after and run down some of the troopers, certainly any wounded and stragglers, probably making derisive comments about wasichu courage as they went about their bloody business.

"Reno's panic spread through most of the command," writes James Donovan. "Desperate troopers jumped on any horse they could find, leaving others without mounts. Through thick underbrush and suffocating clouds of dust, those men who had found horses followed the Major."

Instead of escape, however, the fleeing soldiers rode into a new force of warriors. They parted to let the terrified troopers through, then from both sides, they fired their rifles. The gruesome gauntlet took its toll. A fortunate few died instantly. Others whose horses were shot out from under them or were merely wounded and toppled over were set upon by seething warriors and hacked to death with knives or smashed into pulp with stone clubs.

Two of the Seventh Cavalry civilians who would not return at all were "Lonesome Charley" and Isaiah Dorman. Reynolds, who had been plagued by gloomy premonitions, proved prescient.

As Doctor H. R. Porter later testified: "I was tending to a dying soldier in a clump of bushes just before the retreat to the bluffs when it happened. The bullets were flying, and Reynolds noticed that the Indians were making a special target of me, though I didn't know it. He yelled at me, 'Look out, Doctor, the Indians are shooting at you,' and I turned to look and just in time to escape. Then I saw Reynolds throw up his hands and fall."

Thanks to Reynolds's warning, Dr. Porter survived—in fact, he was the only Seventh Cavalry surgeon who made it.

The African American interpreter Dorman's finish was especially grisly. He had dismounted and fired his rifle until he was out of ammunition, or he had been wounded too seriously to continue fighting. Lying on the ground, he was approached by a Hunkpapa woman on a black horse. She was the twenty-three-year-old Moving Robe Woman, and her face was painted red. Dorman said to her, "Do not kill me because I will be dead in a short while anyway."

He had reason to hope for some mercy. Dorman was married to a Hunkpapa woman living at the Standing Rock Agency and was known by some members of the tribe. But Moving Robe Woman had been told by her parents, Crawler and Sunflower Face, that her brother, Deeds, only ten years old, had been one of those killed at the river by the Arikara and Crow scouts. She had plunged into the battle seeking vengeance. And in her right hand was a pistol.

She said down to Dorman, "If you did not want to be killed, why did you not stay home where you belong and not come to attack us?" Then Moving Robe Woman shot and killed him. She rode on to find another victim.

The interpreter was not shown any mercy, even in death. When his body was later discovered, beside it were his coffee kettle and cup. Both were filled to the brim with Dorman's blood. His hacked-off penis was in his mouth, and his testicles had been staked to the ground. There were at least a dozen bullet holes in him. An Arikara scout found near him had been stripped and sliced open, and a willow branch protruded from his chest.

47

MEN LEFT BEHIND

The river—the Greasy Grass, as the Sioux called it—beckoned to Reno. It would, somehow, provide the escape he desperately sought. Abandoning the wounded and those on foot, the shaken major led a disorderly gaggle of troopers for a mile, searching in vain for a ford to cross the river. He made no attempt to engage the Indians to prevent them from picking off men in the rear. And there was no hesitation when he reached the west bank—horse and rider jumped in and barreled through the rushing water.

Dozens of troopers followed, with the reunited and expanded force of warriors hot on their heels. A few men drowned after their horses threw them. Others were shot with arrows or bullets and killed or were finished off by the pursuers. Some of them were reminded of a buffalo hunt.

Reno, with maybe half his command left, did escape. He emerged from the river and urged his horse up the east bank. After a mad dash across a hundred or so yards of even ground, the major had his horse push up a ravine. When he was some two hundred feet above the river, he finally came to a halt.

On foot or still on their mounts, troopers ascended to the summit. Gasping and shuddering, they gathered around Reno. For once, they were grateful for the late-afternoon sun—it was about four o'clock—warming them and beginning to dry their clothes. Horses snorted and breathed heavily, exhausted and by now famished. The men hoped the major had collected himself and could dictate what to do next—most important, how to stay alive.

Not bothering to hide it, Reno had a few jolts of whiskey as he observed the carnage below—the remaining wounded men of his command who were being brutally dispatched by Sioux and Cheyenne. They were also ransacking the dead for clothing, ammunition, and other possessions and carving scalps. On the summit, morale was already low, but it plunged further as the survivors witnessed this ghastly display. A few prayed it would not be a preview of their own fate.

48

A STARTLING SIGHT

When the wheezing Dr. Porter arrived at the summit, he found Reno dismounted. The straw hat was gone, replaced on the major's head by a red bandanna. Nonsensically, Reno proclaimed to the physician, "That was a charge, sir!"

There was nothing to say to that, so Dr. Porter began to set up a site where he could treat the wounded who had been hauled to or somehow had managed to ascend to the summit. From what he had seen below, Dr. Porter did not expect any more to arrive.

Not that another few troopers would make a difference. It appeared that only half the battalion was left. Many were spent and terrified, isolated and low on ammunition atop bluffs with a sea of warriors lapping at the bottom. And the commanding officer was clearly unable to command. Dr. Porter wondered why he was bothering to help the wounded—it was unlikely the remnants of the battalion could withstand an attack by over a thousand Sioux and Cheyenne.

Then, disbelieving their eyes, the soldiers saw many of the Indians cleave off from the crowd below and go in a direction different from uphill. Gesturing and shouting to each other, they hurried north along the river.

Another sight roused Reno's men further. Heading toward them along the bluffs was a column of troopers—Benteen's battalion.

ACT V

THE AVENGERS

Hoka hey! Today is a good day to fight! It is a good day to die! Strong hearts, brave hearts to the front. Weak hearts and cowards to the rear.

—**CRAZY HORSE**

49

CAUTIOUS CUSTER

Compared to the desperate actions involving Major Marcus Reno and his men, the experience of the white-haired Captain Frederick Benteen had been almost serene. And useless. His three companies had been assigned by Custer to detour out to the left to a line of bluffs two miles distant where, supposedly, the captain could get a better look down into the Bighorn Valley—or be attacked.

He was, after all, leading only three companies into unknown territory, where some of the Seventh Cavalry's scouts claimed there was a very large number of Indians. If a strong force fell on Benteen and his battalion, would Custer come to his aid?

The captain was convinced that his commander did not give a damn about him. Why had Custer sent a fifth of his overall command in a direction that took it farther away from Sitting Bull's village? To Benteen, the obvious answer was so that Custer and his larger battalion would engage the enemy and garner the glory of routing the Sioux and Cheyenne.

Though Benteen had ample reason for believing this, given his fractious history with Custer, it was not necessarily true. Yes, of course, the glory of victory was the Seventh Cavalry commander's goal, but a more immediate issue was lack of information. Advancing at a frustratingly cautious pace, Custer still could not see where the Native village was. For an encampment reportedly so large, why was it so difficult to find? Bluffs and other physical features kept blocking his view ahead, as though they were moving to aggravate him.

Maybe Benteen would be of some use. But if he demonstrated the same initiative as the blundering Major Reno, the left-wing battalion might arrive at a point where, still not having seen anything, they paused and waited for orders. Well, Custer would give him one: He had a messenger set off after the captain to tell him to keep going forward until he sighted the village.

Almost by accident, Custer had created an encouraging scenario. If Reno could occupy as many warriors as possible on one side, the five-company central battalion could attack the village head on. This would send its residents scrambling to dismantle their lodges, allowing for troopers to kill more residents and take hostages—the biggest prize, of course, would be Sitting Bull—and the warriors would be in a defensive mode. While they retreated slowly to buy time, villagers would flee with what they could carry—and possibly run into Benteen's battalion.

Even better, if they were adhering to the general's plan and schedule, Terry's force and Colonel Gibbon's Montana column would soon be arriving at the mouth of the Little Bighorn River. If Sitting Bull's village could be encircled, the large combination of Sioux and Cheyenne tribes would have no choice but to surrender.

And that would be General Sherman's "final solution" become reality.

50

MORE DIVISION

To confirm Custer's surmising, a messenger from Major Reno arrived to inform him that instead of warriors scattering from a bold charge, his battalion was under attack. That was good news—a rough spot for Reno, of course, but it meant Sitting Bull's warriors were advancing to cover the fleeing of their families. The village must be close, and in increasing disarray. Time to prepare for an attack of his own.

Custer had his men halt at a tributary of Sun Dance Creek so their horses could drink. As they were doing so and the men were refilling their canteens—in more than a few cases, the fresh water replacing the whiskey they had already consumed—Custer issued instructions to yet again divide his command. He appointed Captain Myles Keogh to lead a small battalion of three companies that would comprise the right wing of the anticipated assault.

Keogh certainly had one of the most unique backgrounds of any of Custer's senior officers. He and some of his family survived the Great Famine; then, in 1860, at age twenty, he had a way out: Keogh and over a thousand of his countrymen responded to a call to arms by the Catholic clergy in Ireland to go to rally to the defense of Pope Pius IX, who was in a struggle with Italy.* In August, Keogh was appointed second lieutenant of his unit in the Battalion of St. Patrick, Papal Army.

He was posted at Ancona, a central port city of Italy. The following month, the papal forces were defeated in the Battle of Castelfidardo, and Ancona was surrounded. After the soldiers in the city surrendered, Keogh was imprisoned at Genoa. There was a quick release by exchange, and Keogh went to Rome. There, he was invited to wear the spirited green uniforms of the Company of St. Patrick as a member of the Vatican Guard. During his service, the Holy See awarded him the Medaglia for gallantry—the Pro Petri Sede Medal—and also the Cross of a Knight of the Ordine di San Gregorio.

Bored by the mundane duties of the Vatican Guard, Keogh responded to another call to arms—this one from U.S. Secretary of State William Seward, who was seeking experienced European officers to serve in the Union army. In March 1862, Keogh resigned his commission in the Company of Saint Patrick and, after a brief return to Ireland, took the steamer *Kangaroo* to New York. Before long, he was fighting in the Civil War.

Probably his most notable duty came on June 30, 1863, when he accompanied General John Buford into the small town of Gettysburg. The officers realized that the Army of the Potomac, under its brand-new commander, George Meade, was about to face a superior force of rebels. They set about creating a defense against the Confederate advance, acutely aware of the importance of holding the tactically important high ground.

---

* The pope would eventually lose this struggle and become a virtual prisoner of Italy in the Vatican. Still, at thirty-two years, Pius IX has thus far had the longest reign of anyone in papal history, with the possible exception of Peter the Apostle.

Buford's defensive troop alignments, coupled with the bravery and tenacity of his dismounted men, allowed the First Corps, under General John Reynolds, time to come up in support and thus maintain a Union foothold. Myles Keogh received his first brevet for "gallant and meritorious services" during the battle and was promoted to the rank of major.

There were more battles, and Keogh survived them. After the war, he remained in the U.S. Army. In July 1866, he was promoted to captain and assigned to the Seventh Cavalry at Fort Riley and soon was a member of Custer's inner circle.

The captain's horse would become one of the more notable footnotes in the Battle of the Little Bighorn. The gelding had been purchased by the U.S. Army in 1868 in St. Louis and brought to Fort Leavenworth in Kansas. There, Keogh, impressed by his size of fifteen hands, bought him for his personal mount, to be ridden only in battle.

That same year, while the army was fighting the Comanche tribe in Kansas, the horse was wounded. Though an arrow protruded from his hindquarters, the horse continued to carry Keogh in the fight. He renamed the horse "Comanche" to honor his bravery. The gritty gelding was wounded several more times in battles but always exhibited the same toughness.

The left wing would be an even smaller contingent, just two companies, under the command of Captain George Yates.

Sandwiched between his first and last names was Wilhelmus Mancius, who had been born in Albany, New York. His army service had begun in June 1861, when he enlisted in the Fourth Michigan Infantry. Yates compiled a long war résumé, including being in the First Battle of Bull Run, Seven Days Battles, Sharpsburg, Antietam, Fredericksburg (where he was wounded), Chancellorsville, and Gettysburg. He not only survived these and other battles but married well, too, to Annie Gibson Roberts, whose father, Milnor Roberts, was the chief engineer for the Northern Pacific Railway.

Once the horses had their fill of water from the glittering tributary, the five companies directly under Lieutenant Colonel Custer's command re-formed into imposing columns of four and rode up the slope to the top of the bluffs. After a mile of hot and dusty riding, Custer halted the columns. He had one of his trumpeters, John Martin, and the Crow scouts accompany him to the top of a high ridge.

Finally, Custer could see what the Seventh Cavalry faced. From the height of what would later be dubbed Sharpshooter Ridge, the Little Bighorn Valley could be seen, with the undulating river snaking through it.

"Suddenly they saw it: the flat and seemingly endless expanse of the Little Bighorn Valley through which wandered the sparkling blue-green ribbon of river," writes Nathaniel Philbrick. "And there, two miles to the northwest, was the largest Indian village any of them had ever seen: hundreds of gleaming white teepees beneath the soaring transparent canopy of the sky. Beyond the lodges to the west was a swirling sea of reddish brown that the soldiers only gradually realized was the village's herd of fifteen thousand to twenty thousand ponies."

Against all that, Custer realized, he had a regiment of fewer than six hundred men. To its commander, that was more than enough.

51

"PLENTY FOR ALL OF US"

Clouds of dust indicated to Lieutenant Colonel Custer where Major Reno and his battalion probably were and had begun their attack. To his surprise, none of the people in Sitting Bull's village appeared to be fleeing, as many Indian inhabitants had done before when white soldiers approached their encampment. This was good, actually—the opportunity still existed for Custer's command to make a direct assault on the largest concentration of hostiles.

There was already a joyous sensation of accomplishment. Once again beating the odds, in the middle of a bright day, Custer had found and for the most part surprised the epicenter of Sioux and Cheyenne resistance.

However, that also meant that Sitting Bull had numbers on his side. He could have a thousand, even two thousand warriors to call on. The Crow scouts were nervous—their fears were being realized. Most likely, another commander would have taken heed of this as well as the evidence before his own eyes and called off the attack. Wisdom dictated waiting for General Terry and his column or trying to get a message to Colonel Gibbon to close in and do it fast.

But to Custer, this was the Washita scenario all over again. What made more sense was a bold strike that would avenge the deaths of Captain William Fetterman and his eighty men. Any actions afterward during the summer would be little more than mop-up operations. The worst move would be to retreat or be immobilized by indecision while Sitting Bull was informed by scouts of their predicament and bands of Indians packed up and scattered in all directions.

No, attack. Capture or kill Sitting Bull. As at Washita, the hostiles would be too shocked and frightened to offer much resistance. And take as many hostages as possible to reduce the risk of counterattacks and increase the odds of a surrender. Hopefully, Colonel Gibbon's column was, at least, in position to gather up Indians trying to escape west and north. Plus, there were the companies below. If indeed Major Reno had engaged the enemy, Custer would have to hurry to support him, and the best support would be a bold and strong thrust into the massive compound.

"For the first time," explains Robert Utley, "Custer had reliable knowledge of enemy location, enemy strength, and the battle terrain. He must now have determined to hasten to the next ford downstream and launch his own assault on the village. Of compelling urgency, Benteen and the packtrain had to be hurried forward. To fight a village of this size, Custer needed every man of the regiment and the twenty-six thousand rounds of reserve ammunition carried on the mules."

After telling his brother Tom and other senior officers of his intention, Custer ordered an advance. Sensing excitement, a few horses wanted to gallop. "Boys, hold your horses," Custer called out. "There are plenty of them down there for all of us."

Continuing in columns of fours, the companies rode until they came to a coulee where several ravines converged. (It would later come to be known as Medicine Tail.) After a moment's consideration, Custer led the columns left into the coulee. He believed it would lead to a ford to allow crossing of the Little Bighorn River and then they could aim at the village.

That prospect made Custer anxious once more about not having enough men or ammunition. He needed to send a courier, and he gestured to John Martin. Lieutenant Cooke had the presence of mind to take into account the Italian trumpeter's fractured English, and he wrote Custer's instructions on a sheet of paper, though his writing was also a tad garbled: "Benteen. Come on. Big Village. Be Quick. Bring Packs. W.W. Cooke. P. bring pacs."

As Martin turned his horse and rode away, Custer released his Crow scouts, with the exception of Curly, who was away with Mitch Boyer. The scouts were obviously terrified and would be of little if any good in a battle. As much as the Crow scouts would love to kill Sioux and Cheyenne, there were simply way too many of them. The Crow riders remained at the Medicine Tail Coulee, where they could watch the battle unfold.

On his hurried mission, the courier Martin halted when he encountered Boston Custer. The commander's younger brother had been with the packtrain, but fearing he might miss out on the drama unfolding up ahead, he had climbed atop a horse and rushed forward. Boston was relieved to learn that in only a few minutes, he would reunite with his brother's battalion.

Back at that column, Boyer and Curly arrived. The news they conveyed was not good: Reno and his command were already in retreat. Perhaps an attack should be postponed. Custer did not give this a second's thought. He plucked the wide white hat off his head and waved it about while exclaiming, "Hurrah, boys, we've got them!"

According to Philbrick, "Hindsight makes Custer look like an egomaniacal fool. But as Sitting Bull and many other Lakota and Cheyenne realized that day, he came frighteningly close to winning the most spectacular victory of his career."

52

FALLING BEHIND

The Civil War general in Custer probably required that he attack anyway. But at the same time, the somewhat more mature cavalry commander recognized that doing nothing could be even more dangerous. With Reno having withdrawn and Benteen and the precious packtrain not yet having arrived, the Sioux and Cheyenne warriors could soon be on his troopers from three sides. And Custer being Custer, retreat was unthinkable.

The two companies led by Captain Yates were dispatched to descend the Medicine Tail Coulee. The aggressive forward motion of this force, bugles blaring and shining in the merciless afternoon sun, might dissuade the warriors from approaching. Captain Keogh and his three companies would occupy a ridge that separated Medicine Tail from what was called Deep Coulee. Now, this would be the perfect time for Benteen and his troops to appear. With more men and ammunition and the Indians nonplussed, a concerted attack on Sitting Bull's village itself would be most effective.

However, Captain Benteen, whose behavior historians have puzzled over for many decades, did not share his commander's urgency. His battalion was ambling along so leisurely that instead of gaining on the companies ahead, he had fallen farther behind. It was only when the trumpeter, Martin, rushed up to Benteen with Cooke's hastily scrawled message that the captain had his men break into a trot.

To make Custer's predicament worse, Benteen's battalion did not join him but joined Reno's battalion atop the hill to which the remainder of the major's men had retreated. According to Robert Utley, "The demoralization of Reno's shattered battalion, combined with the indecision of the two ranking officers, kept seven companies and the packtrain, which also reached the bluff tops, out of action at the most critical moment" for Custer's immediate command.

Feeling especially stranded were Yates and his two companies. Being at the mouth of the Medicine Tail Coulee, they were the closest soldiers to the impressive village—and, thus, the most exposed. As Sitting Bull would later describe the action, "Our young men rained lead across the river and drove the white braves back."

Making the situation even hotter for the withdrawing Yates was that with Reno and Benteen effectively sidelined, many of the warriors who had chased the former up the hill now arrived to join the attack at the coulee. Additionally, warriors who had run to the pony herd during the initial attack were now mounted and arriving in large batches. Within minutes, Yates's undersized battalion was even more outnumbered.

The beleaguered captain tried to maintain an orderly retreat. He had his troopers dismount to form a skirmish line—three out of every four firing their rifles, while the fourth man held the horses. They backed uphill as the Indians pressed the assault. The frightened horses dragged soldiers about, impairing their accuracy. That, and there were simply too many targets coming at them. If Yates's command could get to the high ridge above Deep Coulee, they might survive.

53

BLOODY AND PERSONAL

While in many ways Sitting Bull was ready to fight whatever the U.S. Army threw at him, he hoped he would not have to put his people at that risk. He told those around him outside his lodge, "I don't want my children fighting until I tell them to."

That Reno had not only paused his attack but withdrawn in haste suggested to Sitting Bull that there was a chance to make peace. His nephew, One Bull, was standing beside him. Sitting Bull took the rifle from the young warrior and replaced it with his shield. It was an almost holy item among the Hunkpapa—the same shield had protected Sitting Bull two decades earlier during the battle to the death with the Crow chief. He told One Bull and his good friend, Good Bear Boy, to "go up and make peace."

They mounted their horses and approached the wasichu troopers. But a peace overture was not made. There was the crack of a rifle, and a single bullet struck both of Good Bear Boy's legs. He reeled atop his horse until One Bull looped a lariat around his friend's chest. He turned both horses, and they hurried back to the safety of the village.

To better see what was about to transpire, Sitting Bull had climbed onto his favorite horse. As the two warriors dashed back toward him, more rifle shots were heard. Two bullets hit Sitting Bull's horse, and he had to jump clear. That was it.

"Now my best horse is shot!" he announced as loudly as he could. "It is like they have shot me. Attack them!"

Often overlooked in accounts of the Battle of the Little Bighorn were the women warriors who were part of Sitting Bull's army, such as Moving Robe Woman. "I sang a death song for my brother who had been killed," she told an interviewer years later. "My heart was bad. Revenge! Revenge! For my brother's death. I thought of the death of my young brother. I painted my face with crimson and braided my black hair. I was mourning. I was a woman, but I was not afraid."

Nor were other Indian women who rode with other determined warriors out of the village. Among them were the Cheyenne Calf Trail Woman, Pretty Nose of the Arapaho, and the Oglala Minnie Hollow Wood and One Who Walks with the Stars.*

The elders in the tribes, most of whom were too old to fight themselves, prepared the village for the battle being brought to it. The half-blind Inkpaduta dispatched his grandsons and other youngsters as sort of town criers, warning that more soldiers were on the way and advising residents to keep their horses close and to begin to pack up the lodges. He shouted encouragement to the warriors as they found and mounted their ponies and rode toward the soldiers.

Everyone wondered where Crazy Horse was. There was no more

---

* Moving Robe Woman lived the rest of her life at the Standing Rock Agency and may have known Isaiah Dorman's widow, who also lived there. Moving Robe Woman died in 1935 at age 81, one of the last survivors of the Little Bighorn battle. Outliving her, though, was Pretty Nose. She was able to welcome the return of a descendant, Mark Soldier Wolf, to the Wind River Reservation in 1952 after his service as a marine in the Korean War before she died at 101.

admired warrior in the Sioux and Cheyenne nations. But no one had to look for the man who was a close second: Gall. When the enraged Hunkpapa appeared before Sitting Bull, that is when he learned that there had already been Indians killed—and they were women and children.

Gall had discarded his rifle. His chest heaving, he stood before Sitting Bull with only a hatchet in his hand. His vengeance would be very bloody and very personal.

54

WELL-ARMED WARRIORS

While Yates's undersized battalion was clearly in deep trouble, the battle was going a bit better for Captain Keogh. His men were in the heights between the Deep Coulee and the Medicine Tail Coulee. Here, the warriors were also attacking with superior numbers, but the battalion's dismounted skirmish lines were positioned so that they had a clear line of fire into the charging Indians. Organized volley fire proved especially effective.

Meanwhile, Custer sized up the situation. He had to make sure that his two outlying wings did not become isolated. More of an advantage would be gained if they could be united into a combined force of five companies. The place to pull them together became known as Calhoun Hill.

James "Jimmi" Calhoun had become part of his commander's inner circle by virtue of marrying Maggie Custer. His thirty-first birthday was two months away, and he was a lieutenant in command of Company L.

He and the other company commanders knew they were in serious jeopardy. A flat hill summit overlooked Deep Coulee and was the southern end of a half-mile-high ridge, eventually to be known as Battle Ridge. Steep hills and deep ravines led down to the Little Bighorn River. Here, Custer tried to organize a defensive position.

"Custer must have recognized how desperate his plight was," writes Robert Utley. "Faced with overpowering numbers of well-armed warriors, caught in rough terrain unsuited to cavalry, and with no trace of Benteen or the packs on the hills to the south, even Custer's robust self-confidence surely wavered."

Adding to the jeopardy was—to the surprise of Custer and other veteran Indian fighters—that the Sioux and Cheyenne were so well armed. More warriors than to be expected were firing carbines, so hundreds of bullets vied with hundreds of arrows for air space and targets.

And their tactics were different. For many years on the Great Plains, battles between tribes were not European-model confrontations between grand armies but small groups competing against each other to count coups and gain prestige while stealing ponies or just for the sheer joy of fighting. Sometimes, a "battle" could be one warrior challenging another to the Indian equivalent of a duel. While destroying an entire village would be a sensational victory, it was rarely the goal.

But here at Little Bighorn, there were coordinated attacks. And in many instances, warriors massed together, supporting each other's assaults and withdrawals. That unusual mindset of every warrior working for the good of all, coupled with more modern weapons and arrows being shot with furious rapidity, meant that a weary and thirsty wasichu force twice the size of the Seventh Cavalry, or even larger, could not have prevailed.

But for Custer, there was no time to analyze the situation. He had soldiers to save.

55

NOT QUICK ENOUGH

With both of Custer's left and right wings under siege, this would have been an especially opportune time for Captain Frederick Benteen and his battalion to show up on the scene to at least relieve some of the pressure. But he was nowhere near the action.

Custer's orders to him were to circle around to the left to where the captain could get a good look into the Little Bighorn Valley. And this was what he had been doing for almost two hours, but the wandering battalion never reached that desired vantage point. Benteen, however, finally thought they had when one of his lieutenants glimpsed a tributary of Sun Dance Creek and mistook it for the Little Bighorn River. What was not glimpsed were any of Sitting Bull's people. It was time for this futile foray to end.

Benteen had his column turn around and begin the trek back to the main force. One of his lieutenants, Edward Godfrey, later reported, "Our march was very leisurely."* Making the return journey even more

---

* Lieutenant Godfrey would not only survive the battle but remain in the

leisurely was a lengthy stop to water the horses. Yes, this was a prudent thing for cavalry to do—a fatigued and dehydrated horse does not make for an effective fighting trooper. But the stop delayed Benteen's return to Custer's main force even more.

Several of Benteen's officers became impatient as the horses slowly filled their bellies. They could hear firing in the distance. They could not know what was happening with Custer's and Reno's battalions, but obviously there was a battle underway. They noted that Benteen appeared unfazed by the prospect of missing out on a dramatic victory.

One of the anxious officers was Captain Thomas Weir, who commanded D Company. Finally, he could not wait anymore. Pointing vaguely, he declared, "They ought to be over there." He spurred his horse ahead, and the men of his company followed him.

Benteen watched them go. Then he was distracted by the surprise arrival of the packtrain under the command of Captain McDougall. This threatened a humiliation: The rest of the Seventh Cavalry accomplishes its goal of defeating and possibly killing Sitting Bull and Crazy Horse while Benteen and his battalion are in self-exile with the clumsy and safe packtrain. It was time to move, and move faster.

Benteen led his column away from the water hole. Soon a messenger sent by Custer, Sergeant Daniel Kanipe, galloped up and confirmed the fears of Benteen's battalion: "We've got them, boys!" Kanipe chortled. The lackadaisical captain was even more abashed when Kanipe resumed his gallop, the message he bore intended not for Benteen but

---

U.S. Army for another thirty-one years, having an especially distinguished career. Despite being severely wounded at the Battle of Bear Paw Mountain against Chief Joseph and the Nez Percé in September 1877, he continued to lead his men in battle, later receiving the Medal of Honor. He rose up the ranks while serving in Cuba during the Spanish-American War and then saw action in the Philippine-American War. Godfrey retired from the army in October 1907 with the rank of brigadier general.

for McDougall. The packtrain, apparently, was more urgently needed than Benteen's column.

Two miles later, however, it was finally Benteen's turn. The second messenger he encountered was the wayward trumpeter John Martin, who almost by accident had found the battalion. Along the way, he had dodged a few potshots by distant warriors.

Benteen read the "Be Quick" note written by Lieutenant Cooke and asked, "Where is the general now?"

Martin replied that by now, Custer was probably "charging through the village" and had the Sioux and Cheyenne "skedaddling."

Ignoring the urgency expressed in the note from his superior officer, Benteen kept chatting with the perplexed trumpeter. Finally, Benteen wondered aloud how he could rush to Custer and bring the packs and ammunition that were behind him in the slow-moving supply train. The orders appeared contradictory. Eventually, the dawdling captain determined that his troopers with their own full loads of ammunition arriving at a crucial time would be of more benefit to the attack—if it was not already concluded—than the balky packtrain.

Benteen had his column resume their trek at a trot, dust kicking up in their wake. Then, as if to vex him further, they arrived at a point where the trail divided. Who knows how long Benteen would have pondered this dilemma, but three of the Seventh's Crow scouts heading away from the battle—Hairy Moccasin, White Man Runs Him, and Goes Ahead—appeared and advised that the column should climb the bluff on the right.

The scouts also kept stating, "Too many Sioux," but were dismissed.

After reaching the bluff, the soldiers of the Seventh at last could look down into the Little Bighorn Valley. However, they did not see Sitting Bull's village in the midst of being destroyed or dismantled. Instead, Benteen observed hundreds of warriors attacking soldiers left behind at the river. He spurred his horse down, and the battalion followed.

No doubt Captain Benteen wondered anew: Where was Custer?

56

A WISP OF SMOKE

While some of the wasichu soldiers were wondering where their greatest warrior was, some of the Lakota and Cheyenne were wondering: Where was Crazy Horse?

The answer as the battle progressed was seemingly everywhere.

Crazy Horse had been swimming in the river with his friend Yellow Nose when they heard the first shots exchanged between Reno's battalion and the village. Moments later, horseless, he met his wife's brother, Red Feather, bridling his pony. "Take any horse," said Red Feather as he prepared to dash off, but Crazy Horse waited for his own mount.

Once he had his favorite horse, the gelding, Crazy Horse prepared himself for battle. In the emergency of the moment, many men grabbed their weapons and ran toward the shooting, but not all. War was too dangerous to treat casually; a man wanted to be properly dressed and painted before charging the enemy.

According to Thomas Powers in *The Killing of Crazy Horse*, "Without his medicine and time for a prayer or song, he would be weak. A 17-year-old

Oglala named Standing Bear reported that after the first warnings Crazy Horse had called on a *wicasa wakan* (medicine man) to invoke the spirits and then took so much time over his preparations" that many of his warriors became impatient.

Ten young men who had sworn to follow Crazy Horse anywhere in battle were standing nearby. He dusted himself and his companions with a fistful of dry earth gathered up from a hill left by a mole or gopher. Into his hair, Crazy Horse wove some long stems of grass. Then he opened the medicine bag he carried about his neck, took from it a pinch of powder, and burned it as a sacrifice on a fire of buffalo chips that another warrior had prepared. The wisp of smoke, he believed, carried his prayer to the heavens. Crazy Horse then painted his face with hail spots and dusted his horse with the dry earth. Now, he was ready to fight.

His first act of leadership was to organize the resistance to Reno's stumbling advance and then to give chase when the wasichu soldiers ran to the river. "As soon as these troops were driven across, he went at once to General Custer's front and there became the leading spirit," reports Ambrose.

There, Crazy Horse would rendezvous with Gall for the first last stand.

57

"PLENTY OF FIGHTING"

For a time—as long as forty-five minutes—George Armstrong Custer was nowhere. The man who had charged one enemy after another with reckless abandon became virtually motionless as the battle intensified.

"Something happened up in the hills above the Little Bighorn," notes Nathaniel Philbrick. "Custer, the officer of seemingly perpetual motion, had paused at the most crucial stage of the battle."

Presumably, since no soldier in Custer's main battalion survived, we will never know what transpired.* While it is true that by the end of the day on June 25, 1876, Custer's immediate command was annihilated,

* Some accounts contend that there was a white survivor of the battle—the trumpeter, John Martin, because he had been a member of one of the companies directly under Custer's command. In the ensuing decades, over two hundred men came forward to falsely claim to have survived the Battle of Little Bighorn. One historian observed, "If as many men who claimed to have survived the battle were actually with Custer that day, he might have prevailed."

there were three men who had accompanied the regiment until being told to leave—the three Crow scouts.

Decades later, when he was compiling his monumental twenty-volume *The North American Indians*, the photographer Edward Curtis visited the Little Bighorn battlefield. Through an interpreter, he interviewed White Man Runs Him, Goes Ahead, and Hairy Moccasin. (The fourth scout, Curly, was not interviewed by Curtis during the 1907 visit.)

According to the scouts' recollections, Custer led his column to a high hill, where he halted and had his senior officers dismount. From there, they could observe Captain Reno's aborted charge and the fighting mostly on foot of the smaller battalion's skirmish line. The passive minutes of observation piled up until finally, White Man Runs Him asked Custer why he was not attacking in support of his besieged major.

The Crow claimed that Custer responded, "No, let them fight. There will be plenty of fighting left for us to do."

All three Crow scouts were puzzled by this behavior, but there was nothing to do but wait along with the idle troopers.*

Custer continued to watch impassively the battle below. Ultimately, it became obvious that Reno's force not only was being repulsed by warriors streaming out of the village but was in a chaotic retreat. Too late to stem that tide, Custer finally gave the order to his men to move out.

Historians not fond of Custer have contended that the commander was waiting for the field to clear so he could make a direct assault on Sitting Bull's stronghold. This is indeed a damning view, but other

* White Man Runs Him's status as a Little Big Horn participant made him a minor celebrity late in life, and he even played a small supporting role in the 1927 feature film *The Red Raiders*. He lived the remainder of his life on the Crow Reservation in the Bighorn Valley region, just a few miles from the site of the famous battle. He died there in 1929 at age seventy-one.

explanations will always be nothing more than conjecture. The fact is, once Custer put his column in motion, there was nothing for Reno to do but keep running right out of the picture frame of an anticipated victory.

58

TRAPPED IN THE TIMBER

Major Reno's pell-mell retreat to the river had left behind a dozen or so men who had sought the shelter of the timber. For at least an hour, they hunkered down. During that time, they were much relieved when the thousand or so Lakota and Cheyenne warriors made their own pell-mell dash, not in retreat but to the north, in the direction of where the firing of weapons had become incessant.

The men concealed in the timber were not under the command of George Herendeen, a civilian, but they deferred to the cooler head of the veteran scout—who was still just twenty-seven years old. By rank, the senior soldier was Sergeant Charles White. But being wounded and impressed by Herendeen's calm demeanor, he was happy to let him take the reins.

Several times, Herendeen crept to the edge of the timber to look for any returning Natives. Finally, he suggested to the soldiers that rather than wait until warriors did reappear, they make an attempt for the river and try to find what, if any, remained of Major Reno's battalion. Herendeen told them not to run, as that might attract attention, and when the scout stepped out of the safety of the trees, the others cautiously and anxiously followed.

Given what they had experienced an hour before, the trek to the river was blissfully uneventful. At the river itself, they encountered a small cluster of Indians. Herendeen raised his rifle and fired a single shot, and the warriors scattered out of sight.

An encouraging sign was that looking atop the bluffs on the other side of the river, the dozen men could see guidons. This told them that at least some of Reno's battalion had survived and established a position they could protect.

As the soldiers crossed the river from west to east—the cold, streaming water up to their chests felt bracing on such a hot afternoon—Herendeen and White stayed back to provide cover. This was reciprocated when the scout and the wounded sergeant waded across. Revitalized by the water, they reassembled as a group and began to make their way up the bluffs.

HARPER'S WEEKLY.
A JOURNAL OF CIVILIZATION

Vol. VIII.—No. 377.] NEW YORK, SATURDAY, MARCH 19, 1864.

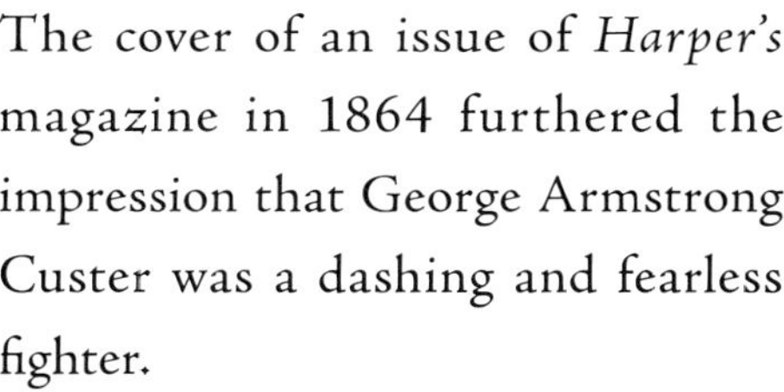
The cover of an issue of *Harper's* magazine in 1864 furthered the impression that George Armstrong Custer was a dashing and fearless fighter.
(Courtesy of the Library of Congress)

A formal portrait of the "Boy General" done the month after the Civil War ended.
(Courtesy of the Library of Congress)

The posing newlyweds George and Libbie Bacon Custer.

(Courtesy of the Library of Congress)

Sitting Bull was a powerful and charismatic leader who united the northern plains tribes to try to preserve their way of life.

(Courtesy of the Library of Congress)

There is no public image of Crazy Horse other than this memorial in Custer County, South Dakota, which has been under construction since 1948.

(Courtesy of the Library of Congress)

Red Cloud had been the leader of the Lakota Sioux until he retired to a reservation, and the role fell to Sitting Bull.

(Courtesy of the Library of Congress)

Spotted Tail was Red Cloud's chief rival for Lakota leadership. He too chose not to fight the U.S. government.

(Courtesy of the Library of Congress)

A sketch depicting prisoners taken by the Seventh Cavalry during the Washita River Valley attack in November 1868.

(Courtesy of the Library of Congress)

George, Tom, and Libbie Custer. Tom Custer was the recipient of two Medals of Honor during the Civil War.

(Courtesy of the Library of Congress)

Major Marcus Reno had a troubled U.S. Army career and often was at odds with Lieutenant Colonel Custer.

(Courtesy of the Denver Public Library Special Collections)

The "Custer Clan," who accompanied their commanding officer on his expeditions, included favored senior officers as well as family members.

(Courtesy of the Denver Public Library Special Collections)

Captain Frederick Benteen's heroic actions during the Little Bighorn battle saved what was left of the Seventh Cavalry.

(Courtesy of the Denver Public Library Special Collections)

Several members of Sitting Bull's extended family stand outside their tipi.

(Courtesy of the Library of Congress)

Unable to stem the tide of white miners and settlers into the Black Hills, President Ulysses S. Grant instituted a policy that all Plains Indians be confined to reservations.

(Courtesy of the Library of Congress)

General William T. Sherman, the top military officer during the Grant administration, sought a "final solution" to the "Indian problem."

(Courtesy of the Library of Congress)

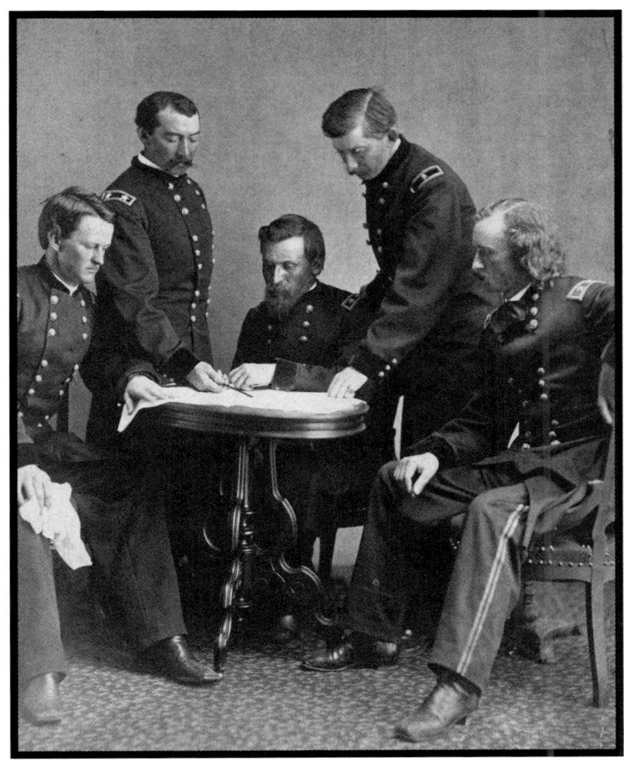

Philip Sheridan confers with his generals, including George Crook (seated) and Custer (right).

(Courtesy of the Library of Congress)

General Alfred Terry was tasked with carrying out Sheridan's plan to find and capture Sitting Bull.

(Courtesy of the Library of Congress)

General George Crook was no match for Crazy Horse during the Battle of the Rosebud in June 1876.

(Courtesy of the Library of Congress)

Colonel John Gibbon led an army column that arrived too late to save Custer's command.

(Courtesy of the Library of Congress)

The Hunkpapa Gall and Crazy Horse were Sitting Bull's most aggressive warriors.

(Courtesy of the Library of Congress)

Rain-in-the-Face had his vengeance against Tom Custer at Little Bighorn.

(Courtesy of the Library of Congress)

Curly was one of the several Crow scouts who accompanied the Seventh Cavalry into the Little Bighorn Valley.

(Courtesy of the Library of Congress)

The army scout "Lonesome Charley" Reynolds was correct in predicting he would not survive the campaign against Sitting Bull.

(Courtesy of the Denver Public Library Special Collections)

This is just one of the many depictions of Custer and his last stand.

(Courtesy of the Library of Congress)

Though severely wounded, Comanche survived the Little Bighorn battle. The horse's owner, Captain Myles Keogh, did not.

(Courtesy of the Library of Congress)

A monument to the steamboat captain Grant Marsh in Yankton, South Dakota, overlooks the Missouri River.

(Courtesy of the Library of Congress)

Soon after the Little Bighorn battle, markers—including this one for Lieutenant John Crittenden—were placed where it was believed troopers fell.

(Courtesy of the Library of Congress)

The ambitious Nelson Miles succeeded where previous field commanders had failed in subduing the northern plains tribes.

(Courtesy of the Library of Congress)

The Indian agent James McLaughlin had a contentious relationship with Sitting Bull at the Standing Rock Reservation.

(Courtesy of the Denver Public Library Special Collections)

Sitting Bull was a star attraction in Buffalo Bill's Wild West extravaganzas.

(Courtesy of the Library of Congress)

Crow Foot, a son of Sitting Bull seen here in 1881, was murdered along with his father nine years later.

(Courtesy of the Library of Congress)

Many of the victims of the Wounded Knee massacre were left to freeze in the snow. *(Courtesy of the Library of Congress)*

A modern-day view of the Little Bighorn battlefield in Montana. *(Courtesy of the Library of Congress)*

59

A DIFFERENT RIVER

Custer did not have the regimental band with him as he had at the Washita River battle, so instead he resorted to bugles blaring as Captain George Yates and his two companies descended the Medicine Tail Coulee. Custer and his companies remained on the bluffs overlooking the valley. Why didn't all the troopers descend the coulee? Because Boston Custer had just joined his brother and no doubt informed him that Captain Benteen's column was maybe twenty-five minutes away. Such additional forces would make for an even more powerful thrust into the village.

However, the warriors under Sitting Bull's command were not inclined to be immobile, waiting to be attacked. The remaining men of Reno's battalion who had made it across the river were being chased up a hill like hunted animals being treed and trapped. And Sitting Bull knew that Long Hair was close.

After boldly galloping down Medicine Tail Coulee, the left wing of Custer's main battalion neared the Little Bighorn River. They began to cross the free-flowing water. Suddenly, warriors appeared on the west bank and began firing. This had not happened at the Washita River, so in case Custer needed any further convincing, this attack on the attackers demonstrated this battle would not be another Washita rout.

Captain Yates needed no further convincing. He shouted to his men that the river crossing was to be abandoned. They turned around and rode uphill to rejoin Custer.

With Yates back, the lieutenant colonel convened his officers. Captain Benteen's battalion might never arrive if it, too, had run into an attack. It was time, now that the shot-up left wing had caught its breath, to reconsider the regiment's plan of attack. Another attempt to cross the river at that particular point would be foolish. There could be hundreds of Lakota and Cheyenne concealed behind the west bank, begging for the wasichu soldiers to reappear.

It was here when Custer made one of his most critical decisions. He would not wait for Benteen to arrive or for Captain Keogh's right wing, which had been assigned to wait for Benteen. Custer determined to take the troops he had on hand to the north. They would find a less dangerous river crossing and attack Sitting Bull's village.

He was not as concerned about killing warriors as he was about taking hostages. With enough captives, especially women and children, the Lakota and Cheyenne warriors would not attack. Perhaps Sitting Bull would offer to surrender to save the hostages. And the best fighters, like Crazy Horse, would be neutralized.

With Custer in the lead, his battalion set off to the north.

60

SEEKING SAFETY

Perhaps Custer's Luck would strike again. After a mile of travel, he discerned a buffalo trail that allowed passage down from the ridge to the Little Bighorn River. As the column rode down it, the troopers were harassed by hostile rifle fire coming from the hills behind them.

And then from in front of them: Warriors who had been hiding in the thick brush alongside the river suddenly popped up like prairie dogs and began shooting arrows and bullets. The battalion reversed itself and again sought the safety of the ridge.

Custer may have wondered about the whereabouts of Mark Kellogg. If so, this might have been out of genuine concern for the ingratiating man or because he was fretting about not having the reporter on hand should the Seventh Cavalry triumph. When last spotted, Kellogg had been atop a mule, urging it across the river. Since then, nothing.

The reporter apparently made it across the river but not much farther before he was killed. According to James Donovan, "Save for a missing scalp and ear, he was untouched, probably dying so far from the main action and so early in the battle that he was forgotten and undiscovered when the mutilation and plunder began."

Custer could count well enough to realize he simply did not have a sufficient number of men to break across the river, let alone attack a village that was like an angry hornet's nest of Indians. He would have to wait for Benteen's battalion.

According to Nathaniel Philbrick, "By this point, Custer must have seething with impatience and indignation. Just as Reno and Benteen were sitting on their hill to the south raging against Custer, Custer and his staff were, no doubt, raging against Reno and Benteen."

By this time, the Seventh Cavalry was dangerously fragmented. The packtrain with its attending civilians and soldiers and thousands of rounds of ammunition was far behind, plodding along at a pace set more by the mules than the human overseers. As far as Custer was concerned, Major Reno's portion of the regiment was somewhere and Captain Benteen's battalion was somewhere else. Captain Keogh was in charge of three companies left behind on the ridge to protect Custer's rear, to be visible to Benteen when he finally drew close enough and, if necessary, serve as a high-ground defensive position should Custer's advance be repulsed.

Thus, the rash lieutenant colonel's immediate command consisted only of the eighty or so men in Captain Yates's two companies, the Seventh's headquarters staff, Tom and Boston Custer and their nephew Autie Reed, the interpreter Mitch Boyer, and the thirty-year-old physician George Lord. To advance against a clearly superior force of warriors—who had shown no sign of being intimidated by wasichu soldiers—was ill-advised, at best.

Custer thought that too much time had already been wasted—but his options were rapidly becoming more limited.

61

EXPOSED POSITION

Captain Myles Keogh's strategy for occupying—and, if necessary, holding—the hill at the end of the ridgeline was a sound one. With forty-four members, L Company under Lieutenant Jimmi Calhoun was the closest to full strength, so Keogh had them line up across the crest of the ridge. Behind them, C Company, with the fewest men with combat experience, was placed behind Calhoun's company. Keogh's own I Company was a bit farther back, kept in reserve.

The strategy was good, but the battalion's position was not. On three sides there were places in the hills where warriors could remain concealed and fire at the troopers. Also, leading up to the ridgeline were gullies and ravines that hid the progress of dismounted warriors stealthily crawling upward. The soldiers hid as best they could, popping up from time to time to return fire, though most of their bullets struck rocks and trees.

What had to be especially maddening was the ability of the warriors not using guns to send arrows aloft on a trajectory that had them dropping down on the soldiers' exposed backs and limbs. And the screams of the wounded horses were agonizing. Keogh hated to think that one of the horses being heard was Comanche.

After about forty minutes, Captain Keogh decided to not just sit there and take it. He ordered the twenty-seven-year-old second lieutenant Henry Harrington to lead a contingent from C Company to advance down the hill. Surprisingly, the gambit worked. Stunned by the attack, the Indians retreated and hid where they could. Harrington and his men returned to the edge of the ridgeline.

But the warriors must not have been very impressed by the swift assault because within minutes, they were back. To Keogh, there appeared to be even more of them scrabbling uphill. There was nowhere to go, and another bold advance would probably not work. And it would dilute the number of troopers he had left.

Whatever was going to happen, it would happen here.

62

HIGHER GROUND

On what would be known as Calhoun Hill, Custer arrived in a spinning cloud of dust. As hordes of warriors closed in, he had some of his troopers dismount and form a skirmish line. For now, the troops led by Captain Yates would have to fend for themselves.

With the rest of the men under his immediate authority, Custer hurried along Battle Ridge to find even higher ground. With Keogh's meager force clinging to the ridge to guard the rear of the ridge, Custer was left with E and F Companies and members of the headquarters group.

Below, hundreds of Lakota and Cheyenne slowly but relentlessly made their way up the ravines. Other warriors remained at a distance yet close enough that they could fire away with arrows and rifles. Some of them who might not previously have had guns or had older ones like muskets had upgraded thanks to Reno's dead and wounded. Troopers on the high ground were being targeted and were trapped by the firing of Winchester and Henry repeating rifles.

And the rain of arrows was relentless. There was an almost limitless supply because as the attackers moved about, especially closer to the centers of action, arrows that were not embedded in the ground or a tree or a trooper or a horse could be picked up and again sent on their way.

Soon, despite Captain Keogh's best efforts, his small command was being further exposed. Warriors suddenly appeared at the rear. Facing them were only those troopers designated to hold the horses. Some tried to fire their guns with one arm while the other arm struggled to keep the horses under control. The troopers were overwhelmed, and the petrified animals bolted down the coulee.

There would be no help from other companies. From a nearby ridge, Lakota and Cheyenne took aim and picked off troopers. And at this point in the battle within a battle, Crazy Horse burnished his reputation as unkillable.

63

"A GOOD DAY TO DIE"

Crazy Horse sought his best opportunity to join the fighting, and that was to the north, where Long Hair was. On his ride there, wherever he saw soldiers, Crazy Horse fired at them with his Winchester. As he expected, wasichu bullets whistled past him.

Also on the attack was Crow King, the Hunkpapa warrior. He would have been one of the bravest and fiercest fighters on the field that day anyway, but he had added incentive—earlier in the battle, two of his brothers had been killed. They would be avenged.

Also accompanying Crazy Horse was his friend Low Dog, who had been only fourteen when bestowed the honor of being an Oglala war chief. Pointing to a wasichu position up ahead, he called out to the warriors following him, "This is a good day to die—follow me!" He later recalled: "We massed our men, and that no man should fall back, every man whipped another man's horse and we rushed right upon them. As we rushed upon them the white warriors dismounted to fire, but they did very poor shooting. Their horses were so frightened that they pulled the men all around, and a great many of their shots went up in the air and did us no harm."

With Keogh's command under siege, Crazy Horse saw an opportunity. He was riding beside White Bull, and he challenged Sitting Bull's nephew to join him on a brazen escapade—ride right through the wasichu troopers on the ridge.

The astonished soldiers were subjected to a display of classic Crazy Horse. With White Bull right behind him—and seemingly under his protective shield—the Oglala galloped through Keogh's ranks. Bullets appeared to have no effect. Not only did the two warriors ride through to the other side of the ridge, they cut a path that divided the troopers into two, smaller groups. Thus they were even less able to resist the inspired warriors in Crazy Horse's wake.

According to Low Dog, "The white warriors stood their ground bravely, and none of them made any attempt to get away."

There was nowhere to go anyway. Still, Keogh gamely tried. He found Comanche—the horse had indeed been wounded more than once—and climbed atop him. In contradiction to Low Dog's recollection, some and possibly most members of Keough's command abandoned their positions and ran for the rear. The captain considered that the only real chance of survival was to rally his remaining troopers and have them fight their way north, to join up with Custer's column, which could be faring better.

But a warrior's bullet foiled what ultimately would have been a futile effort. It went through his left leg at the knee and passed into his horse. Both Keogh and Comanche collapsed on the ground.

Troopers gathered around Keogh. Though in agonizing pain, he managed to resume issuing orders. However, he could not be heard over the gunshots and shouting and warriors' whoops, all combining into an incessant roar. As James Donovan succinctly put it, "The bulk of I Troop was still clustered around its captain when the wave of Indians swept over them all."

They seemingly came from every direction, led by Crazy Horse. Though an easy target atop his horse, still none of the dozens of bullets fired touched him. According to Red Hawk, a nineteen-year-old Oglala warrior, "The Indians kept coming like an increasing flood which could not be stopped. The soldiers were swept off their feet, they could not stay, the Indians were overwhelming."

Soon, Lakota and Cheyenne were all along the ridgeline, attacking every soldier on it. The troopers atop the hill lasted just a few more minutes. Only several horses—including Comanche—survived the onslaught. Among the troopers shot and hacked to death was Custer's handsome brother-in-law, Jimmi Calhoun.

Evidence at the hill where he died showed that he and his men fought ferociously before they were killed. Lieutenant Calhoun and his second in command, Lieutenant John Crittenden, fought back-to-back, and their bodies were found within a few feet of each other.*

There were still more wasichu to hunt down. According to James Donovan, "Scores of exulting Lakotas and Cheyennes joined in from the south. Warriors stopped to grab rifles, pistols, and ammunition from the dead and their horses. Then it was another buffalo stampede as they chased soldiers fleeing northwest along the ridge. Some escaped their pursuers, but most of them were brought down before getting too far, shot or chopped or bludgeoned."

Custer and Yates were the only senior officers still left.

---

* The frail, one-eyed Crittenden would not seem cut out for a military career, especially after leaving West Point before graduating. However, he was the son of General Thomas Crittenden, the grandson and namesake of former Kentucky U.S. Senator John Crittenden, and the great-grandson of Virginia politician John Crittenden Sr. In 1875, with such connections trumping a diploma, he successfully petitioned President Grant for a commission and was assigned to an army unit as a second lieutenant.

64

NOWHERE TO GO

Anywhere a soldier or small clusters of them could be found in what had become a widespread battlefield, death was swift. Some were so petrified that they were too frozen to even fire a gun and just waited for death. Some others, fearing what might be done to them before death, shot themselves.

One of the Lakota fighters interviewed years later, Stephen Standing Bear, a Miniconjou who was seventeen in June 1876, recalled of the beleaguered soldiers, "I really felt sorry for them. They looked so frightened. Many of them lay on the ground with their blue eyes open, waiting to be killed."*

The Lakota and Cheyenne warriors were in such a fighting frenzy

---

* Fourteen years after the battle, Stephen Standing Bear's wife and daughter were killed in the Wounded Knee massacre. At the time, he was in Austria, touring with the *Buffalo Bill Wild West Show*. He later remarried and became known for his artwork, including illustrating the 1932 edition of *Black Elk Speaks*.

that they were killing each other as well as troopers. Some were felled by arrows that were flying almost indiscriminately through the hot air roiling with dust and gun smoke. The prominent Cheyenne headman Lame White Man had donned the coat of a dead soldier, and that cost him his own life when a Sioux warrior killed him, thinking Lame White Man was an Arikara scout.

Unlike on Calhoun Hill, there were soldiers who survived the overwhelming attack on the rest of Keogh's command. Of the 115 soldiers who had comprised the right wing, some twenty escaped. On horses and on foot, they rushed away, in the general direction they hoped Custer's battalion might be. Miraculously, most also survived the gauntlet of bullets and arrows launched by the warriors and found Custer's command, which had joined up with Captain Yates's column.

It was a rather tattered left wing by now. Atop the hill were the commanding officer, his regimental staff, and F Company under Captain George Yates. E Company under Lieutenant Algernon Smith remained in a skirmish line on the north side. Several soldiers may have recognized that there was little time left if there were no reinforcements—and the remnants of Keogh's command were not enough. There was nowhere to go, and all around the slopes of the hill hundreds of warriors swirled and inexorably climbed.

65

DREAM SCENARIO

In a surreal way, Sitting Bull was watching a replica of his Sun Dance dream—and Libbie Custer's ominous mirage. The wasichu soldiers led by Long Hair had indeed come from the east and had sort of fallen into his camp.

At this point in the fray, Sitting Bull was two miles away, observing what he could from the west side of the Little Bighorn River. Like Custer had been, the headman was dressed in buckskin. He did not wear war paint, and his only adornment was a single feather in his dark hair. His field generals, Crazy Horse and Gall, were closing in on Long Hair.

Sitting Bull had already done his part by being the better battlefield tactician. According to Nathaniel Philbrick, "Whereas Custer had frantically divided his regiment, Sitting Bull had sought to consolidate his forces from the start. Rather than seek out the enemy (as the young warriors had forced him to do at the Rosebud Fight), his intention all along had been to let the soldiers come to him. In the face of Custer's hyperactive need to do too much, it had proven a brilliant strategy."

Next to feel the full force of Sitting Bull's successful strategy was what remained of Captain George Yates's battalion at the northern end of Battle Ridge. The troopers in his two companies, E and F, fought off the warriors as best they could; then it was time to run for it. The former left wing rejoined Custer, who deployed them on a small, flat-topped hill.

There were some men of Company E who tried a different avenue of escape. They sought the shelter of a shallow ravine and fired at their attackers from it. But there were more warriors than bullets. Soon, at that particular ravine, there was silence.

66

FIGHTING FOR THEIR LIVES

A short time earlier, George Armstrong Custer had to be wondering: Where was Benteen? Though Lieutenant Clarke had written it in haste, the message was clear: Hurry up!

This would be a perfect time for that battalion to arrive. The sound of gunfire and the clouds of dust indicated that Captain Keough was keeping the warriors busy at one end of the high ridge. Yates and his troopers had to be engaged in battle, too, occupying the attention of more warriors, and then they could retreat to add to Custer's immediate command. Were Custer and Benteen to combine their columns, they could deliver a direct and powerful punch to the vulnerable village.

Waiting around was gaining nothing. In fact, it was worse than nothing because while Custer's column stayed put, more and more Lakota and Cheyenne were gathering around it. The main battalion could certainly not eventually combine with Keough and Benteen and possibly Reno, wherever he had gone to, if it was hemmed in on all sides.

Some action was better than none at all. Custer told Lieutenant

Algernon Smith to take E Company survivors two hundred yards to the south to a ravine where warriors could be seen approaching. There were more Indians nearing from other directions, but slamming that exposed doorway closed would buy some time.

As Smith set up a skirmish line that extended to the ravine, Custer had the rest of his command move up to higher ground. The position would not hide the soldiers from bullets, but the poor marksmanship of the warriors made distant rifle fire the least of his problems. Still, if enough bullets were fired, some were going to strike flesh, human and horse.

Custer may have questioned how the Indians seemed to have an unlimited amount of ammunition and noted that with the packtrain nowhere to be seen, his own men had to be running low. And on water too. Having had a meager amount of sleep the night before and spending the entire day active under a merciless sun, the troopers had to be parched as well as exhausted. Same for their horses. The Little Bighorn River seemed to be so far away.

Being on high ground trumped any other concerns. Custer grudgingly realized that until he was reinforced by at least one of the other Seventh Cavalry units, an assault on Sitting Bull's village was a fantasy. The priority was establishing and maintaining a defensive position.

Custer did so on a narrow flat area. Around him were his brothers, his nephew, and his regimental staff. Sergeant Robert Hughes planted Custer's personal guidon, its red and blue swallowtails fluttering in the sporadic breeze.

Everywhere Custer looked, warriors were on their way to him. He ordered his men to shoot their horses. He hated using the bullets, but breastworks were most needed now.

"The men on the side of the hill and on its crest threw themselves down behind dead horses and resumed firing," writes James Donovan. "They were now fighting for their lives, and they knew it."

67

DEATH IN THE GULLY

It was soon clear to Lieutenant Algernon Smith that his company was not going to rid the ravine of warriors. The death cries of horses told him what was happening up above, and it was unlikely that help was on the way. Smith's men fired into the ravine, but it appeared that for every warrior felled, three took his place. It was time to withdraw, if it was not already too late.

A moment later, before Smith could shout to his soldiers, the skirmish line was disrupted by an attack of about two dozen mounted warriors. They killed several troopers and routed the horses. There would be no concerted withdrawal—it was every man for himself.

Some soldiers ran down into the ravine, apparently intending to bull their way past warriors and outrun them to the river. What being at the river would do to save them probably did not enter their panicked minds. They simply rushed—or in a few cases, galloped—downward.

When they reached a gully, they were easy targets, stuck together in a mostly confined area. Jubilant warriors fired rifles and shot arrows down into the gully and stopped only when all the soldiers and the few remaining horses were dead.

Except for one trooper. Maybe he had not been hit or had been shot several times, it did not matter: He burst out of the gully and made for the river. Astonished warriors hesitated—perhaps they had just seen a dead wasichu with powerful enough medicine to come back to life—then several took off. The trooper was no match for them—he was caught and killed. And this time, he stayed dead.

Above, Lieutenant Smith managed to lead several soldiers uphill to the fragile safety of his commanding officer, Custer's, position. There, they joined the others hiding behind the ghastly breastworks. Even Custer and his inherent confidence could not get past the observation that his battalion had forty, maybe forty-five men left, and almost on all sides of them, there could be as many as a thousand Lakota and Cheyenne.

And then Myles Keogh's battalion showed up.

Or what was left of it. Apparently, when Crazy Horse and his fellow warriors overwhelmed the captain's position on the ridge, several soldiers had managed to wriggle out of the frantic scrum. In the swirling dust clouds, they may have become invisible to the warriors focused on finishing off Keogh's command.

They suddenly appeared on the slope leading up to Custer's fragile perimeter, with Lakota and Cheyenne close behind. Soldiers shot down at the pursuers, and they scattered, allowing the fatigued and frightened fellow troopers to ascend the rest of the way.

Their gasping report told Custer that there would be no help coming from Captain Keogh.

68

RAINING ARROWS

The tactic of shooting arrows in a high arc so that they rained down on huddled wasichu had been so effective elsewhere on the battlefield that it was used here too. The horseflesh breastworks that were good for stopping bullets were of no help against the downpour of arrows.*

The disadvantage to this was friendly fire. A furious Gall led warriors up one side of the hill while a determined Crazy Horse led warriors up the other side. The columns of warriors were drawing closer to not only Custer but also each other. Their arrows and bullets found the flesh of Lakota and Cheyenne as often if not more than U.S. soldiers'. As many as half of the Indian casualties that day were from accidental shooting.

* It has been configured that if there were two thousand Sioux and Cheyenne warriors involved in the fighting and if half of them shot ten arrows each, ten thousand arrows were fired at the Seventh Cavalry. Sitting Bull's army may not have possessed ten thousand arrows when the battle began, but some of the arrows, after being yanked out of the ground, tree trunks, and human and horse flesh, were put back into service.

One exception was the death of Lame White Man, which was deliberate, but likely a mistake. Before the battle started, the thirty-nine-year-old Cheyenne had been taking a sweat bath in the village. When Major Reno's battalion neared the village and shooting began, Lame White Man did not take the time to put on his proper war clothing. Instead, he grabbed his weapons, mounted his horse, and rushed into battle.

When his body was found after the battle, he had been scalped, and it is thought that he was killed by Lakota warriors. Because he was not wearing distinctive Cheyenne warrior regalia, he may have been mistaken for an enemy army scout.

Meanwhile, writes Mark Lee Gardner in *The Earth Is All That Lasts*, "Warriors stealthily crawled up ravines and ditches on all sides, creeping ever closer with a seemingly endless supply of cartridges and arrows. Efforts to drive them back simply saw them regroup and come again with even more fighters. An expanding haze of black powder smoke turned sweaty, scared men into gray silhouettes, horses kicked and plunged with arrows sticking out of their bleeding rumps, and soldiers fell."

Such was the carnage closing in on Custer. And it was being witnessed by Sitting Bull.

Earlier in the battle, the Hunkpapa headman had crossed to the east side of the Little Bighorn River to exhort his warriors to kill those who had brought violence to the village. Then he had returned to the west side and now from two miles away he continued to observe the desperate fighting of the dwindling wasichu army.

Sometimes the action was obscured by swirling clouds of dust and gun smoke. But nothing interfered with hearing the incessant sounds of battle. Even from that distance, Sitting Bull heard the screaming of men and horses, the pop-pop-pop of gunshots, and the high-pitched shrieking of the eagle-bone whistles of his warriors.

Then, suddenly, Sitting Bull was startled by what he heard: nothing.

69

THE SILENCE

Of George Armstrong Custer's right wing, left wing, and immediate command, no one was left to fight except the tightening circle of men who surrounded him. The Arikara scouts who had survived had fled the valley. The Crow scouts who had been released had repaired to high ground, where they could safely watch the rest of the battle unfold. The Lakota French interpreter and scout Mitch Boyer was dead, one of those slaughtered in the ravine. Every Seventh Cavalry officer not with Reno's or Benteen's commands was dead.

The exceptions, of course, were those atop the hill. There were, at most, perhaps forty soldiers left, who were outnumbered by at least forty to one. They included Custer; his brothers Tom and Boston; his nephew Autie; his adjutant, Lieutenant Cooke; and Captain Yates.* The defenders

* George Yates left a widow and three children. His wife would spend many years as a teacher at the Carlisle Indian School in Pennsylvania. She would later be crushed to death in a New York City subway accident in 1914. Yates's

were probably low on ammunition, but that really did not matter—even if the packtrain had miraculously appeared in their midst, the outcome was inevitable. It was only a question of how quickly it would come.

The Miniconjou warrior Standing Bear recalled: "Everywhere our warriors began yelling, 'Hoka hey! Hurry! Hurry!' Then we all went up, and it got dark with dust and smoke. I could see warriors flying all around me like shadows, and the noise of all those hoofs and guns and cries was so loud it seemed quiet in there and the voices seemed to be on top of the cloud. It was like a bad dream."

A few of the soldiers turned their guns on themselves, preferring to die fast than be tortured and probably mutilated while still alive. Some soldiers essentially gave up and awaited the killing bullet or blow from a club. A few continued to fight.

Custer fired his bulldog pistols until they were empty. Most likely, his self-confidence had been replaced by seething defiance, or deflating despair. And guilt. Even if not for his military decisions but for Boston and Autie. It was one thing for Custer and his brother Tom to die in battles—they were army officers who had sworn an oath. But not these civilians, and Autie barely being eighteen years old.

Crazy Horse on one side and Gall on the other drew closer. The battle was reaching its crescendo. There could be only one outcome. Then there was silence on the hill.

"The sudden quiet after so much chaos was surreal," notes Mark Lee Gardner, "made even more so by the low moaning of wounded and dying Long Knives."

The moaning would last only a few moments longer.

---

brother-in-law, Richard Roberts, had accompanied the Custer column as a civilian herder and part-time correspondent for the *New York Sun* but had to drop out seventy miles from the Little Bighorn when his pony gave out, thereby sparing his life.

ACT VI

THE LAST STANDS

I warned my people not to touch the spoils of the battlefield. Many did not heed, and it will prove a curse to this nation. Indians who set their hearts upon the goods of the white man will be at his mercy and will starve at his hands.

—**SITTING BULL**

70

THE FIRST LAST STAND

In the 150 years since the Battle of the Little Bighorn, there have been several theories of how George Armstrong Custer died, gleaned from forensic evidence and interviews with Lakota and Cheyenne participants.

Losing credence over the years is that Custer was killed or severely wounded during the attempt to ford the Little Bighorn River. There were a few accounts by participants years later of an officer resembling Long Hair being shot at the river. While it is possible that a lucky shot struck Custer and the wounded or dead commander was then transported by troopers up to where his body was eventually found on Last Stand Hill, it is not likely.

It has also been contended that Custer was killed by his brother Tom. Sometime in the waning minutes of the fighting on the hill, Custer was shot in the chest and probably fell to the ground. He was also shot in the left temple. This fatal wound might have been administered by Tom to spare his brother the pain and humiliation of being captured and tortured or killed in a more gruesome way.

Supporting this scenario is that the bodies of George and Tom Custer were only a little more than a dozen feet of each other. Also, there is evidence that Tom Custer may have been the last to die after a mighty struggle. Apparently, his bravery elicited no mercy: His body was slashed and pounded so severely—including his head smashed into jelly by stone clubs—that it was identified as Tom Custer only by a tattoo on his arm.

The perpetrator may well have been Crazy Horse. He had fought his way up the hill. He saw soldiers with their backs to the top of the hill, most of them horseless by now, many wounded, hard-pressed by Gall's force on the other side.

"The troopers were badly strung out," writes Stephen Ambrose. "Hot, tired, dusty, thirsty, afraid, they were slowly working their way up the hill, trying meanwhile to maintain a steady volume of fire in order to hold back Gall's warriors. Just below Crazy Horse there was a small knot of men. Tom Custer was there, and Bos, and most of Custer's staff. Custer was at their head, not much more than twenty yards away from Crazy Horse. The officers were making their way to the top, probably looking in that direction, so it is possible that Crazy Horse and Custer looked into each other's eyes."

And this time, each knew who the other was. And it would have been fitting that the greatest warrior on the field delivered the final blow. After all, Joseph Marshall III points out, "Crazy Horse was the Lakota battle leader who, in the span of eight days, got the best of two of the United States Army's field commanders: Brigadier General George Crook and Lieutenant Colonel George Custer."

The scenario accepted by most historians is the one that has been reflected in popular culture for decades—from films like *They Died with Their Boots On* to the famous Budweiser print that adorned an untold number of saloons across the U.S.: There finally was no last soldier standing.

As Gall recalled years later: "The dust and smoke was black as evening. Once in a while we could see the soldiers through the dust, and finally we charged through them with our ponies. When we had done this, the fight was over."

The Long Knives and their reviled leader were dead. But there was still more to do. According to Robert Utley, "The hot June sun hung low over the Bighorn Mountains when the last man fell. Exultant warriors raced their ponies around the battlefield, killing wounded men, firing their rifles in triumph, and raising great clouds of dust. Women and children made their way up the slopes from the village to rob, strip, and mutilate the bodies."

71

THE DESECRATIONS

Very soon after quiet again descended on the battlefield, women and boys too young to be warriors and a few elderly men arrived. It was their role to finish off the wounded and mutilate the bodies.

One of them was the sixteen-year-old Black Elk. He would later recall that when a couple of companions found a moaning white man on the ground with arrows protruding from him, they not only pushed the shafts in farther but shot the soldier with a few arrows of their own.

Mark Lee Gardner recounts one bizarre scene: "Women plunged knives into soldiers' bodies to make sure they were dead before stripping them of clothing. Two women neglected to stab one body." The naked trooper jumped up and grappled with the two women, who screamed for help. "Finally, another woman rushed up and stabbed the man, causing a stream of bright red blood to spew out of the wound. The trooper collapsed, and this time he was truly dead."

There was the obligatory scalping, but this was not as satisfying as usual because so many of the soldiers had close-cropped hair. There was still much to do: As with Tom Custer, heads were mashed beyond recognition; hands and feet were hacked off, the body parts flung aside; some heads were cut completely off; penises were sliced off and in some cases thrust into white men's mouths; and any other butchery previously practiced or thought of in the moment.

There were two notable exceptions to the mutilations. One was Captain Miles Keogh. The former fighter for Pope Pius IX wore an Agnus Dei (Lamb of God) medal around his neck. It is believed that out of respect for this medicine that Keogh's body was spared desecration.

And George Custer. His body had been stripped naked, and several warriors were about to begin their bloody work, when two women strenuously objected. They insisted that he was married to the Cheyenne woman Monahsetah and they'd had a child together. Thus, Long Hair was a relative. Frustrated at being denied such a prize, the warriors cut off one of Custer's fingers.

And there was to be one more humiliation. The Cheyenne women recalled the wasichu chief's visit with the headman Rock Forehead two years earlier. They had smoked a pipe together, and as far as the Cheyenne were concerned, Custer had agreed to Rock Forehead's request to not make war against them.

Obviously, he had not listened. To help him hear better in the afterlife, the women pushed the metal needle of a sewing awl deep into one ear and then the other.

The work continued on the battlefield as the dust settled and the sun set closer to the horizon. But warriors began to leave by the dozens, and then the hundreds. There was another last stand about to take place. Surely on this glorious day, there would be the same outcome.

72

EMPTY VALLEY

As much as the two men detested each other, their only common ground being the Seventh Cavalry and their mutual loathing of Custer, Major Marcus Reno was much relieved when Captain Frederick Benteen and his battalion arrived at the summit.

The red kerchief almost distracted the captain from what Reno had to say: "For God's sake, Benteen, halt your command and help me. I've lost half my men. We are whipped!"

Given all the wearying wandering around his column had done in the last couple of hours, Benteen was certainly not about to go anywhere. Staying put made the most sense. Their combined commands were now around three hundred men, and Benteen's troopers had a lot of unused ammunition. And unless there was a mishap, the grinding mules of the packtrain led by Captain McDougall and carrying more ammunition and supplies could show up not long after Benteen had.

Whatever the two senior officers discussed next, apparently engaging the enemy was not part of it. Instead, they were mesmerized by the astonishing sight below of the last warriors leaving the valley. Was Custer's battalion charging in force and the Indians needed every fighter they could get to defend the village?

But after a couple of minutes when there was no sign of any troopers, and especially no sign of their commanding officer, Reno and Benteen noticed that it was not so much that the warriors were attempting to escape an attack as they were heading away to initiate or join one. This was disturbing to the two veteran officers because in all the fighting for decades on the Great Plains, the tribes were not known for initiating coordinated attacks. This was a rather ominous development.

Reno later claimed that he did not know that Custer's command was in such dire straits, let alone being annihilated. Even if he had, it is doubtful that he would have led his battalion in relief of his commanding officer. That afternoon, he had shown that he would only lead away from fighting—and in disarray.

From the hilltop where his beaten-up battalion had sought refuge, the troopers could stare at the horror below. "In the river, the pale bodies of the soldiers floated like dead fish," writes Nathaniel Philbrick. "But as their moans and cries for help indicated, many of the soldiers scattered across the hillside and valley below were still very much alive."

Reno seemed unable to comprehend his deadly failure: "Instead of being the first to safety, the commander should be one of the last. But Reno had led all the way, and in just half an hour, forty of his men—three officers, thirty-two soldiers, two civilians, and three Indian scouts—had been or were about to be killed."

At best, half the regiment was left to put up a fight. With luck, they would not have to. Sitting Bull's warriors were either being defeated or at least dispersed by Custer's troopers. Or, though less likely, they were closing in on a victory and then would be occupied by celebrations. With luck, General Terry would arrive with his battalions before the Lakota and Cheyenne turned their attention elsewhere.

Further cheering the morose Reno was another arrival—Captain Thomas Weir and the remnants of his company. But the major reacted in an odd way. Apparently annoyed by the sporadic firing of warriors from bluffs as far as a thousand yards away, Reno felt compelled to fire back. After discovering that sometime during the harried retreat he had lost his own pistol, he yanked one out of a trooper's holster and emptied it, though everyone witnessing this gesture knew that the bullets would fall far short.

Weir did something more practical: He set up a skirmish line on the river side of the bluffs. The Indians could return at any moment.

73

ONE MORE SIGN

As the senior officer, Reno had the authority to decide what to do next. One option was to take his newly combined command and turn east to begin to get away from Sitting Bull's village as quickly as possible. He did not do this, possibly because his confused mind could not comprehend any advantage to leaving the safety of the summit. Or, to give him some credit, while Reno was not about to stick his head in the lion's mouth by trying to find Custer and his battalion, he was not going to fully abandon his commanding officer either—even though, by staying where he was, he was not doing Custer any good.

Again, to be fair, the soldiers in Reno's and Benteen's battalions were exhausted and dehydrated, and the same could be said for their horses. Though it was now late in the afternoon, the blistering day showed no signs of cooling. Even those men who could still stand or ride might not necessarily be effective fighters. Some were close to being out of ammunition, and that plodding packtrain was nowhere to be seen.

And many of Reno's troopers had been traumatized by their narrow escape and the comrades they had left behind, some to face agonizing deaths. Lieutenant Myles Moylan, who had first joined the U.S. Army nineteen years earlier and was an experienced Seventh Cavalry officer, had been seen bawling like a baby, distraught by the warriors' ferocity. He was not about to lead troops anywhere.

But Captain Benteen's column was another story. The futile foray ordered by Custer might have made the men and horses weary, but they were otherwise ready to fight. They had plenty of ammunition, and there were simply more men, and not scarred ones like in Reno's command. However, Benteen did nothing but speculate as to where Custer was and what was happening.

Reno was not listening anyway. Instead, he wondered whether his adjutant, Benjamin Hodgson, one of the very few friends he had, was still alive. The lieutenant was last seen struggling to reach the other side of the river. As it turned out, the only productive advance Major Reno made that day was to lead a few troopers downhill to search for the twenty-seven-year-old lieutenant. He was back soon, after finding Hodgson's body. It was like another sign to stay put.*

And just in case the troopers needed one more sign: From their vantage point, they could see what was happening by the river, and it nauseated them. Women and old men were busy desecrating the bodies of all those who had fallen. Some of them smashed in skulls with stone hammers, and some used knives to hack off heads, limbs, and penises.

Captain Weir was still motivated to learn the whereabouts of Custer. He saw plumes of dust rising to the north and believed—correctly—that it signaled where the main battalion was fighting. Weir approached Reno and Benteen and suggested that the combined battalion hurry in that

* Lieutenant Hodgson's watch would later be found in Sitting Bull's campsite and given to General William Carlin, who returned it to the family.

direction. The relief column could arrive in time to save Custer or, much more optimistically, be in on and share the rewards of a glorious victory.

Reno would have none of it. He might not have been any drunker than before, but that did not make him any bolder. He was not about to budge, and Benteen concurred. Weir declared, "Well, if no one else goes to Custer, I will go."

He climbed onto his horse and set off north. The men of D Company dutifully followed.

Soon after their departure, the tardy packtrain and its tired mules finally arrived.

74

IMMINENT DANGER

The farther Captain Weir got from Reno Hill, the louder was the sound of gunfire. Arriving at a high point—which would later share the names of Weir Point and Sharpshooter Ridge—the captain and his troopers strained to see the battle below.

Weir was handed a pair of binoculars by Sergeant James Flanagan, who advised, "You better take a look. I think those are Indians."

Because of the clouds of dust, the captain could not see much, but what he did discern was disturbing: Many warriors on horses were firing rifles at the ground, at who were probably wounded soldiers. And then, either having spotted Weir's company or it was just time for the next phase of the battle, the warriors turned their horses toward the observation ridge.

In imminent danger were Lieutenant Winfield Edgerly and a contingent of troopers who had been leading the company forward. When they dipped into a hollow, they were unable to see the hundreds of warriors who were now rushing toward Weir Point. However, the captain could see this threat quite clearly. He got Edgerly's attention and signaled for him to lead his men back uphill, and do it fast.

Those soldiers atop the ridge watched with increasing apprehension as the fast-riding warriors drew closer and the horses of Edgerly and his men struggled uphill. As soon as they did reach the ridge, they dismounted. With all the company's horses in the rear, Weir had his men form a skirmish line.

The situation looked dire indeed. Soon, only a few dozen men would be under attack by hundreds of evidently bloodthirsty Lakota and Cheyenne warriors. A siege was probably the only chance of survival—but the numbers told Weir the chance was slim. The captain made sure his men were locked and loaded, and they faced north.

Suddenly, there was commotion to the south—right behind them.

75

THE APPROACH OF GRASSHOPPERS

Back on Reno Hill, a crate of ammunition was broken open and distributed to the troopers. The newly arrived Captain McDougall, after a minute of observation, told Major Reno, "We ought to be down there," meaning to the north, where the dust and firing of weapons were still being seen and heard.

Reno, sucking on a bottle of whiskey that was still half-full, ignored the suggestion. He'd already had enough fighting against superior odds for one day. And with the battle being waged there having siphoned off hundreds of warriors, riding toward the battle would be like approaching an angry beehive.

But Benteen heard McDougall and reacted differently. Perhaps more out of shame than concern for Custer, the captain had his two remaining companies climb up on their horses, and he led them down off the hill and northbound. The small battalion pretended not to hear the sound of Reno's trumpeter ordering a halt.

Captain Weir and his men were no doubt relieved to discover that the commotion was not an attack from behind them but Benteen's battalion arriving. The combined force did not stay long. Benteen determined that it would be much more difficult to defend this ridgetop than the position he had just left. Best get back to it, and quick, because as one of the men, Private Edward Pigford, later testified, the approaching Lakota and Cheyenne were "as thick as grasshoppers in a harvest field."

Benteen might have stuck it out longer on the ridge if he knew his command was about to be reinforced.* Galvanized—or, more likely, shamed—by Benteen's advance to the north, Major Reno unhappily directed that his battalion be on the move. He had, at least, a few more men with him, as George Herendeen, Sergeant Henry Wright, and the ten or so others suddenly appeared, having sweated and gasped their way up the hill.

Given how hesitant Reno was to once more engage the Indians, he had to give thanks when he encountered Benteen and his men on the way back. The two senior officers conferred briefly and then had their by now further confused and weary troopers return to Reno Hill. It is not known if Custer's name was even mentioned.

Left on their own was Lieutenant Edgerly and the soldiers who had ridden into the hollow. They advanced to a higher vantage point and were shocked to see a large horde of warriors riding at them. The lieutenant did not hesitate—he had his men about-face and head for the hill. There were exchanges of gunfire with the warriors behind them, but only one man, a blacksmith named Vincent Charley, was wounded and left behind.† The rest of the troopers were able to rejoin Benteen's scrambling battalion.

---

* A map of the Little Bighorn battlefield and its immediate surroundings displays a number of sites named after Seventh Cavalry officers—Custer, Weir, Calhoun, Reno, etc. Captain Benteen, third in command, alas, was not so recognized.

† Later, Charley's body was found with a stick rammed down his throat.

According to Nathaniel Philbrick, "It was a pathetic, even absurd way to begin what was about to become one of the greatest sieges in the history of the American West."

It was also one of the more peculiar sieges anywhere.

76

A COMPANY OF FOUR

The rush of the troopers to get back up Reno Hill became something of a mad dash of men, horses, and discarded equipment. Captain Weir's company joined the panicky parade, and behind him was M Company, led by Captain Thomas French. Left to provide rearguard protection was K Company, under Lieutenant Edward Godfrey.

Near the top of the hill, Captain Benteen pointed men to take up the defensive position he had selected. It was a shallow hollow with a bluff on one side that eliminated one direction from which the Indians could attack. Benteen called for G Company to advance and help Godfrey's efforts to retreat in a slow, orderly fashion. But when their interim commander, Lieutenant George Wallace, informed the captain that there were only him and three other men left in the company, Benteen instead plugged that remnant into the perimeter being formed.

When the arc of men was completed as best as could be expected in desperation, of the seven companies ostensibly under Major Reno's command, five faced north and the majority of the onrushing warriors. The firing of bullets and arrows became more intense, but the line held.

Not faring as well were the troopers' horses and mules. There were no natural rock formations or man-made breastworks shielding them. They shared the center of the battalion's position with the aid station that Dr. Porter had quickly created. The wounded, being less exposed, were not as vulnerable, and the physician scuttled between them. However, dozens of bullets and arrows found four-legged flesh. The screaming and groaning animals collapsed when their bodies bled out from too many wounds.

The one advantage the dead animals offered to the soldiers was that the carcasses could be dragged to the perimeter and become effective breastworks.

11

DIGGING IN

To the surprise and delight of the troopers, most of them were still alive after sunset. The cessation of shooting offered an opportunity for the men to better protect themselves. They supplemented the forty or so dead horses and mules on the perimeter by digging depressions in the ground and piling up hardtack boxes and saddles. Dirt was scraped up around the dead animals. Writes Mark Lee Gardner, "Troopers were more than happy to put up with the stench on the chance the carcasses might stop a bullet."

This might have been all for naught if Reno's command had moved out. Captain Benteen later insisted that the major had proposed trying to slip away in the dark. This was actually not a bad idea—it could save the battalion rather than spend the following day trying, and likely failing, to fend off an overwhelming force of Indians. But Benteen rejected the suggestion because it would mean abandoning the more seriously wounded soldiers.

Captain Weir and Lieutenant Godfrey also proposed being on the move—not to escape but to find Custer and his command. If what was left of the Seventh Cavalry's companies could be reunited, there was a better chance of survival. Maybe even victory, if Custer had one more bold charge left in him. But this idea was also rejected, for the same reason.

Then, keep digging in. For Reno, that meant resting near the horses and sucking from a whiskey bottle. By default, command of the beleaguered battalion fell to Captain Benteen.

78

WARRIORS WEARING BLUE

It was not yet dawn on the morning of Monday, June 26, when the Lakota and Cheyenne warriors resumed shooting their guns and arrows. Benteen—who had not slept for the second night in a row—told the trumpeters who were left to sound reveille. Such defiance might make Sitting Bull think twice about sending his warriors on an attack.

Then, as light began to illuminate the horizon, the Indians displayed some defiance of their own, and it was both frightening and deflating for the troopers. At first, they were ecstatic to see at least two dozen mounted soldiers bearing the regiment's guidons. As they advanced from the north in the expanding rosy light of approaching sunrise, Reno's command believed they were seeing the forefront of Custer's battalion. They were saved!

And then, not. The "troopers" halted a few hundred yards away and began firing. From that distance, the shooting was not deadly, but the emotional effect was close to it. That these had to be Indians in soldiers' clothing implied the worst for Custer and those under his command. The men probably had to pin their hopes on the columns of Terry and Gibbon arriving.

And that required surviving as long as they could hold out. Shooting from the surrounding hills increased. An exhausted Benteen chose this time to stretch out and take a nap, apparently oblivious to the bullets kicking up dirt around him, including the one that knocked off one of his boot heels. With Reno continuing to keep the remaining horses and mules company, the battalion was virtually leaderless.

Lakota and Cheyenne warriors gathered in one of the ravines. They were about to attack one particular spot on the depleted line. The soldiers of H Company, perhaps sensing they had been targeted, left the line and retreated to where the horses and mules were tethered. If the warriors selected that abandoned position, the entire battalion could be overrun.

And it almost was.

79

BORN FOR THIS

Frederick Benteen awoke, and just in time. An attack had indeed begun where H Company had been.

"The warriors were so close that they were pelting the soldiers with rocks and clods of dirt," reports Nathaniel Philbrick. "Some were even *throwing* arrows at them. [Benteen] must stop the retreat of soldiers to the corral."

This he did. After hoisting himself up off the ground, Benteen went to the makeshift corral and chased the hiding troopers back to the perimeter. Then he went to find Reno to request more men.

He discovered the major and Captain Weir lying side by side in a hole in the ground. It was like they had already buried themselves. And with a bottle of whiskey. Reno, refusing to take any action himself, gave Benteen permission to reorganize the battalion to bolster the more vulnerable spots.

That done in haste, the most pressing assault was beaten back by volleys of rifle fire. For the rest of the morning, Benteen roamed along the perimeter, exhorting the troopers, pointing out targets, and no doubt frustrating the warriors because they could not kill him. Unlike his soldiers, Benteen stood and strolled, cheering on the battalion's sturdy defense, and it was almost as if he had borrowed Crazy Horse's medicine because except for his boot heel having been shot off, bullets did not touch him. Shouting, striding, gesturing, and inspiring his men, it was like Captain Benteen had been born for this moment.

And walking about also gave him the best view of anyone in the battalion. Nathaniel Philbrick notes, "As Benteen stood on his hill amid a shower of bullets, he was suddenly taken with the sheer number of Indians gathered not only in the ravine but all around their little saucer of grass."

One might reasonably ask: If the Lakota and Cheyenne fighters outnumbered the wasichu soldiers by five to one, or more, why didn't they simply attack en masse and overwhelm the perimeter, which had to be weakening through attrition?

There were at least two reasons. One: With apparently neither Crazy Horse nor Gall—the latter mourning his slain wife and children—available, no one with enough authority could try to coordinate such an unfamiliar tactic. Two: Topography. Reno may not have recognized how good a position defending the top of the hill was. There was no open plain to attack across. Warriors could approach upward in small clusters and be exposed to rifle fire. The majority of the warriors looked on from the hills surrounding the siege.

The battalion now under Captain Benteen's rather dramatic command could hold out indefinitely. Or until their ammunition ran out. Or the men became too weak from dehydration. From noon on, the merciless sun of a typical northern plains summer day beat down on the battalion trying to hold a shadeless hill.

80

"GIVE THEM HELL!"

Wizened Lakota and Cheyenne elders issued advice to the warriors: Watch the approaches to the Greasy Grass. The white soldiers had to have used up all the water in their canteens, there was no source of water in the hills, and it was another torrid and dry day. The wasichu had no choice but to risk runs for water.

The old men were right. Soldiers carrying canteens, buckets, and kettles, as many as a dozen men, scooted down Reno Hill via a ravine, and when they reached the bottom of the gulch, they raced for the river. Covering fire came from the top of the hill, but the more furious firing was launched by the warriors. Still, with just one man wounded in the leg, the soldiers made it back safely from the river, though several of the containers had water spouting through bullet holes.*

---

* In 1878, the army awarded twenty-four Medals of Honor to members of Reno's and Benteen's combined battalion for bravery, many of them for risking their lives to fetch and carry water from the river up the hill to the wounded and parched men.

With the troopers somewhat recovered thanks to fresh water, Benteen decided to attack. At some point, he expected, the warriors crowded in the ravine were going to try an attack themselves. They were probably almost waiting for distant rifle fire and wasichu exhaustion to take enough of a toll. The white-haired captain was about to turn the tables.

Benteen pointed to the men to accompany him, who nervously stood. They probably thought the captain was mad. He *was* mad—not out of his senses but, as he would later testify, angry mad. The warriors would not let him *sleep*.

With Benteen leading the way and many of them screaming, the men surged over the hill and ran about a hundred yards down into the ravine, firing furiously. Startled warriors turned and ran as if they were seeing ghosts. Satisfied with the result, Benteen led his men back up the hill.

Soon, however, he was informed that warriors were amassing on the opposite side of the hill. He returned to the hole where Reno and Weir continued to lie. It took some persuading, but finally, with every minute more precious, Benteen convinced the major that another charge was required. Right after Reno sat up—resurrected, in a way—and gave the command, Benteen announced, "Ready, boys: Now charge and give them hell!"

Once more, he charged down the hill, his soldiers like banshees behind him. Once again, the warriors scrambled away as fast as their legs could carry them. This time, the soldiers had to go only fifty yards before returning to the perimeter. Again, mission accomplished.

The disheartened Lakota and Cheyenne fired sporadically from the hills during the rest of the afternoon. Benteen and many of the men were buoyed—and probably mystified—by the lack of aggressive action. Still, at nightfall, the siege had not ended.

It was a tense night for the battalion, and a third sleepless one for Benteen. Most likely, with dawn the Indians would renew the gunfire and maybe finally try to storm the top of the hill. As the sun made its first appearance, what remained of the Seventh Cavalry was locked and loaded.

But the spreading sunlight revealed that surrounding hills were empty of warriors. For a while, anyway: There were dust clouds to the north. A fresh batch of Lakota and Cheyenne fighters? But as they drew closer, the riders were seen to be wearing blue uniforms. Another trick by the warriors, wearing the clothing of the dead?

No. The mounted men were the advance guard of General Terry's column.

81

THE MOVING VILLAGE

Both impressed and frustrated by the durable defense of the remaining troopers, Sitting Bull decided to withdraw his fighters. And it was time to go before more wasichu soldiers arrived in the valley. The entire village had to be on the move.

And he was angry, despite the great victory. His dream had also included not plundering the possessions of the wasichu dead, yet that had happened. It not only tainted the triumph but also Sitting Bull feared there would be consequences from Wakan Tanka, the Great Spirit. He told his people that he feared they would "starve at the white man's door [and] they will be scattered and crushed by troops."

And it might happen sooner than later if they did not get moving. Scouts rushed into the village, their ponies heaving, to report to Sitting Bull that many more soldiers were approaching from downstream—Colonel Gibbon's column, now joined by General Terry's.

The soldiers who were still alive at the Little Bighorn would remain so. Sitting Bull proclaimed, "Let them go now so some can go home and spread the news."

Late in the afternoon of Tuesday, June 27, the Indians set fire to the prairie grass. Already by the first week of summer, the grass was dry enough that it kindled easily. Burning the grass would destroy food the wasichu horses would need, slowing, if not preventing, any pursuit. And the waves of flames and dark smoke at least partly shielded the men, women, and children as they packed up their utensils and other possessions, dismantled their lodges, and hauled their travois and lodgepoles up the slope on the west side of the valley and then southwest to the Bighorn Mountains. They were leaving the field of a stunning victory rather than risk it becoming a disastrous defeat.

The column of Indians, with Cheyenne in the lead and Hunkpapa bringing up the rear, stretched for two miles. Part of the caravan was as many as twenty thousand ponies.

"The troopers on the bluff, puzzled by the long lull in the fighting, watched in awe as the mass of Indians and animals emerged from the cloud of smoke, slowly snaking up the valley," reports Mark Lee Gardner. "With the sun sinking to the west, the smoke and dust turning the enormous sky to a blood-red hue, the incredible procession seemed like it would never end."

82

"IT'S HIM!"

On its way toward the Little Bighorn Valley, Alfred Terry's advance guard had encountered White Man Runs Him, Hairy Moccasin, and Goes Ahead. The three Crow scouts had witnessed the battle and, when they thought it was safe, had set off for home.

They told the terrible tale to Little Face, one of Terry's scouts, who in turn communicated it to his commander. Thus, it is quite possible that Lieutenant James Bradley was the first white soldier to learn of the Custer calamity. A messenger was sent back to inform Terry.

By the time the column led by Terry and Colonel Gibbon descended into the valley, Bradley had ridden around the battlefield. He reported to his superior officers that he had counted 197 dead soldiers. For now, the lieutenant spared them the details.

Still, Terry was affected enough that he was weeping when he met with Major Reno and Captain Benteen. Their first query: Where was Custer?

The general responded, "He lies on the ridge about four miles below here with all his command killed."

Benteen declared that he did not believe that Custer was dead. Terry told the captain to take some men and ride down into the valley and look for himself. The search was a short one. A private, pointing at a body on the ground, called to Benteen, who dismounted and walked up to it.

He stared at the body in shock. "My God, it's him!" he exclaimed. Perhaps at that stunning moment, the irony occurred to Benteen: As Major Joel Elliott had been forsaken at the Washita River, he and Marcus Reno had done the same to Custer at the Little Bighorn River.

83

BLOATED MASKS

Including those who were not under Custer's immediate command, the Seventh Cavalry's total casualty count was 268 dead, including several Arikara scouts, and 55 wounded, 6 of them so severely that they would perish.

Estimates of Native American casualties have differed widely, from as few as 36 dead to as many as 300. The Lakota headman Red Horse told an army officer in 1877 that the Lakota and Cheyenne suffered 136 dead and 160 wounded during the battle. In 1881, Red Horse told Dr. C. E. McChesney the same numbers, but in a series of drawings done by the headman to illustrate the battle, he drew only 60 figures representing Lakota and Cheyenne casualties. In the last 150 years, historians have been able to identify multiple Indian names pertaining to the same individual, which has greatly reduced previously inflated numbers.

According to Peter Cozzens in *The Earth Is Weeping*, "The asymmetry in losses [was] largely a consequence both of Custer's splitting his outnumbered command in the face of a much larger force and of the

Indians' having refrained from exposing themselves unnecessarily. The Lakota-Cheyenne alliance had achieved a great victory in a battle they had not sought."

Though publicly outraged by the massacre, privately General Terry was not surprised. And the high cost did serve a desired purpose: Public opinion would turn overwhelmingly against the northern plains tribes. And the country mourned its fallen hero.

The army public relations campaign that would portray Custer as peacefully dead—even smiling—next to his horse with but two tidy bullet wounds in his temple and chest began that summer. Writing to his wife, Captain Benteen falsely claimed that the bodies of Custer and those around him "were as recognizable as if they were in life."

Elaborating in the same untruthful vein, Lieutenant Edward Godfrey rather ludicrously recorded that the stripped-naked Custer "was not mutilated at all. He laid on his back, his upper arms on the ground, the hands folded or so placed as to cross the body above the stomach: his position was natural and one that we had seen hundreds of times while taking cat naps during halts on the march."

It would be decades before the ugly truth was accepted—that almost all of the Seventh Cavalry troopers under Custer's direct command had been severely butchered and dismembered.

The families of the slain soldiers were fortunate to be living at a time when the queasiest of details could be literally covered up.

"More than two hundred bodies and about seventy animal carcasses had been exposed to the June sun for two or three days when burial parties went to work," reports Evan S. Connell. "Soldiers detailed to hide the remains were overcome by nausea, vomiting and retching while they tried to dig graves, so the business was simplified. Bodies thought to be those of officers were nudged into shallow trenches. Those thought to be enlisted men were hastily concealed beneath sagebrush and a few shovels of dirt. Some attempt was made to identify them, although not much. Few could be recognized. Very often the features were distorted by fright or anguish. The faces of some had been pounded with clubs or stones until they were bloated masks of congealed blood encrusted with feeding insects."

84

INCREDIBLE NEWS

Outside of the Seventh Cavalry and General Terry's column, the first people to hear the news of the Custer defeat were those aboard the steamboat *Far West*, which had brought supplies for the expedition. Curly, one of Custer's scouts, rode up to the docked steamboat and tearfully conveyed the information to Captain Grant Marsh and the army officers on board.*

When the wagons carrying the wounded arrived, Marsh quickly converted the *Far West* into a floating field hospital and welcomed aboard the fifty-two men from Reno's and Benteen's battalions. As soon as they were secured, the boat aimed for Fort Lincoln.

Traveling night and day, with a full head of steam, Marsh brought the *Far West* downriver to Bismarck, Dakota Territory, making the 710-mile

---

* In one of history's tantalizing coincidences, in late April 1883, Grant Marsh's packet boat, the *W. J. Behan*, would transport Sitting Bull and his remaining followers from Fort Yates to Fort Randall, where they had been detained after their return from Canada.

run in the record time of fifty-four hours. Something like a virus that would rampage through the U.S. population, the news of what came to be called the "Custer Massacre" disseminated, spreading from the people aboard the *Far West*. The editor of the Bismarck paper kept the telegraph operator busy for hours transmitting information to *The New York Herald*, for which he served as a stringer.

News of the defeat arrived in the East as the United States was observing its centennial. "General" Custer had been scheduled to appear in the July 4 Centennial Parade in Philadelphia as the grand marshal. The glamorous role of returning war hero would have helped his chances at a presidential run. When Custer did not arrive in Philadelphia in time to prepare for the parade, his absence was rationalized as the dashing cavalry commander being unable to leave the campaign out west.

Instead of through official channels, Generals William Sherman and Philip Sheridan, attending centennial ceremonies in Independence Square, were informed of the debacle in Montana by the screaming headlines in the Philadelphia newspapers. Reporters wanting details from the senior army officers were instead told that the reports had to be false. The newspapers were irresponsibly reporting nothing more than fanciful rumors.

With exquisite timing, as the generals were holding court, Sherman was handed a telegram. With incredulity, he read: "Dispatches from General Terry confirm the newspaper reports of a fight on the 25th of June, on the Little Big Horn, and of General Custer's death."

What had seemed at first a preposterous notion morphed into grim reality with each passing hour as more messages arrived in other major cities.

85

"SUPREME MOMENT"

The Battle of the Little Bighorn had far-reaching consequences. It was the beginning of the end of the Indian Wars and was, albeit longer, as much a last stand for the western tribes as it had been for George Armstrong Custer.

According to Stephen Ambrose, "The battle of the Little Bighorn had been a supreme moment in the life of the Sioux nation. Never before had the Sioux people been so united, nor would they be again. Never before had the Sioux warriors been so ably led, nor would they be again. Crazy Horse counted up the losses. He mourned for them, of course, but not too deeply, because it had been a good day to die."

Out of necessity as well as fear of quick retribution, within forty-eight hours of the battle, all the Sioux and Cheyenne had left the former encampment on the Little Bighorn River. According to the young Black Elk, "We fled all night, following the Greasy Grass. My two younger brothers and I rode in a pony-drag, and my mother put some young pups in with us. They were always trying to crawl out and I was always putting them back in, so I didn't sleep much."

In smaller congregations, and with no sign of pursuit by the U.S. Army, the Lakota and Cheyenne feasted and celebrated during July. Once the celebrations ceased, many of the Indians returned to their agencies and reservations. They had not only killed many soldiers but taught the wasichus in general a lesson: Leave us alone. Soon the number of warriors under Sitting Bull amounted to only about six hundred.

They were right not to have worried about their safety. Both Generals Crook and Terry remained immobile for seven weeks after the Little Bighorn battle. They were waiting for reinforcements, unwilling to venture out against the Lakota and Cheyenne until they had at least two thousand men. Apparently, they were unaware of Sitting Bull's reduced force. It was not until mid-August when Crook and Terry took to the field.

"Finally, more troops were on the way," writes Robert Utley in *Cavalier in Buckskin*. "The Little Bighorn had shocked and outraged the American people," who did not even know most of the sordid details. "Newspapers cried for swift reprisal."

The first big reprisal was not a military one but legislative vengeance enacted two thousand miles from the northern plains. As a direct consequence of the Custer catastrophe, Congress attached what the Lakota Sioux called a "sell or starve" rider to the Indian Appropriations Act of 1876. This rider cut off all rations for the Sioux until they terminated hostilities and ceded the Black Hills to the United States.

86

SMALL VICTORIES

By the time General Terry was ready to return to the field, the Seventh Cavalry had been assigned new officers, and recruiting efforts had begun to fill the depleted ranks. The regiment, reorganized into eight companies, remained part of Terry's column, to be joined by Colonel Gibbon's troopers, who were idling on the Yellowstone River at the mouth of the Bighorn.

On August 8, after Terry was further reinforced with the Fifth Infantry, the expedition finally moved up Rosebud Creek in pursuit of the Lakota. It met up with Crook's command, similarly reinforced, and the combined force, almost four thousand strong, followed the Indians' trail northeast toward the Little Missouri River.

And that was about as far as they got. Persistent rain and lack of supplies forced the column to pause, and then the units returned to their varying starting points. For the Seventh Cavalry, that meant back to Fort Abraham Lincoln. Colonel Sturgis, probably prompted by the death of his son, Lieutenant James Sturgis, in the Little Bighorn battle, traveled from St. Louis to take field command of the regiment.

The limp late-summer campaign further emphasized to Terry and Crook—and by extension, General Sheridan, who was back in Chicago—that large, lumbering columns of soldiers blundering about the northern plains were not likely to catch the more nimble and knowledgeable Sitting Bull and Crazy Horse. Even entire villages could fold up their tents and move faster than army forces, who often did not know where they were and what waited for them.

Also demonstrated was that even with the strenuous efforts of Grant Marsh and other steamboat captains, the bigger the force, the harder it was to keep it supplied. Both Napoleon and Frederick the Great have been credited with saying that "an army marches on its stomach," and on the northern plains, the U.S. Army could not forage and improvise like the Lakota and Cheyenne could.

There was another harsh revelation about the ineffectual campaign of Terry and Crook: After Custer's death, none of the remaining commanders knew how to fight Indians, at least plains Indians.

Still, there were small victories that began to have a cumulative impact. Before the Centennial summer of '76 was over, the last stands of northern plains tribes had begun.

87

LAST MOMENT OF GLORY

On September 10, Captain Anson Mills, who had distinguished himself under Crook in the Rosebud fight, led two battalions of cavalry that captured a Miniconjou village of thirty-six tepees in the Battle of Slim Buttes in South Dakota. Crazy Horse and his followers attempted to rescue the camp and its headman, American Horse, but they were unsuccessful. The soldiers killed American Horse and much of his family after they were found holed up in a cave.

The onslaught of retributions the Lakota and Cheyenne expected did not come to pass in the autumn. With the onset of winter, many of them, including Sitting Bull, began to feel safe. He had not counted on a new field commander with the same tenacity as Long Hair.

On January 8, 1877, though winter had a strong hold on the northern plains, Crazy Horse's warriors fought the U.S. Army in what would be their last major engagement—and the last moment of glory for Crazy Horse—the Battle of Wolf Mountain in southern Montana.

With the other commanders unable to deliver a knockout blow, the War Department believed it had found another George Armstrong Custer—without the recklessness—in Nelson Appleton Miles. The twenty-two-year-old Massachusetts native had enlisted in the Union army a few months after the Civil War began, and though he was not a West Point alum, like Custer, his rise was meteoric. Starting out in September 1861 as a lieutenant, soon after he survived the Battle of Antietam in September 1862, his latest promotion made him a colonel. Miles survived other hellscapes too—though he was wounded four times in them—and by the war's end, he was a brevet major general.* Postwar, he would become a colonel in the regular army.

After uninspiring administrative positions, in the mid-1870s, Miles was back in the saddle. After Crook, Terry, and Gibbon were essentially sidelined, the ambitious colonel was tasked with successfully ending what newspapers referred to as the Great Sioux War. Miles eagerly accepted the challenge. His first priority was to capture or kill Crazy Horse.

Miles was well aware that in November, another ambitious colonel, Ranald Mackenzie, had led 1,400 troops in an attack on a Cheyenne village in the Bighorn Mountains in Wyoming. Its headman, Dull Knife, organized a delaying action that allowed his people to escape, but it was a victory nonetheless, eliciting high praise for Colonel Mackenzie, another officer wounded several times in the Civil War who had previously earned praise for conducting the Red River War in Texas.†

---

* Two of those wounds, in the neck and abdomen, came in the Battle of Chancellorsville, and for his actions, Miles was awarded the Medal of Honor.

† Attrition, lack of food, and a concern for the Cheyenne women and children would persuade Dull Knife to surrender at Fort Robinson, Nebraska, in the spring of 1877.

Seeking safety from the soldiers, Dull Knife and his followers trekked as best they could through snow and icy conditions to join the camp of Crazy Horse in the Tongue River Valley. Concerned with the approaching winter and the destitute condition of Dull Knife's band, Crazy Horse decided to negotiate peace with the army. This first peace foray ended quickly when Crow scouts murdered Crazy Horse's delegation.

Seeking revenge, Crazy Horse led a series of small raids in an effort to draw out Colonel Miles from the army's nearby cantonment. The strategy worked. In December, Miles led most of nine companies in pursuit of Crazy Horse, heading south along the Tongue River Valley. On January 7, 1877, Miles and his force of 436 men camped by the Tongue just south of present-day Birney, Montana. During that night, a fresh layer of deep snow fell and temperatures dropped—not good conditions for a surprise attack, but Crazy Horse almost did it.

After shots were fired in the early morning hours, Miles reacted quickly. He set up a defensive perimeter along a ridgeline, with its most prominent feature being a small conical-shaped knoll later called Battle Butte. Miles positioned two pieces of artillery beside it, in front of a clear field of fire. At 7:00 A.M., Crazy Horse and the Cheyenne leader Two Moons began a series of attacks.

Frustrated by wasichu firepower, the warriors regrouped several times to begin attacking again. Attempts to flank the army's line also proved to be futile when Miles shifted his reserves to fill critical positions. Finally, Miles ordered several Fifth Infantry companies to advance to a series of hills occupied by warriors. The soldiers struggled in taking the hills, the matter being further complicated with deep snow. After soldiers secured seven of the hills, the Sioux and Cheyenne withdrew as weather conditions deteriorated.

The Battle of Wolf Mountain was considered a draw. Colonel Miles had been bloodied and a bit humiliated that Crazy Horse had led charge after charge against his troops yet had emerged untouched. And the combined Lakota and Cheyenne force had gotten away.

But the Indians had won only a reprieve. That Miles would not hesitate to mount a campaign in the most difficult northern plains weather conditions was disturbing. There might not be anywhere safe, even for their greatest warrior.

88

"NOT A WHITE MAN IS LEFT."

In June 1877, a Sun Dance was held in honor of Crazy Horse and in commemoration of the Little Bighorn triumph. Crazy Horse attended but did not take part in the dancing. Five warrior cousins sacrificed blood and flesh for Crazy Horse at the Sun Dance—three brothers, Flying Hawk, Kicking Bear, and Black Fox II, all sons of Chief Black Fox, also known as Great Kicking Bear; and two other cousins, Eagle Thunder and Walking Eagle. For Crazy Horse and many other Lakota, it would be their last Sun Dance.

To the shock of many wasichu as well as Indians, Crazy Horse had already surrendered.

Crazy Horse and other northern plains leaders had arrived with their emaciated and barely clad families and followers at the Red Cloud Agency near Fort Robinson in Nebraska on May 5. With He Dog, Little Big Man, Iron Crow, and other elite warriors, Crazy Horse met in a solemn ceremony with First Lieutenant William Clark as the first step in a formal surrender.

For the next four months, Crazy Horse resided in his village near the agency. The admiring attention that the legendary Lakota warrior received from the army and many residents at the agency sparked the jealousy of Red Cloud and Spotted Tail, who did not want another rival for power. Perhaps not coincidentally, rumors of Crazy Horse's desire to slip away and return to the old ways of life—which included reteaming with Sitting Bull to fight the despised wasichu—started to spread at the Red Cloud and Spotted Tail Agencies.

The rumors added to the warrior's woes. Notes Joseph Marshall III, "Nearly four months had passed since Crazy Horse and his seven-feet-tall people had arrived at Camp Robinson, 900 people in all, with over 1500 horses. The soldiers had taken their horses first, and then their guns, and then their hope."

Late that summer, officers at Camp Robinson received word that the Nez Percé led by Chief Joseph had broken out of their reservation in Idaho and were fleeing north through Montana toward Canada. When asked by Lieutenant Clark to join the army against the Nez Percé, Crazy Horse and his seven-foot-tall Miniconjou friend Touch the Clouds objected, saying that they had promised to remain at peace when they surrendered.

But Crazy Horse might have changed his mind. Frank Grouard was now a scout and interpreter at Fort Robinson—albeit not a very good interpreter. When Crazy Horse told him that he would fight "till all the Nez Percé were killed," that was translated as the vaunted warrior was about to "go north and fight until not a white man is left." More rumors raced throughout the fort and the agency that Crazy Horse was soon to resurrect the war against the army.

To get to the bottom of the escalating tension, General George Crook was ordered to visit Fort Robinson. A council of the Oglala leadership was called and then was canceled when Crook was incorrectly informed that Crazy Horse had said the previous evening that he intended to kill the general during the proceedings. Crook ordered Crazy Horse's arrest and then departed.

Stuck with carrying out the order was the post commander, Lieutenant Colonel Luther Bradley. To prepare for a rebellion at the Red Cloud Agency, additional troops were brought in from Fort Laramie.

89

END OF THE JOURNEY

On the morning of September 4, 1877, two columns moved against Crazy Horse's village, only to find that its inhabitants had scattered during the night. Crazy Horse had fled to the Spotted Tail Agency with his wife, Black Kettle Woman, who was ill with tuberculosis.

It was a fleeting escape. After meeting with military officials at Camp Sheridan, the adjacent military post, Crazy Horse agreed to return to Fort Robinson with Lieutenant Jesse Lee, the Indian agent at the Spotted Tail Agency.*

The next morning, Crazy Horse prepared to return to Fort Robinson. "He dressed himself in the plain clothes of everyday life: a white

---

* In 1861, at the age of eighteen, Lee had enlisted in the Fifty-Ninth Indiana Volunteer Infantry as a private. By the time he retired forty-six years later, he had achieved the rank of major general. In addition to the Civil War and the Indian Campaigns in the west, he saw action in the Spanish-American War, the Philippine Insurrection, and the Boxer Rebellion in China.

cotton shirt with blue stripes, deer-hide leggings, and beaded moccasins," reports Thomas Powers in *The Killing of Crazy Horse*. "Around his waist or over his shoulder was a red wool trade blanket. Somewhere on him he carried a trade knife much worn with use for cutting tobacco."

Escorted by Lieutenant Lee and a contingent of army Indian scouts as well as an entourage of Indians, including Touch the Clouds, Crazy Horse began the seven-hour journey to Fort Robinson. Arriving soon before sunset outside the adjutant's office, Lieutenant Lee was informed that he was to turn Crazy Horse over to the officer of the day.

Lee protested and hurried to Lieutenant Colonel Bradley's quarters to protest the order. But the post commander had received his own order—Crazy Horse was to be arrested and taken under the cover of darkness to Division Headquarters.

A reluctant Lieutenant Lee turned the Lakota war chief over to Captain James Kennington, in charge of the post guard, who accompanied Crazy Horse to the guardhouse. Once inside, Crazy Horse, realizing he was to be imprisoned, struggled with the guard and Little Big Man. It was a sad sign of the times that Little Big Man, a cousin of Crazy Horse and his lieutenant in many battles, including Little Bighorn, was now acting as a tribal policeman.

Angry at being manhandled so disrespectfully—or at all—Crazy Horse attempted once more to escape. "Let me go!" he shouted repeatedly. For a mighty warrior who had roamed the Great Plains with impunity, this doorway was his last stand.

Just outside the guardhouse, Crazy Horse was stabbed with a bayonet by one of the members of the guard detail. "They have killed me," he was heard to say as he collapsed.

According to Thomas Powers, "On the ground Crazy Horse was bent in on himself, convulsing with pain." Touch the Clouds picked up the red blanket that had fallen off Crazy Horse's shoulders during the struggle and spread it over him. After much discussion, he was carried into the adjutant's office.

Crazy Horse, even when dying, refused to lie on a white man's cot. He insisted on being placed on the floor. Armed soldiers and tribal police stood by until he died, shortly before midnight.

According to Joseph Marshall III, "Touch the Clouds reached over and laid a palm against the scars on the left side of his face, then withdrew his hand to wipe the tears sliding down his own face. Worm reached slowly down and laid his hands on top of his son's head. Since childhood, his son's hair had always been soft and fine. Moving a hand down, he gently closed the eyes, and wept. So ended the journey."

The following morning, Crazy Horse's body was turned over to his parents, Worm and Rattling Blanket Woman, who took it to a place near Camp Sheridan and placed it on a burial scaffold. The following month, when the Spotted Tail Agency was relocated to the Missouri River, Worm and Rattling Blanket Woman moved the body to an undisclosed location.

To this day, the final resting place of Crazy Horse remains unknown.

90

CROSSING INTO CANADA

It can be said that Sitting Bull had two last stands—one ended in surrender, the other ended in death.

After the huge village that had been so solidly united by the Little Bighorn River split apart, Lakota and Cheyenne families fled west, south, and north. Sitting Bull and the Hunkpapa went in the latter direction. For months they gradually put more distance between themselves and any possible pursuers.

In October, they crossed the Yellowstone River, and having heard that buffalo ranged on the plains north of the river, they made camp, planning on staying a while. The Hunkpapa were joined by some Miniconjou and Sans Arc.

The sojourn turned out to be shorter than they would have liked. After just a few days, a hunting party arrived at Glendive Creek and spotted a U.S. Army camp filled with supply wagons. This was too irresistible a target to resist. The warriors attacked but were driven off by soldiers and their effective rifles. Another group of warriors led by One Bull tried again during the next couple of days while the wagon train was on the move, with the same frustrating result.

Now, the army knew of the presence of Indians. Because of this, Sitting Bull and his people moved on.

On October 20, they were delighted to discover a herd of buffalo grazing near a confluence of the Yellowstone and Missouri Rivers. A new camp was hastily set up, and the hunt began.

It was a brief one. Word arrived that wasichu soldiers were closing in. Rather than prepare for battle, Sitting Bull sent two men toward the column of troopers with a white flag. The commanding officer, the persistent Colonel Nelson Miles, agreed to meet. He and several officers advanced, though keenly aware that he was about to confront a chief who only four months earlier had crushed almost half of a well-armed cavalry regiment.

Sitting Bull and several of his senior warriors also advanced along flat ground. He was about to parley with an army officer who was a much better field commander than Terry, Crook, and possibly even the impetuous Custer. On that day, Miles was given the nickname "Bear Coat" by the Hunkpapa because he wore a long coat of bear fur and his head was topped with a fur hat.*

The talks between the two leaders lasted two days—time wasted, as it turned out. Miles refused Sitting Bull's demand that the soldiers go away and leave his people in peace, and Sitting Bull refused to surrender.

The troopers attacked the Hunkpapa and their allies and kept at it for the next two days. Leaving some possessions behind in their hurry, the Indians fought a rearguard action as they traveled over forty miles north, hoping the soldiers would give up. Miles did call a halt when he accepted

* Though Miles was a good enough soldier, with Civil War experience, to rise through the ranks on his own abilities, it did not hurt that his wife's uncle was General William T. Sherman.

the surrender of the Miniconjou and Sans Arc bands who had been with Sitting Bull.

No winter on the northern plains is easy, but the one of 1876–77 was particularly brutal for Sitting Bull's people, as it had been for Crazy Horse's. In addition to snowstorms and subzero temperatures, they had to stay one step ahead of Bear Coat's tenacious pursuit. This sometimes meant that in their haste to pack up and go, they left possessions, even food, behind. It was already evident that few buffalo remained in the area.

After learning that several Lakota leaders had taken their followers across the border into Canada, Sitting Bull pondered doing the same. He waffled for weeks. Meanwhile, his people became more hungry and desperate. Even the approach of spring did not help. Reports Robert Utley in *The Last Sovereigns*: "On March 17 they crossed the Missouri River and pitched their shelters on the north bank. That night the winter's ice pack broke up and sent a giant wall of water down the river. It swept over the Lakota camp and damaged or destroyed nearly all their possessions."

Still, Sitting Bull hesitated. But Bear Coat was not giving up, and spring did not bring with it an influx of buffalo. The mostly Hunkpapa village of about a thousand people kept moving north. Finally, during the first week of May 1877, almost eleven months after his greatest victory, a beleaguered Sitting Bull and his followers crossed into Canada.

They knew that the wasichu soldiers could not follow them. But Canada had wasichu soldiers too.

91

STILL A FORMIDABLE FIGHTER

At last, Sitting Bull experienced some luck. Supervising the Lakota camp being established at Pinto Horse Butte would be the North-West Mounted Police, and the liaison between the two would be its leader in West Canada, Major James Walsh. Unlike most American officers, he had no animosity toward Sitting Bull and Indians in general.

James Morrow Walsh, about to turn thirty-seven, was born in Prescott, Ontario, and was one of the original officers of the North-West Mounted Police when it was formed in 1873. Two years later, he was tasked with constructing a post in the Cypress Hills in Saskatchewan. Rather immodestly, once completed, he named it Fort Walsh.

Lakota had sought safety across the Montana border in Canada as early as the summer of 1876, one of the immediate fallouts of the Little Bighorn battle. Walsh had greeted them and had them settle near the Wood Mountain post, also in Saskatchewan. By the time Sitting Bull's people arrived, there were several thousand Lakota in the area.

Major Walsh developed a strong friendship with the famous Hunkpapa exile, and the two successfully kept peace in the region. As soon as that summer, Walsh shifted his headquarters from Fort Walsh to the Wood Mountain facility. Detailing the circumstances of the Indian population there, some reporters in the United States referred to Walsh as "Sitting Bull's Boss."

He was indeed, in the sense that Walsh had the on-scene authority to oppose the Indians or accommodate them. He chose the latter. However, during the next few years, he spent less time at Wood Mountain because of other responsibilities and health-related leaves of absence. His protection of Sitting Bull weakened. At the same time, pressure was applied by the U.S. government to coerce the Lakota leader to leave Canada.

Adding to that pressure, in October 1877, a commission established by President Rutherford B. Hayes entered Canada to resolve what had become a somewhat embarrassing cross-border standoff. It was headed by General Alfred Terry.

Sitting Bull and his senior leaders met with the commission at Fort Walsh. With Sitting Bull adamantly refusing to return to the United States to surrender, there was not much to talk about. "Go home where you came from," he told Terry. "This country is mine and I intend to stay here."

In case that was not clear enough, reports Utley, "Four more chiefs made similar speeches. The wife of one of the chiefs also made a speech. Although Terry would not have known it, simply to have a woman in such a venue, and furthermore to have her speak, was a grave insult that the Indians ironically foisted on the U.S. commissioners."

General Terry and his team left. Sitting Bull and his followers continued as guests of the Canadian government and, by extension, Queen Victoria. Over time, their numbers swelled. Late in 1877, there was a surge of Lakota crossing the border in the wake of the death of Crazy Horse. A rough count by Major Walsh revealed that there were as many as eight thousand residents in Sitting Bull's camp.

This caused some concern in the government. It was not about the risk of hostilities but a fear that the Indigenous people from America could become something like wards of the state. As in the northern plains, in that section of Canada, the population of buffalo had seriously dwindled. And officials were also concerned about conflict with the United States. Unofficially, the Hayes administration would leave Sitting Bull alone as long as he stayed in Canada. And the Canadians would allow the Lakota to stay where they were, as long as they did not cross the border back and forth.

But in an increasingly desperate search for buffalo, Indian hunting parties roamed far and wide, including into Montana. And often while they were there, they stole horses and cattle and fought with furious ranchers. Sitting Bull's leadership was unquestioned, but the gap between him and young warriors had grown, and he had less influence on them. Plus, being idle in a camp in Canada did not present opportunities for counting coups and earning prestige as a warrior. And the camp needed food and hides.

It was an uneasy situation for everyone involved, yet it lasted several years. During that time, one event demonstrated that Sitting Bull, though now in his late forties, was still a formidable fighter.

In July 1879, Sitting Bull himself was part of a hunting party that had slipped across the border into Montana. After a sufficient number of buffalo had been killed, many of the hunters rode back across the border. Sitting Bull and some other men stayed behind to help the women pack the meat. Natives appeared on the other side of the Milk River. They wore red bandannas, indicating they were army scouts. One of them, brandishing a white flag, made his way across the river.

His name was Magpie, a Crow warrior. He told the Sioux who had ridden up to meet him that he wanted to challenge Sitting Bull in personal combat. Though several of his followers advised against it, the Hunkpapa headman accepted.

The fight did not last long. Both men faced each other on horses and then began to ride toward each other, like jousting knights with rifles instead of lances. Magpie's rifle misfired, but Sitting Bull's did not. Magpie was knocked off his horse. Sitting Bull dismounted, approached the slain Magpie, and scalped him. The other army scouts turned and rode away. Sitting Bull kept his opponent's horse.

92

"THE LAST MAN OF MY TRIBE"

During that long and predictably harsh winter, more and more Lakota chose to take their chances on the American side of the border. Reservation life, even with its indignities, had to be better than starvation. An exodus got underway, with one band after another packing up and leaving. By the summer of 1880, a Lakota village that had peaked at one thousand lodges had been reduced to fifty. Sitting Bull was deep into a dilemma.

Writes Robert Utley in *The Last Sovereigns*, even after several years of hardship, "Sitting Bull treasured his freedom and his adherence to the old way of life. If he went back, he feared that the Americans would punish him for killing Custer and his soldiers. He was a wanted man, and he knew that they would confine him to a reservation where he would lose his freedom."

By the beginning of the 1880–81 winter, almost all the Lakota leaders had surrendered. One of them was Gall, a major hero of the Little Bighorn battle, and still close to Sitting Bull. This betrayal and his followers barely surviving put even more pressure on Sitting Bull. And Walsh had made him aware that the Canadians were tired of the tension with the United States.

Still, Sitting Bull dithered, and more of his followers abandoned him. Finally, Sitting Bull had his Hunkpapa pack up their lodges and few possessions and travel south and east. In July 1881, they arrived at Fort Buford in North Dakota. A count made by one of the officers there revealed that only 44 men and 143 women with their children remained with Sitting Bull.

A surrender ceremony took place on July 20. Major David Brotherton, commander of Fort Buford, explained to Sitting Bull that he and his family and a few close followers would be put on a steamship and taken to Fort Yates at the Standing Rock Agency in North Dakota, where they could live in peace.*

For a full five minutes, Sitting Bull said nothing. Perhaps, though surrounded by soldiers, he was considering changing his mind. More likely, he was reflecting on the significance of his surrender. He was aware that for almost fifteen years, he had been the face of the Lakota Sioux and the chief antagonist of the U.S. Army on the Great Plains. Giving up would, as described by Utley, "mark the end of Lakota resistance, the end of Lakota freedom, and the end of the last Lakota sovereign."

Reflecting on all this, Sitting Bull may have felt the urge to go down fighting and be remembered as a mighty warrior.

But there would be no last stand at Fort Buford. Instead, Sitting Bull signaled to his son Crow Foot to hand the headman's Winchester rifle to Major Brotherton. Once that was done, Sitting Bull made a brief speech. It included: "I wish to be remembered that I was the last man of my tribe to surrender my rifle."

---

* Yes, a bit ironic: In 1878, the fort had been renamed for Captain George Yates, who had died at Little Bighorn.

93

SHOW BUSINESS AND BUFFALO BILL

It did not surprise Sitting Bull that what the U.S. government had said it was going to do, it did not. The military decided to transfer Sitting Bull and his band to Fort Randall in southern South Dakota. The group of 187 Lakota did stay for a time at Fort Yates, but then they were put on the *General Sherman* and steamed three hundred miles down the Missouri River. They arrived in September 1881.

They would spend twenty months outside Fort Randall as prisoners of war. The camp of some thirty tepees was a half mile west of the river and was constantly patrolled by guards. There would be no stealing an enemy's ponies or hunting buffalo. They subsisted on army rations.

During that time, there were increasing efforts to end Sitting Bull's imprisonment. A sympathetic ear was Secretary of War Robert Lincoln, who made a plea to fellow cabinet member Henry Teller, the secretary of the interior.* Finally, in May 1883, Sitting Bull and his entourage steamed back upriver, to live at the Standing Rock Agency.

At the reservation, authority rested with James McLaughlin, a career U.S. Indian agent. He enjoyed a good relationship with the tribes and was married to a woman of mixed blood. Unlike the many incompetent and corrupt Indian agents at that time, McLaughlin managed his agency honestly and with firm authority.

His relationship with Sitting Bull became cordial enough—though the agent favored Gall—that he allowed the Hunkpapa headman to enter show business. In 1884, the promoter Alvaren Allen asked McLaughlin to grant permission for Sitting Bull to tour parts of Canada and the northern United States. The strung-together show was called the *Sitting Bull Connection*. Though it was little more than putting Sitting Bull on display and having him say a few words, audiences were eager to see the killer of Custer, and the fifteen-city tour was a success.

It was during this tour that he met Annie Oakley in Minnesota. Sitting Bull was so impressed with her skills with firearms that he hired a photographer to take a photo of the two together. Sitting Bull felt that she was "gifted" by supernatural means in order to shoot so accurately with both hands. As a result of his esteem, he "adopted" her as a daughter. He named her "Little Sure Shot," a name that Oakley used throughout her career.

The following year, he met Buffalo Bill, and Sitting Bull truly became a showman.

Born in February 1846, William Cody had been a Pony Express rider and a U.S. Army scout, mentored by his older good friend, Wild Bill Hickok. After the Civil War, Cody cemented his reputation and earned

---

* Robert Todd Lincoln was the eldest son of Mary and Abraham Lincoln. He was the only one of their four children to survive past the teenage years.

his nickname as a prolific killer of buffalo to feed railroad construction crews. It was also when he had his share of fighting Indians, with one action leading to him being awarded the Medal of Honor. In another action, so Cody claimed, in July 1876, he killed a Cheyenne conveniently named Yellow Hair. After using his knife, Cody waved his prize aloft, shouting, "The first scalp for Custer!"

Four years earlier, Cody had traveled to Chicago to make his stage debut with his friend Texas Jack Omohundro in *The Scouts of the Prairie*, written and produced by the frontier embellisher Ned Buntline, The effort was panned by critics—one writer compared Cody's acting to a "diffident schoolboy"—but the play was a hit with the sold-out crowds.

Noting the robust box office, in 1873, Cody invited Hickok to join the group in a new play called *Scouts of the Plains*. Wild Bill did not enjoy acting and often hid behind scenery; in one show, he shot at the spotlight when it focused on him. But he stayed with the touring show through a successful Broadway run in New York. Then Cody founded the *Buffalo Bill Combination* in 1874, in which he performed for part of the year while scouting on the prairies the rest of the year. Beginning two years later, Buffalo Bill included a reenactment of the fight at Warbonnet Creek where he had killed and scalped Yellow Hair.

In 1883, finally finished on the plains, Cody founded the show that would bring him his greatest fame: *Buffalo Bill's Wild West*, a circus-like attraction that toured annually. It became so popular that he wasted no time in expanding the production. He included a sharpshooting performance by an English big-game hunter. The Buffalo Bill Cowboy Band was put into action. Cody hired Annie Oakley and her husband, Frank Butler, for more sharpshooting fun.

Performers reenacted Pony Express rides, Indian attacks on wagon trains, and stagecoach robberies. The finale was typically a portrayal of an Indian attack on a settler's cabin. Cody would ride in with a cadre of cowboys to defend the settler and his family. The onetime teamster in General Crook's column, Calamity Jane, would join the show in 1893.

Sitting Bull, though his fame rested on having killed over two hundred U.S. troopers and the legendary Long Hair—or, because of this—was again greeted enthusiastically by audiences. It was a pretty easy gig: He earned $50 a week for riding once around the arena. The Hunkpapa also charged for postshow autographs.

And there were side jobs. One of the more unusual ones took place in 1884. Sitting Bull gave an opening address at a celebration of the completion of the once-bankrupt Northern Pacific Railway. Probably prompted by the irony of praising the Iron Horse, Sitting Bull departed from the remarks written for him and instead said: "I hate all White people. You are thieves and liars. You have taken away our land and made us outcasts." The audience smiled and cheered—not only were the words spoken in Lakota, but the translator read to the crowd the original address, which had been written as a "gracious act of amity."

When he'd had enough of show business and wasichus fawning over him, Sitting Bull returned to the Standing Rock Agency, intending to spend the rest of his days there. There would be fewer of them than he anticipated.

94

GHOST DANCE

In 1889, Sitting Bull had an unexpected addition to his lodge. Caroline Weldon, a member of the National Indian Defense Association, reached out to him from Brooklyn, offering to be his secretary, interpreter, and advocate. Sitting Bull accepted. Weldon arrived with her young son, Christie, and moved into the family home.

She would stay only a little more than a year. The split with Sitting Bull was prompted by her opposition to the growing Ghost Dance movement. Weldon warned that it would give the government a pretext to harm him and to summon the military for intervention, which would destroy what remained of the Sioux Nation. Frustrated, Weldon and her son left Sitting Bull and the Standing Rock Agency in November 1890.*

---

* While traveling via riverboat, Christie died of tetanus near Pierre, South Dakota. His mother would die alone back in Brooklyn at age seventy-six in March 1921 from a fire in her apartment sparked by a candle. Weldon was portrayed by Jessica Chastain in the 2017 film *Woman Walks Ahead*.

Weldon would prove prescient. "By 1889 the Lakotas had fallen into despair," writes Robert Utley. "Land agreements had cost them half of the Great Sioux Reservation, sixty million acres. Scorching dry winds had killed their crops, and Congress had delayed appropriations for so long that their rations had to be severely cut. Sickness swept the reservations."

The following year, word spread among the reservations of a Paiute prophet named Wovoka, whose expanding fame was due to the founding of the "Ghost Dance." Wovoka claimed to have had a vision that the Christian Messiah, Jesus Christ, had returned to Earth in the form of a Native American. Though a rather confusing concept, it proved alluring to an impoverished and despairing people.

Furthermore, according to Wovoka, the white invaders would disappear from Indian lands, ancestors would lead them to good hunting grounds, the buffalo herds and all the other animals would return in abundance, and the ghosts of their ancestors would appear to them on Earth. They would then live in peace. All this would be brought about by the slow and solemn Ghost Dance, performed as a shuffle in silence to a single drumbeat.

After learning the dance from Wovoka, two Lakota leaders, Kicking Bear and his brother-in-law Short Bull, taught others in the tribe.* They also wore specially made Ghost Dance shirts. Kicking Bear misunderstood the meaning of the shirts and contended that they had the power to repel bullets. Another claim by Ghost Dance proponents—which had to be particularly appealing—was that the power of the Ghost Dance would produce a great earthquake and flood that would drown all the wasichu.

Surrounding settlers were alarmed by the sight of the northern plains tribes performing the Ghost Dance, and they worried that such brazen

---

* The following year, Short Bull would assume the role in *Buffalo Bill's Wild West Show* that had been performed by Sitting Bull, and he made several trips to Europe with the ensemble.

defiance might be a prelude to armed resistance. Among them was the U.S. Indian agent James McLaughlin. He and other officials decided to take some of the chiefs into custody to quell what they called the "Messiah craze." At the top of the list was Sitting Bull.

"Sitting Bull had gone with zest into the business of promoting the new religion," McLaughlin alleged. "Knowing his people, and utilizing the mysticism with which he habitually preyed on their superstitions, he established himself as the high priest of the cult."

On December 14, 1890, McLaughlin ordered the arrest of Sitting Bull in a letter to Lieutenant Bull Head of the Indian police. "PS," McLaughlin added. "You must not let him escape under any circumstances."

The next morning, Sitting Bull was awoken by as many as forty Indian police officers arriving at his cabin on the Grand River. He let in Bull Head and several others. Bull Head told Sitting Bull that he was under arrest. Sitting Bull acquiesced, dressing and coming quietly out of his cabin. But one of his wives began to shout, and his son Crow Foot berated him for simply going along. Dogs in the village, woken by the dawn raid, barked, waking dozens of people who began to coalesce into a crowd at their headman's home.

Sitting Bull changed his mind about complying. The police were ordered to force him out of the cabin. Like Crazy Horse, his last stand was in a doorway. Sitting Bull resisted until forced outside.

The Lakota in the village were enraged. One of them, Catch-the-Bear, raised a rifle and shot Lieutenant Bull Head, who reacted by firing his revolver into the chest of Sitting Bull. Another police officer, Red Tomahawk, shot Sitting Bull in the back of the head. He and Bull Head fell to the ground. Inside the cabin, Crow Foot was shot to death.

Shortly after noon that day, Sitting Bull died. He was fifty-nine years old. Bull Head would also die from his wound.*

* As quickly as possible, Sitting Bull was buried at Fort Yates, on the North

After Sitting Bull's death and the subsequent skirmish, two hundred members of his Hunkpapa band, fearful of reprisals, fled Standing Rock to join Spotted Elk and his Miniconjou band at the Cheyenne River Indian Reservation. And not feeling safe enough there, on December 23, Spotted Elk and his band, along with thirty-eight Hunkpapa, left that reservation and fled to the Pine Ridge Indian Reservation to seek shelter with Red Cloud.

There would be one more act of vengeance—one of the cruelest in American history.

Dakota side of the reservation. A monument was installed to mark the burial site. However, in 1953, Lakota family members exhumed what they believed to be Sitting Bull's remains, transporting them for reinterment near Mobridge, South Dakota, his birthplace. Another monument was erected there. Every July, the Sitting Bull Stampede Rodeo is held in Mobridge.

95

MASS GRAVE

As the Seventh Cavalry had done in November 1868 in the Washita River Valley and in June 1876 in the Bighorn River Valley, the troopers stealthily approached the Indian encampment on the Pine Ridge Reservation. This time, though, in December 1890, two weeks after the death of Sitting Bull, at Wounded Knee there would be a battle that would punctuate the end of the Great Sioux War and with it the last resistance of Indigenous people in the United States.*

* One could argue that there was one more act of resistance, again at Wounded Knee, in February 1973, when some two hundred Oglala joined members of the American Indian Movement to occupy the town. The action was partly in protest over the U.S. government's failure to fulfill treaties. Protesters demanded the reopening of treaty negotiations, with the goal of fair and equitable treatment of Native Americans. Activists controlled the town for seventy-one days while U.S. marshals, FBI agents, and other law enforcement agencies cordoned off the area.

Finally, fourteen years later, there would be vengeance for the bloody Little Bighorn defeat.

Even with that motivation, that there would be one more military action at all was something of a surprise, given how impoverished the Lakota had become. Their predicament was so bad that they received support from an unlikely source. In Rapid City, South Dakota, on December 19, 1890, General Nelson Miles, the army general most responsible for forcing Indians onto reservations in the American West, wrote a telegram to General John Schofield, the commanding general of the U.S. Army, in Washington, DC. It read in part:

> The difficult Indian problem cannot be solved permanently at this end of the line. It requires the fulfillment of Congress of the treaty obligations that the Indians were entreated and coerced into signing. They signed away a valuable portion of their reservation, and it is now occupied by white people, for which they have received nothing.
>
> They understood that ample provision would be made for their support; instead, their supplies have been reduced, and much of the time they have been living on half and two-thirds rations. Their crops, as well as the crops of the white people, for two years have been almost total failures.
>
> The dissatisfaction is wide spread, especially among the Sioux, while the Cheyennes have been on the verge of starvation, and were forced to commit depredations to sustain life. These facts are beyond question, and the evidence is positive and sustained by thousands of witnesses.

But the ongoing promotion of the Ghost Dance, coupled with the murder of Sitting Bull, had raised tensions between the wasichus and the remaining Lakota and Cheyenne people. Even a small spark could touch off a fire.

It began on December 28. Spotted Elk and 350 of his hungry and freezing followers were making the slow trip to the Pine Ridge Reservation. Southwest of Porcupine Butte, they were met by a Seventh Cavalry detachment under Major Samuel Whitside. John Shangreau, a scout and interpreter who was half Lakota, advised Whitside not to disarm the Lakota immediately, as it would lead to violence. The commanding officer concurred, and his troopers escorted the Lakota column about five miles westward to Wounded Knee Creek, where they told them to make camp.

Later that evening, Colonel James W. Forsyth and the remainder of the Seventh Calvary arrived, bringing the number of troopers at Wounded Knee to 500. The 350 followers of Spotted Elk consisted of 120 men and 230 women and children. Even though they showed no sign of agitation on that very cold night, troopers surrounded the encampment and set up four rapid-fire mountain guns.

At daybreak, Colonel Forsyth ordered the surrender of weapons and the immediate removal of the Lakota from the "zone of military operations" to awaiting trains. A search of the camp confiscated thirty-eight rifles, and more rifles were taken as the soldiers searched the Lakota. None of the old men was found to be armed. A medicine man named Yellow Bird allegedly harangued the young men, who were becoming irritated by the search, and the tension spread to the soldiers.

Specific details of what triggered the massacre are still being debated. According to some accounts, Yellow Bird began to perform the Ghost Dance, reminding the Lakota that their "ghost shirts" were bulletproof. As tensions mounted, Black Coyote refused to give up his rifle. He was not being obstinate—in addition to not speaking English, he was deaf, and thus he was unable to hear or understand the order.

A fellow Miniconjou interceded, informing a soldier that Black Coyote was deaf. The bluecoat persisted in trying to take the rifle, and he was soon assisted by two soldiers, who seized Black Coyote from behind. During the ensuing struggle, his rifle discharged. That was all it took: Five young Lakota men with concealed weapons threw aside their blankets and fired their rifles at Troop K of the regiment, who began to return fire. Within seconds, the firing became indiscriminate.

At first, all firing was at close range. Reportedly, half the Lakota men were killed or wounded before they had a chance to get off any shots. But some of the Lakota grabbed rifles from the piles of confiscated weapons and opened fire on the soldiers. With no cover, and with many of the Lakota unarmed, this lasted a few minutes at most.

While the Lakota warriors and soldiers were shooting at close range, other soldiers used the mountain guns against the rest of the camp full of women and children. It is believed that many of the soldiers were victims of friendly fire from these guns. The terrified Lakota women and children who were not wounded fled the camp, seeking shelter in a nearby ravine. At that point, Forsyth and his senior officers lost all control of their men.

Some of the soldiers fanned out and finished off the wounded. Others leaped onto their horses and pursued the Sioux and Miniconjou women, children, and older men for a mile or more across the frozen prairie, which offered no natural shelters. In less than an hour, at least 150 Indians had been killed and 50 wounded. Other estimates indicate nearly 300 of the original 350 were killed or wounded.

A blizzard blew in, preventing an immediate search following the massacre. Reports indicate that the soldiers loaded fifty-one survivors—four men and forty-seven women and children—onto wagons and took them to the Pine Ridge Reservation. Army casualties were reported to be twenty-five dead. Among the Miniconjou dead was Black Coyote.

Three days later, when the blizzard finally subsided, the military hired civilians to bury the dead Indians. The burial party found all the deceased frozen. They were gathered up—sometimes, limbs had to be broken—and placed in a mass grave on a hill overlooking the encampment. It was reported that four infants were found alive, wrapped in their deceased mothers' shawls.

General Miles denounced Forsyth and relieved him of command. An exhaustive Army Court of Inquiry convened by Miles criticized Forsyth for his tactics but otherwise exonerated him of responsibility. Secretary of War Redfield Procter reinstated Forsyth to command of the Seventh Cavalry. He resumed a long career in the U.S. Army, retiring as a major general.

Incredibly, and no doubt to put a shiny gloss on a cold-blooded massacre, nineteen troopers were awarded Medals of Honor for their actions at Wounded Knee. Some of the citations on the medals bestowed state that the troopers went in pursuit of Indians who were trying to escape or hide. Another citation was for "conspicuous bravery in rounding up and bringing to the skirmish line a stampeded pack mule." Another medal was given in part for extending an enlistment.

Several efforts over the years—the most recent being the Remove the Stain Act introduced in Congress in May 2025—have failed to have any of the Medals of Honor rescinded.

EPILOGUE

By the time of the Wounded Knee massacre, many of the participants of the Battle of the Little Bighorn had died or retired to their lodges and cabins. The only documented and verified survivor of Custer's immediate command was Captain Myles Keogh's horse, Comanche. The wounded animal was discovered on the battlefield by General Terry's troops. Although other cavalry mounts had survived the battle, they had been taken or killed by the Indians. For whatever reason, Comanche was spared.

After being transported to Fort Abraham Lincoln, he was slowly nursed back to health. After a lengthy convalescence, Comanche was retired. In April 1878, the mourning Colonel Samuel Sturgis, still in command of the Seventh Cavalry, issued the following order: "The horse known as 'Comanche,' being the only living representative of the bloody tragedy of the Little Big Horn, June 25th, 1876, his kind treatment and comfort shall be a matter of special pride and solicitude on the part of every member of the Seventh Cavalry to the end that his life be preserved to the utmost limit."

In June 1879, Comanche was brought to Fort Meade, where he was well cared for until 1887, when he was taken to Fort Riley. As an honor, he was made "Second Commanding Officer" of the Seventh Cavalry. He became something of a pet to the fort's residents, occasionally leading parades and indulging in a fondness for beer.

When Comanche died of colic on November 7, 1891, believed to be twenty-nine years old, Colonel Sturgis's order that he be "preserved to the utmost limit" was taken quite literally. He is one of only four horses in U.S. history to be given a funeral with full military honors.* However, his remains were not buried but were sent to the University of Kansas and preserved via taxidermy. Comanche can still be seen today in the university's Natural History Museum.

George Herendeen, whose cool head helped a dozen men of Reno's battalion survive in the timber, remained an army scout for a time, participating in the Nez Percé Campaign the year after Little Bighorn. Then he drifted, living in several places until settling in Harlem, Montana, in 1889, where he worked on the Fort Belknap Indian Reservation. Herendeen was seventy years old when he died there of hypostatic pneumonia in June 1919.

In 1879, while serving in an artillery battery at Fort Schuyler in New York, Giovanni Martino—the trumpeter John Martin—met and married an Irish girl named Julia Higgins. The first of their five surviving children was named George in honor of Custer.

Martin would see combat once more, during the Spanish-American War. He served in the army until age limitations forced his retirement

---

* The other three horses: Black Jack, who was the symbolic riderless horse in four state funerals, most notably the one for President John F. Kennedy, whose widow, Jacqueline, purchased Black Jack upon his retirement in 1973; Sergeant Reckless, who was awarded a Bronze Star for valor while fighting with the Marines in the Korean War; and Chief, who is credited as having been the U.S. Army's last living cavalry mount and who died in 1968 at age thirty-six.

in 1904. Martin remained with his family in Baltimore, where they lived and operated a sweets and candy store. Two years later, perhaps following one of his daughters, Martin moved to Brooklyn and took a job as a ticket agent at the 103rd Street Station of the recently built New York City subway system. As he aged, the long hours and commute of his ticket-taker job forced Martin to take a watchman's job at the nearby Navy Yard in 1915.

In 1922, while crossing a Brooklyn street, Martin was injured by a truck and hospitalized. He died from complications that December. He was buried on Christmas Day in the Cypress Hill Cemetery in Brooklyn.

The fierce Hunkpapa warrior Gall had a quiet rest of his life. After the painful split with Sitting Bull in Canada and bringing his band to surrender at Fort Buford, in May 1881, he and his followers were loaded onto steamers and shipped downriver to the Standing Rock Indian Reservation. The first complete census of the Lakota at Standing Rock, taken in the fall of 1881, listed Gall with a band of 52 families, totaling 230 people.

Becoming a farmer, Gall encouraged his people to assimilate to reservation life. He also converted to Christianity, took the additional name Abraham, and served as a judge on the reservation's Court of Indian Affairs. Gall lived on the Standing Rock Agency until his death at his Oak Creek home on December 5, 1894. He was buried in Saint Elizabeth Episcopal Cemetery in Wakpala, South Dakota.*

Less than a year after trying to run away with Crazy Horse, Black Buffalo Woman gave birth to a pale-skinned daughter. For the rest of the daughter's life—which lasted up to World War II—others on the Pine Ridge Reservation would remark on her unusual light hair and complexion.

After the disaster at the Little Bighorn, the U.S. Congress authorized

* In 1991, Gall's remains were exhumed because a Utah state park museum purported to have his skull. However, the remains were found to be intact.

funds to reinforce the Big Horn and Yellowstone Expedition. Newly determined to demonstrate the willingness and capability of the U.S. Army to pursue and punish the Sioux, General George Crook took to the field late in the summer of '76.

It was not a glorious return to action. Crook embarked on what came to be known as the grueling and poorly provisioned Horsemeat March, named for obvious reasons. A patrol sent to Deadwood for supplies came across the village of American Horse the Elder in September and looted it in the Battle of Slim Buttes. Crazy Horse led an attack against Crook the next day but was repulsed by Crook's superior numbers.

As a consequence of his disappearance after the Rosebud fight and the subsequent Big Horn and Yellowstone Expedition debacle, General Crook was transferred out of the northern plains to become head of the Department of Arizona. While Crook successfully forced some members of the Apache tribe to surrender, Geronimo continually evaded capture. In March 1886, he received word that Geronimo would meet him in Cañon de los Embudos, in the Sierra Madre Mountains. Geronimo, camped on the Mexican side of the border, agreed to Crook's surrender terms.

But that night, a soldier who sold the Apache whiskey alleged that they would be murdered as soon as they crossed the border. Geronimo and twenty-five of his followers slipped away during the night. Their escape cost Crook another command.

The leadership of his replacement, Nelson Miles, finally brought an end to the Apache Wars. He captured Geronimo and the Chiricahua Apache band and detained the Chiricahua scouts who had served the U.S. Army, transporting them all as prisoners of war to Florida. (Furious that the scouts who had faithfully served the army were imprisoned along with the hostile warriors, Crook fired off numerous telegrams to Washington, which were ignored.) They, along with most of Geronimo's band, were forced to spend the next twenty-six years in captivity before they were finally released.

Crook wound up with a respectable-enough career, rising up to major general. In 1888, President Grover Cleveland placed him in command of the Military Division of the Missouri. To his credit, though it was too little too late, Crook spent his last years speaking out against the unjust treatment of his former Indian adversaries. He died suddenly in Chicago in March 1890 and was buried in Arlington National Cemetery.

Though the Little Bighorn tragedy occurred on his watch, as top commander in the field, General Alfred Terry and his advocates were able to deflect most of the blame to Lieutenant Colonel Custer. Terry remained in charge for several more years, and in 1881, a new town in Montana was named after him.

Five years later, he would finally kick the dust off his boots and settle down in Chicago as a newly promoted major general and commander of the Military Division of the Missouri. He performed the role that was formerly Sheridan's until April 1888, when he retired from the army. Terry died two years later in New Haven, Connecticut, and was buried there.

For General Philip Sheridan, the opportunity to move up one more step came in November 1883, when he succeeded General William Sherman as Commanding General of the U.S. Army. He held the position until his death in August 1888 in Dartmouth, Massachusetts, at just fifty-seven years old, and he was buried at Arlington National Cemetery. Two months earlier, Sheridan had been promoted to the same rank as Sherman and Ulysses Grant, equivalent today to five-star general. One of his four children and only son, Philip Sheridan Jr., also had a distinguished army career, which ended abruptly when he had a heart attack at only thirty-seven years old.

The general's wife, Irene, just thirty-five at Philip Sr.'s death, never remarried, saying, "I would rather be the widow of Phil Sheridan than the wife of any man living."

The thirty-eight-year-old Captain Thomas Weir, who had begun serving under Custer during the Civil War, was deeply affected by the Little Bighorn battle—or, more specifically, his inability to come to his commander's aid and his hiding with Major Reno in a hole in the ground.

Drinking heavily and showing symptoms of post-traumatic stress disorder, Weir's mental health declined rapidly. He wrote letters to Libbie Custer, hinting at untold matters regarding her husband's death. Posted to New York City on recruiting duty, Weir refused to go outside, continued to drink heavily, and in his last days was said to be extremely nervous to the point of being unable to swallow.

He died at his home in New York on December 9, 1876, reportedly in a state of extreme depression. He was buried on Governors Island, but in the 1880s, his remains were transferred to a cemetery in Brooklyn.

Captain Frederick Benteen stayed on duty on the northern plains, participating in the Nez Percé and other campaigns. As a member of the Ninth Cavalry in December 1882, Benteen was promoted to major. His career had further ups and downs. The latter was illustrated by his being convicted of drunk and disorderly conduct in 1887. He would have been dismissed from the army if not for President Grover Cleveland, who ordered a one-year suspension. During it, Major Benteen retired.

He and his wife, Kate, had five children, four of whom died in infancy. When Benteen died in Atlanta in June 1888, his only surviving child was Frederick Jr. He had by then joined the army and would retire as a lieutenant colonel. Major Benteen was buried at Arlington.

For Marcus Reno, the rest of his career was a shambles. In December 1876, while commanding Fort Abercrombie in Dakota Territory, he was charged with making unwanted advances toward the wife of another officer of the Seventh Cavalry, Captain James Bell, while Bell was away. After a general court-martial, Reno was found guilty on six of seven charges and ordered dismissed from the army. He, too, benefited from presidential intervention when Rutherford Hayes ordered a two-year suspension instead.

Responding to charges of cowardice and drunkenness at the Little Bighorn, Reno demanded and was granted a court of inquiry. The court convened in Chicago in January 1879 and called as witnesses most of the surviving officers who had been in the fight. After twenty-six days of testimony, Judge Advocate General Dunn concluded, "I concur with the court in its exoneration of Major Reno from the charges of cowardice which have been brought against him." He added, "The suspicion or accusation that Gen. Custer owed his death and the destruction of his command to the failure of Major Reno, through incompetency or cowardice, to go to his relief, is considered as set to rest."

Back on duty in 1879 and while commanding officer at Fort Meade in the Dakota Territory, Reno again faced a court-martial, charged with conduct unbecoming an officer, including a physical assault on a subordinate officer. He was convicted and dismissed from the service. The disgraced major took an apartment in Washington, DC, where he doggedly pursued restoration of his military rank while working as an examiner in the Bureau of Pensions.

The apple did not fall far from the Reno tree. He married in October 1882, and immediately there was friction between the new Mrs. Reno and her eighteen-year-old stepson, Robert. On Christmas night 1883, Robert Reno, without invitation, entered the room of actress Carrie Swain through a window. Swain refused to press charges, but the management insisted that young interloper leave. Reno sent his son to live with an uncle in Pittsburgh. Still, the marriage failed.

So did several business ventures, and Reno became a traveling salesman. In March 1889, he was diagnosed with cancer of the tongue. He was admitted to Providence Hospital in Washington and underwent surgery. While hospitalized, he developed pneumonia and died at the age of fifty-four in the early hours of March 30.

No preparations had been made for his burial, so it was arranged that he be temporarily interred at Washington's Glenwood Cemetery until he could be reinterred with his first wife at the Ross family plot in Harrisburg, Pennsylvania. No room could be found for his remains there, so it seemed his temporary, unmarked grave would be his final resting place.

In 1967, at the request of Charles Reno, a great-nephew, a U.S. military review board reopened Reno's 1880 court-martial. It reversed the decision, ruling Reno's dismissal from the service improper and awarding him an honorable discharge. That September, Reno's remains were reinterred with honors in the Custer National Cemetery, on the Little Bighorn battlefield.

There have been claims and counterclaims that Monahsetah, the young Cheyenne woman captured at the Washita, bore Custer a son named Yellow Swallow and about what happened to him. However, it has also been reported that George Custer contracted syphilis while at West Point, which made him unable to sire children.

In any case, after her time with the Seventh Cavalry, Monahsetah married a white man, had several children, and died in 1921.

Soon after their arrival at the Little Bighorn battlefield, General Terry and Colonel Gibbon deployed troops to bury the dead. This was more easily ordered than done because the sunbaked soil was hard, and the soldiers lacked the proper tools for digging graves. George and Tom Custer were interred in the same grave, though not very well.

The only real mutilation that occurred to Lieutenant Colonel Custer's remains was from the wolves and coyotes in the months after the temporary burial. When his remains were dug up a year later, it was difficult to tell which bones belonged to George and which were Tom's. It was said that only "several handfuls of bones" were collected and placed in a coffin that was marked with a note by the surgeon R. G. Read, who stated that these were the remains of Gen. George A. Custer.

In August 1877, the Atlantic Express train pulled into Poughkeepsie from Fort Abraham Lincoln with the handfuls of bones. The destination was supposed to be the cemetery at West Point. Libbie Custer intended an elaborate funeral with the help of Major General Schofield that was to take place at the military academy, but they needed time to plan and time to allow for the travel of all of Custer's military friends abroad.

Since the West Point Cemetery had no receiving vault to store the remains, Libbie reached out to Philip Hamilton, the son of Alexander Hamilton, whose son at died at the Washita River attack. He offered a temporary place to secure the remains within the receiving vault at the Poughkeepsie Rural Cemetery. He even went so far as to reuse the same American flag that had draped his son's casket in 1868.

When it was finally time for the funeral at West Point, there was a grand procession through the streets of Poughkeepsie. The march moved from the cemetery to the steamboat *The Mary Powell* waiting at the riverfront, with the streets lined with mournful faces. The boat sailed down the river to West Point, where what was left of George Armstrong Custer was laid to rest.*

On July 6, upon hearing of her husband's death, the thirty-four-year-old Elizabeth Bacon Custer did not immediately give in to knee-bending grief but accompanied the army messengers to personally comfort the other twenty-six women at Fort Abraham Lincoln who were being informed that they were widows.

Libbie soon found herself deeply in debt, thanks to the Custers' lifestyle when not in the field and the army's meager remuneration. She received a Federal Widow's Pension, but that was hardly enough to be comfortable. Thanks to the sympathy of the American public, she achieved her economic security as an author and lecturer.

In best-selling books, Libbie built the bigger-than-life legend of Custer as the greatest Indian fighter ever. And she always referred to him

* What were believed to be Tom Custer's remains were interred in the Fort Leavenworth National Cemetery in Kansas. Boston Custer's battered remains were buried in Monroe, Michigan.

as General Custer. Libbie was largely responsible for creating Custer as a national hero and muting criticism of his military actions in Oklahoma and on the northern plains.

She never remarried. And despite spending much of her life traveling extensively throughout the United States (including winters in Florida) and the world, she never visited the Little Bighorn battlefield. Libbie was said to treasure a letter from President Theodore Roosevelt, who stated that her husband was "one of [his] heroes" and "a shining light to all the youth of America."

As a result of her literary career and lecture tours, she amassed an estate of over $100,000 (about $2.45 million today). Libbie Custer died in New York City in April 1933, four days before her ninety-first birthday. She was buried next to her husband at West Point.

A few years before her death, Libbie told a writer that her greatest disappointment was that she never had a son to bear her husband's honored name.

ACKNOWLEDGMENTS

As I touched on in the Author Note, I am indebted to the thorough research and vivid writing of people who have previously written books on the Battle of the Little Bighorn. This is especially true of the best of the best: James Donovan, Mark Lee Gardner, Nathaniel Philbrick, and the late Robert Utley and Stephen Ambrose. (Details can be found in the bibliography.) I am not implying that my book rises to the level of their books, just expressing my gratitude for the trails they blazed.

As I have done before, once again I want to stress that without the dedicated staffers at various research centers, I would not have a career. This time around, with *Vengeance*, my thanks go to those librarians and curators and others at various institutions who helped me along the arduous research road and whose unflagging courtesy made the journey an enjoyable one. I am always both delighted and humbled by the expertise and enthusiasm of such learned and good-hearted professionals.

Particularly helpful were staffers at the Library of Congress and Kellen Cutsforth at the Denver Public Library. Closer to home, I am also grateful for the efforts of staffers at the John Jermain Memorial Library, especially Susan Mullin, for their long-standing assistance and kindness. Extra thanks, too, to Lisa Cowley, who keeps bailing me out—well, writing-wise.

This book would not have originated, let alone been completed, without the encouragement and steadfast support of my editor, Marc Resnick. Others at St. Martin's Press who have also made *Vengeance* a focused and productive adventure include Sally Richardson, Andy Martin, Laura Clark, Rebecca Lang, Lily Cronig, Rob Grom, Steve Erickson, Julia Turner, and Steve Wagner. Another big supporter of this book is Nat Sobel, a friend as well as agent, and I appreciate everything done for me by him and his team at Sobel Weber Associates.

My dear friends continue to wait for me to not work so much so we can get together more often. Their support, especially while *Vengeance* was being written, was a big reason why every day still mattered. And finally, my love to Leslie, Katy and James, Vivienne, and Brendan.

BIBLIOGRAPHY

Adams, George Rollie. *General William S. Harney: Prince of Dragoons*. University of Nebraska Press, 2001.

Ambrose, Stephen E. *Crazy Horse and Custer: The Parallel Lives of Two American Warriors*. Doubleday, 1975.

Andrist, Ralph K. *The Long Death*. Macmillan, 1964.

Bailey, John W. *Pacifying the Plains: General Alfred Terry and the Decline of the Sioux*. Greenwood Press, 1979.

Barnard, Sandy. *I Go with Custer: The Life and Death of Reporter Mark Kellogg*. Bismarck Tribune, 1996.

Barnett, Louise. *Touched by Fire: The Life, Death and Mythic Afterlife of George Armstrong Custer*. Holt, 1996.

Beck, Paul N. *Columns of Vengeance: Soldiers, Sioux, and the Punitive Expeditions, 1863–1864*. University of Oklahoma Press, 2013.

Bradley, James H. *The March of the Montana Column*. University of Oklahoma Press, 1961.

Bray, Kingsley M. *Crazy Horse: A Lakota Life*. University of Oklahoma Press, 2006.

Brill, Charles J. *Custer, Black Kettle, and the Fight on the Washita*. University of Oklahoma Press, 2001.

Buell, Thomas. *The Warrior Generals*. Three Rivers Press, 1997.

Carroll, John M., ed. *Custer's Chief of Scouts: The Reminiscences of Charles A. Varnum*. University of Nebraska Press, 1987.

Clavin, Tom. *Wild Bill: The True Story of the American Frontier's First Gunfighter*. St. Martin's Press, 2019.

Connell, Evan S. *Son of the Morning Star: Custer and the Little Bighorn*. North Point Press, 1984.

Coughlin, Colonel T. M. *Varnum: The Last of Custer's Lieutenants*. J. M. Carroll, 1980.

Cozzens, Peter. *The Earth Is Weeping: The Epic Story of the Indian Wars for the American West*. Knopf, 2016.

Custer, Elizabeth Bacon. *"Boots and Saddles," or Life in Dakota with General Custer*. Harper and Brothers, 1885.

Custer, George Armstrong. *My Life on the Plains, or Personal Experiences with the Indians*. Sheldon, 1874.

Day, Carl. *Tom Custer: Ride to Glory*. Arthur H. Clark, 2002.

Donovan, James. *A Terrible Glory: Custer and the Little Bighorn*. Back Bay Books, 2008.

Drury, Bob, and Tom Clavin. *The Heart of Everything That Is: The Untold Story of Red Cloud, an American Legend*. Simon and Schuster, 2013.

Frost, Lawrence. *The Court-Martial of George Armstrong Custer*. University of Oklahoma Press, 1968.

Gardner, Mark Lee. *The Earth Is All That Lasts: Crazy Horse, Sitting Bull, and the Last Stand of the Great Sioux Nation*. Mariner, 2022.

Gibbon, John. *Gibbon on the Sioux Campaign of 1876*. Old Army Press, 1970.

Gray, John S. *Custer's Last Campaign: Mitch Boyer and the Little Bighorn Reconstructed*. University of Nebraska Press, 1991.

Greene, Jerome. *Washita*. University of Oklahoma Press, 2004.

Hassrick, Royal. *The Sioux: Life and Customs of a Warrior Society*. University of Oklahoma Press, 1962.

Hutton, Paul Andrew, ed. *The Custer Reader*. University of Oklahoma Press, 2004.

Lazarus, Edward. *Black Hills, White Justice*. HarperCollins, 1991.

Leckie, Shirley A. *Elizabeth Bacon Custer and the Making of a Myth*. University of Oklahoma Press, 1993.

Marshall, Joseph H., III. *The Journal of Crazy Horse*. Penguin Books, 2005.

McDonnell, Julia. *Sitting Bull: In His Own Words*. Gareth Stevens, 2015.

Michno, Gregory. *Lakota Noon: The Indian Narrative of Custer's Defeat*. Mountain Press Publishing, 1998.

Monaghan, Jay. *Custer: The Life of General George Armstrong Custer*. Little, Brown, 1959.

Neihardt, John G. *Black Elk Speaks*. University of Nebraska Press, 2000.

Overfield, Lloyd H. *The Little Big Horn, 1876: The Official Communications, Documents, and Reports, with Rosters of the Officers and Troops of the Campaign*. Arthur H. Clark, 1871.

Philbrick, Nathaniel. *The Last Stand: Custer, Sitting Bull, and the Battle of the Little Bighorn*. Viking, 2010.

Powers, Thomas. *The Killing of Crazy Horse*. Knopf, 2010.

Repass, Craig. *Custer for President?* Old Army Press, 1985.

Sanja, Mike. *Crazy Horse: The Life Behind the Legend*. Wiley, 2000.

Scott, Douglas D., P. Willey, and Melissa A. Connor. *They Died with Custer*. University of Oklahoma Press, 1989.

Smith, Sherry. *Sagebrush Soldier*. University of Oklahoma Press, 1989.

Spotts, David L. *Campaigning with Custer and the Nineteenth Kansas Volunteer Cavalry in the Washita Campaign, 1868–69*. Edited by E. A. Brininstool. University of Nebraska Press, 1988.

Standing Bear, Luther. *My People the Sioux*. Houghton Mifflin, 1928.

Utley, Robert M. *Custer Battlefield: A History and Guide to the Battle of the Little Bighorn*. U.S. Department of the Interior, 1988.

Utley, Robert M. *Custer: Cavalier in Buckskin*. University of Oklahoma Press, 1988.

Utley, Robert M. *The Last Sovereigns: Sitting Bull and the Resistance of the Free Lakotas*. University of Nebraska Press, 2020.

Viola, Herman J. *Little Bighorn Remembered: The Untold Indian Story of Custer's Last Stand*. Crown, 2000.

INDEX

ABOUT THE AUTHOR

Gordon M. Grant

TOM CLAVIN is a #1 *New York Times* bestselling author and has worked as a newspaper editor, magazine writer, TV and radio commentator, and reporter for *The New York Times*. He has received awards from the Society of Professional Journalists, the Marine Corps Heritage Foundation, and the National Newspaper Association. His books include the bestselling Frontier Lawmen trilogy—*Wild Bill, Dodge City,* and *Tombstone*—and *Blood and Treasure, The Last Hill,* and *The First to Go West* with Bob Drury. He lives in Sag Harbor, New York.